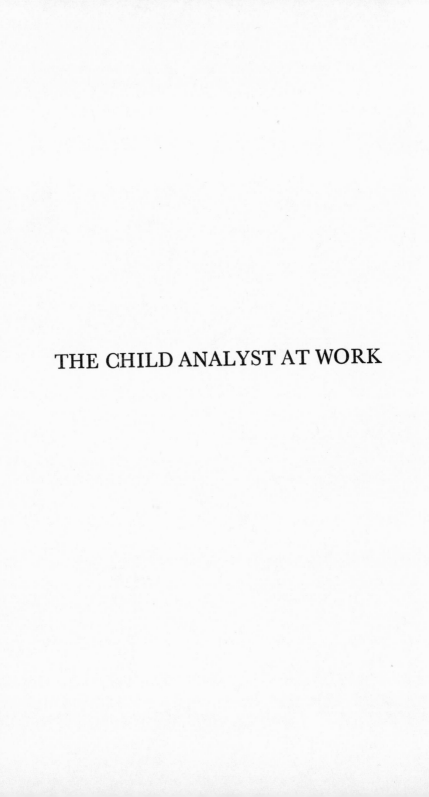

THE CHILD ANALYST AT WORK

THE CHILD ANALYST
AT WORK

Edited by

Elisabeth R. Geleerd

INTERNATIONAL UNIVERSITIES PRESS, INC.

New York   New York

Contents

ELISABETH R. GELEERD, M.D.

Introduction

IN THE LITERATURE on child analysis, the reader finds a
wealth of publications dealing with many facets of child analysis—general problems of technique, the role of the parents
as part of the analytic process, specific aspects of clinical psychoanalysis or child development, and numerous others. When
clinical case material is presented, the authors generally follow Freud's method of reporting, as he first introduced it in
Studies on Hysteria (Breuer and Freud, 1893-1895). One of his
most beautiful case descriptions was "Notes upon a Case of
Obsessional Neurosis" (1909a) (the case of the Ratman), which
has been one of the important contributions to the understanding of obsessional neurosis. The editors of the *Standard Edition* have added to the original publication of the Ratman case
Freud's notes as he recorded them after each session. These
add a new dimension to the understanding of the case material in that they highlight many sides of the relationship between Freud and his patient, although Freud had described
most of them in the original paper.

Freud, in the same year, published the case history of Little
Hans (1909)—another milestone in the recording of case
histories, since this was the first case showing some form of
child analysis. The close cooperation between Freud and
Little Hans' father helped Hans come to grips with the conflicts created by his instinctual strivings as opposed to his need

1

to be loved by his parents. The father was in the role of the analyst. In this work, Freud included much of the actual dialogue which took place between Hans and his father, as it was told by the father to Freud.

There are several ways of reporting sessions from psychoanalytic treatment. The most accurate way is by detailed note-taking during the session or, in rare cases, by recording the sessions on tape. Freud, however, warned the analyst to use great caution since "on-the-spot" note-taking makes the particular form of listening by the analyst—the so-called "hovering attention"—well-nigh impossible. It would seem that the analysts who nevertheless are able to do this tend to record what the patient says but not their own responses and reactions. The introduction of a tape recorder creates almost insurmountable difficulties in the analytic work, although it has proved to be of help for research and teaching purposes.

A patient can only reveal to himself and his doctor what he has hidden from himself when he is sure that the analyst will not divulge his confidences. If the material subsequently is published, some form of disguise is used and, in many cases, the permission of the patient or his parents to publish the material is requested. (Freud also used the additional precaution of waiting for a number of years before publishing his cases.)

In child analysis "on-the-spot" note-taking is incompatible with the relationship the analyst wants to establish between himself and the child, and physically impossible in those cases where the analyst participates in games or is assigned a role in the play of the child.

It is again Freud's example which is followed by most analysts—i.e., if they want to make notes they do so after the session. True, this will, in many cases, lack complete accuracy, but it adds to the reader's understanding of what has transpired in the session. This form of note-taking begins to reflect the filtering through of the material, and whatever seemed important to the analyst in the session is recorded with more precision and is given more weight. In many case reports, we find elaborate recording of sessions, but this is generally not in the form of dialogue. The complete case of a classical child analysis still remains to be written in this form. Since most children in analysis nowadays are in treatment for a number of years, it cannot be undertaken easily. It also requires infinite patience on the part of the reader to follow such detailed description.

For these reasons, I have asked a number of colleagues to join me in a publication of either some aspects of a case of child analysis or a complete description of a case they have treated, with the inclusion of the reporting of some sessions in dialogue.[1] Detailed publication of the analytic treatment of a child or a phase of such an analysis can highlight some of the technical problems encountered in the analytic work with children. Dependent on the aim of the presentation, one can find in such a description many other aspects of the psychoanalysis of children, e.g., those pertaining to the unfolding of the analytic process, development of the transference, the interplay of defenses, development of the superego, and object relationships.

For the uninitiated reader it is not always clear that since the early days of child analysis there have been two separate schools: one, the so-called Kleinian school which was started by the late Melanie Klein, and the other, the classical or Freudian school of which Anna Freud was the pioneer and has remained the leader. Over the years, the two schools have separated more and more. But the workers of both schools

---

[1] Berta Bornstein (1949) presents a case in a form which comes very close to the manner in which the cases in this book are presented.

agree on basic premises of psychoanalysis, such as the existence of unconscious phenomena and processes—the three psychic structures, id, ego and superego, the importance of maintaining the analytic relationship, the role of transference
in psychoanalytic therapy, to mention a few. However, the
analysts of the Kleinian school of child analysis differ in some
of their theoretical views and, therefore, in their technical
applications. A sample of Kleinian technique can be found in
Melanie Klein's book, *Narrative of a Child Analysis* (1960),
which consists of a description of consecutive sessions of a four-
month analysis.[2]

The first book on classical child analysis was written in German by Anna Freud—*Einführung in die Technik der Kinder-
analyse* (1927). It was published in English in 1948 as *Introduction to the Technique of Child Analysis,* with an additional chapter, entitled "Indications for Child Analysis,"
which had originally been published as a paper (1945). This
book no longer reflects exactly our current thinking on the
technique of child analysis, and there is thus far no book
which describes the technique of classical child analysis as it is
practiced today.

However, the fundamental aspects which Anna Freud
thoroughly discusses are still valid. Her theoretical point of
view supplies the foundation for our analytic work with children today. Anna Freud discusses and explains clearly why
changes in the classical analytic technique used with adults
have to be made in the analytic treatment of children in order
to gain access to the child's feelings and thinking and to engage him in the analytic process. I will recapitulate her main
ideas and elaborate upon these.

The adult patient comes to analysis because he suffers. The

---

[2] See also Lebovici and McDougall (1960) for the day-by-day account of the
treatment of a psychotic child.

healthy part of his ego enters into what Richard Sterba (1940) called a therapeutic alliance with the analyst, which is the only means by which the patient is enabled to withstand the stress of analysis. He can then become acquainted or re-acquainted with the feelings and memories which his ego has warded off from consciousness.

Many children, although severely disturbed, do not suffer, or suffer only temporarily. Thus their resistance to being ana-lyzed is far greater than that of the adult patient, since the latter is, at least, consciously aware of his need for it. Thus a child analysis, especially in the beginning phases, could never be sustained if the parents' determination to see it through were not available. Therefore, in the diagnostic work-up of the child and the treatment recommendations, the parents' cooperation has to be assessed in order to determine whether the child can be analyzed at a given time, even if the child's disturbance is such as to indicate that psychoanalysis is the treatment of choice. One might say that to begin a child analy-sis, the therapeutic alliance has to be established with the parents. Later on the child himself becomes a participant in the analytic process. However, if and when the parents cannot cooperate with us for realistic reasons or because of inner re-sistance, the analytic work suffers considerably or ends. Analy-sis of their child is an emotional hardship on the parents beyond the sacrifice in time and money. To stand this stress, a special inner attitude on their part is required. This develops, because of the close relationship between parent and child, into an inner process in the parents, especially the mother, as the analytic work with the child proceeds. Moreover, we know in part how the parents' and child's neuroses are interwoven. Due to the analytic work, the changes in the child reverberate in the parents. The actions and reactions of the child become more meaningful to the parents. In addition, in their regular discussions with the analyst, past events of the child's life may be understood in a different context or recalled if they had been forgotten.

However, sometimes the analysis of the child creates an insight into the parents' neuroses or increases them, and they may require psychotherapy or analysis, especially when the neurotic actions of the child tended to gratify neurotic patterns in the parents. To obtain the information from the parents necessary for the analysis of the child, special skill and tact are required of the analyst. The parents, also, may ask for advice, but in order to keep the analysis of the child as uncontaminated as possible, the child analyst has to refrain from giving advice and furnish it only in special cases or to further the analytic work with the child. A special problem for the child analyst is the situation which develops when the parents compete with the child for the analyst's love and attention. But over and beyond the needed cooperation of the parents, we have to establish a working relationship with the child.

Anna Freud originally suggested complicated ways to make the child dependent on the child analyst. Her thesis before 1936 was that a positive relationship between analyst and child was essential to make up for the deficit in the therapeutic alliance. Since then, thanks to her *The Ego and the Mechanisms of Defense* (1946), we have gained greater insight in the ego's handling of conflicts, and we are able to gain the child's cooperation by analyzing his moods and his defenses.

Before 1936, the establishment of a hyperpositive attachment was the first step in the analysis of a child; now, we obtain his cooperation by verbalizing his most immediate feelings for him—his feelings about "the here and now," encompassing all we can gather about his actions from his play, his verbalizations, and his fantasies. We can also work with the child when he expresses hostility and does not seem to want to enter into any contact with us. These attitudes themselves can be discussed; they are generally part of the child's neurosis. But, especially in the beginning of the analysis, the parents always have to serve as an auxiliary in the analysis of the child insofar as the child is unable to observe himself and report daily happenings.

These actions on our part enhance the child's ego functions of reflection and verbalization and lead to the recall of memories of his recent past. Subsequently, the consistent interpretation of his affects, his defenses, and the transference gradually lead to the uncovering of repressed material. However, to establish and maintain a working relationship with the child, the analyst cannot be a shadowy figure as in the analysis of adults. To treat a child this way would be unnatural and would be a real anxiety-producing event in his life. It would hardly be conducive to helping him face his neurotic anxieties. The analyst thus has to find a way to maintain a certain degree of aloofness and at the same time behave like a normal, friendly adult to the child. Thus a birthday or Christmas present is analytically correct in many analyses of children, or a glass of milk when the child comes to his appointment directly from school and is hungry. There are controversies about such matters in child-analytic circles, but most of us who have contributed to this book feel that this type of friendliness is frequently either in order or essential. We must keep in mind, however, that our actions may become part of the analytic process, and they may need to be analyzed with the child at the time or later.

The whole problem of transference still needs a great deal of reflection, discussion, and clarification among child analysts. Melanie Klein and her followers consider everything which refers to the analyst as a transference manifestation. This leads to a great many symbolic translations. I would like to distinguish different relationships of the child to the analyst:

1. The analyst is another adult, thus a parental figure who sometimes has to set limits, but is also a friend to the child.

2. The analyst is a real transference object, as in adult analysis. Insofar as the child has gone through his developmental stages, the object relationships of the child are past history. Defenses have been erected and the beginning of superego development has taken place. All of these manifestations show up in the relationship to the analyst as transference manifestations and, in some cases, a real transference neurosis can be established.[3]

3. The analyst is used by the child as the anaclitic love object of the earliest phases of object relationship to make up for the residual deficits of need gratification of these early phases. Probably, total need gratification can never be accomplished because in some cases unfortunate circumstances occur, and in others excessive strength of partial drives must be expected. That the analytic relationship can serve to gratify these needs from the past can be clearly observed in work with psychotic and borderline cases, adults as well as children, and with concentration camp victims.[4] In the work with the concentration camp victims, the analyst had to become the representative of the early mother-child relationship and give some sort of gratification before the analysis could proceed. In addition, this relationship has to be analyzed and understood as the patient reacts negatively to the frustrations which automatically arise due to limits of the relationship in place and time. This aspect then becomes an integral part of the

[3] See Harley (1966). In this paper, Harley follows the unfolding transference phenomena, step by step. The child's dog phobia was also transferred onto the analyst and her dog, and could be completely analyzed. See also this volume.

[4] See Alpert (1954), Geleerd (1949), Gyomeroi (1963), Schwing (1940).

regular transference relationship. The same thing takes place in all analytic work, albeit in less dramatic fashion. The amount of gratification and frustration which the analyst has to give depends on his assessment of the stage of object relationship of the child.

4. The assignment of a role in fantasy play is not necessarily transference. However, repetitive assignment in a particular phase of the analysis may indicate transference implications, and this then will need to be analyzed.

Another fundamental difference between the child and adult patient is that we cannot expect the child to free-associate. The adult patient's ego has the capacity for self-observation, reflection, and the vehicle of expression is verbalization. The child lives each moment intensely, and generally this is accompanied either by immediate affective response or none at all. We may observe the latter at the time of a traumatic event. We then may find a gradual but lasting character change instead. One might generalize and say that because the child seeks discharge either directly or in play, reflection about immediate events and recall of the events in words are not easily available. However, even in early childhood, the "mood" which includes degrees of anxiety or mood changes offers important avenues to appraisal. The discussion of these in the sessions leads to important analytic insight for the child analyst as well as for the child. In adolescence, the capacity for reflection develops as an important ego function. Therefore, a new dimension is added because thought and fantasy, verbalization of feelings, and the mood may replace the many avenues of discharge of childhood as the ego develops. These should become more and more the tools and vehicles in the analysis of the adolescent. However, in child analysis, minute observation of the actions of the child in play, his interaction with the analyst, and the information which we gather about

the child through regular contact with the parents have to
take the place of free association.

The analytic work enhances the ego functions of self-observation and verbalization in the child beyond his average
maturational level. When this has been achieved many child
analysts will say "the child now is really in analysis." We tend
to overlook that the preparation for this is an intrinsic
part of child analysis. Actually, what we do here is parallel
to what we do with our adult patients—i.e., the establishment
of a connection in his mind between mood, feeling and anxiety
and recent events. In sum, it is the education of the patient to
the analytic work, as well as analysis of his defenses and affects. Consistent interpretation of these and of the transference will gradually lead to recall of repressed memories or
constructions as in the analytic work with adults. Analysis
of dreams is as important in child analysis as in the analysis
of adults.

Although all these aspects of child analysis are not clear in
each case presented in this book, the individual case high-
lights one or more problems of technique and gives insight
into the analytic process. An advantage of collecting a variety
of cases from different authors is the emergence of certain
trends in analytic work which otherwise might be overlooked
or taken for granted.

In most of the cases reported in this volume, I found that
when the child brought a wealth of material which revealed
the coming to consciousness of important repressed id fantasies, the analyst seemed to disregard and not interpret immediately the obvious references to the primal scene, castration fantasy, or the oedipus complex. Instead, all of the analysts talked about feelings of the child as he expressed them to
the important figures in his life and to the analyst. With the
emergence of id material into consciousness, the child's anx-

iety is heightened, and this is dealt with by the child's ego in the way it had been dealt with in the past. The intensity of the emotion attaches itself to a reality event in the present. At such a point, as id fantasies emerge, the person of the analyst is drawn into the conflict. At this time the analysis of the feelings for the analyst and of the transference manifestations are equally important aspects of the work. The interpretation of the id fantasies generally comes in a later session. How and when id interpretations will be given depends on how the id material has presented itself.

Reviewing the reports of all of these analyses also seems to give an erroneous impression that, especially in the cases of latency age, the analysis of the oedipus complex is not too important. This is only a slant, but it is an observation worthy of note. First of all, in latency the oedipus complex is receding and the defenses and sublimations take the upper hand in the child's development as a transformation of the "dissolution of the oedipus complex" (Freud, 1924.) Thus the analytic work is mainly concerned with tracing the vicissitudes of these transformations. This is done by a step-by-step unraveling of the concomitant affects. The reader will be struck with the dominance of pregenital elements over the phallic oedipal ones, especially the relation to the preoedipal mother.

In most of the cases presented in this publication we can trace the impact of the relationship to the mother from earliest infancy, especially as it is relived in the transference, regardless of the sex of the analyst. We have been fortunate in having a complementary range among our cases from the death of a mother in two cases and the impact of this event on the child's emotional life, the impoverishment and the ways of dealing with guilt feelings concerning her death, to that of a case of a young child whose analysis had to be carried out in the mother's presence; and another case of a young child whose treatment had to be carried out with a minimum of contact with the mother. Three authors specifically highlight different aspects of the relationship of the child analyst to the child as part of the analytic process; two other authors treat psychosomatic illness with classical child psychoanalysis. Between the lines of these case presentations, the reader can gauge the importance of the parent's role in the analytic work and the life of the child. In all cases the analysis of the transference plays a major role.

Although all of us have our own style of working, what transpires in this publication is that all of us try to bring the child to a proper relationship with his own affective life, and our main aim is to help him to cope with his inner striving. The access to these is through analysis of his defenses and affects so that, instead of being frozen in a neurotic conflict, they can be made available to the processes of growth which entail neutralization and sublimation.

I feel most grateful to the contributors. Their generous response has helped me put together a volume which, although unstructured in its selection and choice of presentation, reflects our self-discipline in our work. The cases presented show how each case of child analysis requires a unique approach in order to gain contact with the inner life of the patient. In spite of many actions which would seem "unanalytic" if they were carried out in the analysis of an adult, an analytic process in the child is set into motion, and our interventions are "analytic" since they are geared to the child's stage of ego development. Just as in adult analysis, it becomes an interaction between analyst and analysand where, beginning with an understanding of the daily behavior and feelings of the analysand, we gain access to the warded-off and forgotten feelings, traumata, and memories.

REFERENCES

Alpert, A. (1954), Observations on the Treatment of Emotionally Disturbed Children in a Therapeutic Center. *The Psychoanalytic Study of the Child*, 9:334-343. New York: International Universities Press.

Bornstein, B. (1949), The Analysis of a Phobic Child. *The Psychoanalytic Study of the Child*, 3-4:181-266. New York: International Universities Press.

Breuer, J. and Freud, S. (1893-1895), Studies on Hysteria. *Standard Edition*, 2. London: Hogarth Press, 1955.

Freud, A. (1927), *Introduction to the Technique of Child Analysis*. London: Imago, 1948.

—— (1937), *The Ego and the Mechanisms of Defense*. New York: International Universities Press, 1946.

—— (1945), Indications for Child Analysis. *The Psychoanalytic Study of the Child*, 1:127-150.

Freud, S. (1909), Analysis of a Phobia in a Five-Year-Old Boy. *Standard Edition*, 10:5-147. London: Hogarth Press, 1955.

—— (1909a), Notes upon a Case of Obsessional Neurosis. *Standard Edition*, 10:151-249.

—— (1924), The Dissolution of the Oedipus Complex. *Standard Edition*, 19:173-179.

Geleerd, E. (1949), The Psychoanalysis of a Psychotic Child. *The Psychoanalytic Study of the Child*, 3/4:311-332. New York: International Universities Press.

—— (1963), Evaluation of Melanie Klein's "Narrative of a Child Analysis." *Internat. J. Psychoanal.*, 44:493-506, 1963.

Giomroi, E. I. (1963), The Analysis of a Concentration Camp Victim. *The Psychoanalytic Study of the Child*, 18:484-510. New York: International Universities Press.

Harley, M. (1966), Fragments of the Transference Developments in a Five-Year-Old Child. Unpublished paper presented to American Association for Child Psychoanalysis, April 10, 1966, Topeka, Kansas.

Klein, M. (1960), *Narrative of a Child Analysis*. New York: Basic Books.

Lebovici, S. and McDougall, J. (1960), *Un Cas de Psychose Infantile*. Paris: Presses Universitaires de France.

Schwing, G. (1940), *A Way to the Soul of the Mentally Ill*. New York: International Universities Press, 1954.

Sterba, R. (1940), The Dynamics of the Dissolution of the Transference Resistance. *Psychoanal. Quart.*, 9:363-379.

GRACE McLEAN ABBATE, M.D.

*Notes on the First Year of the Analysis of a
Young Child with Minimum Participation
by the Mother*

THE PARENTS OF JANIE, a two-year, eleven months-old child, sought treatment for her out of desperation and fear. They had reached the point where they could no longer cope with her. The picture which they presented was indeed a disturbing one, both for the child and the parents. They were completely under her control, and were unable to comfort or satisfy her.

Fearful of separation from the mother and constantly in a demanding state, Janie went through cycles of fear reactions, sadness, and violent aggressive outbursts. Any frustration could produce a physical and emotional withdrawal, accompanied by the appearance of intense sadness, distress, and low-key sobbing, or a violent outburst in which she screamed, threw herself around wildly, and vomited. The latter would last as long as forty-five minutes and during it she could not be reached by the parents. She would bite, push them out of the room saying she could not stop, screaming, "I'm suffering." Sometimes these outbursts occurred with no apparent provocation and the parents were extremely frightened by such "fits," as they were called in the family.

Both parents were distressed by the obvious unhappiness of the child, and the mother, in particular, was fearful that the

14

child would repeat her own unhappy pattern. In their attempts to appease and bribe her, she was given into on everything. Toys were bought daily and anything she wanted was
immediately provided for her. The mother not only feared
the angry outbursts, but became depressed when the child
was sad. The intensity of her fear of the child was seen in her
fantasy that the child might knock her to the ground and
plunge a knife into her heart.

The parents were in their thirties, the father a successful
businessman, the mother a schoolteacher. They had had a
stormy marriage and had postponed having children until
they felt that their major emotional disturbances had been
resolved in their own analyses. The mother, however, was
still suffering from moderate depression and was distressed
because of her rage and angry outbursts at the child. She
looked to analytic treatment as the only solution and, in effect,
turned the child over to me.

In contrast to my usual practice of seeing the parents of a
young child weekly, particularly during the first year of treatment, this mother, after a few months, was seen only rarely,
with communication being tenuously maintained by telephone. This routine was established because the mother appeared unable to tolerate the interviews with me. She would
have little to say, would become restless and increasingly hostile. She was aware that she needed more treatment, but felt
that with two small children and one so difficult to manage,
further treatment for herself would be impossible. However,
she was supportive of the child's treatment, faithful in bringing her to the sessions, and sympathetic with her distress
when I was away. She reported dreams and, on a conscious level, was pleased with the child's rapid attachment to the analyst and the analysis. Occasional telephone calls kept me min-
imally informed of current happenings in the family life.

Because this was a child who saw herself as small, almost overwhelmingly threatened by the outer world, unprotected and in constant conflict with her mother, demanding in every way at her disposal love, tenderness, and protection from the mother, I anticipated serious difficulties because of the mother's lack of participation. However, several favorable influences made the analytic work possible. The mother experienced great relief of her guilt feelings as soon as it became apparent that the child welcomed treatment. As treatment progressed, her fear that the child was psychotic was dissipated. The child, on her part, made the exceptionally fast attachment to me seen in children who have had poor mothering experiences, and the treatment sessions became of great importance to her. She was cranky and upset on non-treatment days, complained of missing me, especially during vacation absences, looked forward to her sessions, and talked with her mother about her "work" with me. The mother, who in most areas was an angry, frightening person, was, in the analytic situation, supportive and sympathetic in the child's need to see me.

To the child I was the ideal mother, the helping friend, and the analyst. During the first months of treatment it was important for her to have something "of me" to take home—drawings which I made at her direction, duplicates of cardboard figures cut out for our "games," and other such things had to be taken home. Later, she told me that if she or I went away she would have these things by which to remember me. In the office, as soon as the dramatized stories developed, she had me jot down notes about them, and at the end of a session she would ask me to write down exactly what was happening at the stopping point. We learned to understand in the analysis that this procedure insured for her the continuity of the relationship to me.

It should be noted that I had to read back every word which I had written, and that she watched me and asked questions to make sure that I had not omitted a single word. (Incidentally, this child at the age of six has taught herself to read, although the school has not provided the opportunity for this, and even has discouraged reading at this age.)

CHILD'S HISTORY

Janie was a planned baby. The pregancany caused no discomfort, but the delivery was prolonged and the mother felt as though she were holding the baby back. For several months after the birth there was an increase in the mother's depression and, despite its subsidence, she felt that she could not satisfy or comfort the infant as readily as did the very good housekeeper who stayed with them until Janie was two. The next housekeeper, who has remained with the family, was equally good with the child, providing a warm, comforting relationship which was not easily disturbed.

From earliest infancy, the child was a poor sleeper, vomiting when she was put to bed. At the time of referral she had a major sleep problem. She refused to go to bed because she was frightened, and had violent outbursts when she was put in her crib. The birth of a brother when she was two only accentuated her difficulties. She resented him, objected to any time the mother spent with him, and continued to be very aggressive toward him. Always a big eater, food intake became much greater in the year before entering treatment. She would gorge herself until she complained of a stomach-ache, but, nevertheless, continued to demand and obtain bottles of milk or fruit juice. She refused to give up the bottle, saying that she would do so only when her brother no longer had one. This was, of course, one of the factors which created serious battles between the patient and her mother.

In her home, when a child of her own age visited, she would fight with the child and refuse to share toys. Outside of the home, she was fearful of other children, especially boys. There were many complaints of illness, particularly stomach cramps and headaches, but she refused any medication. She was still not toilet-trained at the beginning of her treatment. She would not use the toilet, announcing that when she was three she would do so. This she did after a furious outburst, without provocation, on the day of her third birthday. However, she continued to wet at night for another year.

TREATMENT

Janie had been prepared for treatment by the mother with the explanation that she would have visits with a doctor who would help her with her troubles and her unhappy feelings. When I met her for the first visit, I saw an attractive, appealing child, somewhat overweight, whose initial shyness was quickly overcome. After a tour through my office with her mother, she offered no objection to having the mother return to the waiting room. She then told me that she had "lots of troubles and fits" and that "Mommy said you would help me." I assured her that this was what I wanted to do, that she would come to visit me often and we would find out what made the troubles. It was as though in the first half-hour, this very intelligent, verbal child entered into a therapeutic alliance with me.

She had been told by her mother that I had a dog. Although I warned her that it was a big dog and might come bounding in, she insisted upon seeing the dog anyway, saying "please, please let her come in. I am not afraid of dogs." When the dog entered and moved toward her, she became pale and retreated to a corner of the room, saying, "I'm not afraid." I responded by saying, "I thought you might be—it is such a big dog." Her response was, "Oh no. I'm a roary, roary lion. I can scare anyone," and with that began to make "lion sounds." She then told me to put her in the lion cage, thus designating the leg space of the desk, and had me complete the cage effect by putting a chair on either side. She continued to make roaring noises and from the safe "cage" inspected the dog who was quietly watching her. We then talked about how frightened she really was when she first saw the dog and of her need not to admit this. Thus, in her first session, we saw the defensive reaction of identification with the aggressor, and a hint of the way in which she handled her reaction to her mother who, when angry, was very frightening to Janie.

Within the first week, activity in the sessions turned to seting up mothering situations with the toy animals. She was the good Mommy and she emphasized good care, cuddling, soothing, and comforting. At times the babies would get into dangerous situations, but the mother always rescued them. She frequently announced proudly, "I am a Mommy." At home, she was fighting more intensely with her mother, demanding from her the same treatment given "her babies" in the sessions. The mother, supported by the child's being in treatment, was able to be more patient with her. The father, who was either away on business or working long hours during these early months, became the recipient of the anger which gradually moved away from the mother.

A typical session in the third month of analysis revealed feelings of being closer to the mother, hostility toward the father, and showed some of the realities of the home situation.

She was friendly and smiling as she walked in carrying her own furry toy kitten. She sat at the work table, rocking the kitten in her arms, caressing and soothing it while singing, "go to sleep, little baby" and repeating frequently, "I will take care of you," and saying to me, "I'm the Mommy and I will take care of her."

I said, "Yes. I know that little girls want their mommies to take care of them." "Yes. That's right," she answered. I added, "They are very unhappy and frightened when they think Mommy doesn't take care of them." She said, "My Mommy gets angry." "And you get frightened," I said. She nodded her head in agreement, looked a bit apprehensive, and walked into the adjoining room saying, "Let's do the cage game." She went under the desk with the kitten, a pillow, and a rug, and ordered me to put out the lights so there would not be "even a crack of light." She curled up, saying, "Now I'm going to sleep." She immediately accused my dog of waking her up and then in a softer tone, said, "Your dog has a problem." She continued speaking to the dog saying, "I'll take care of your problems. Don't make a move," putting her arms around the dog and patting her. Then both "slept." In a few minutes, she said, "There are noises. Noises outside. The baby dog is scared," and she held the dog to comfort it. "My Daddy is bad." I repeated, "Bad Daddy." "My Mommy is nice but sometimes she gets mad because I hit my brother." I said, "And you are worried—you were thinking about being frightened by Mommy." She came out from under the desk, turned on the light, nodded her head, looked thoughtfully at me, and said, "My Mommy really is nice." I agreed with her and said, "Mommy really wants to take care of you and make you happy, but she does get angry and you get afraid that something bad will happen." She nodded. I went on, "And then you get angry and have a fit. She allowed the session to be terminated with great reluctance remarking, "I would like to stay much longer." In a reassuring way, I said, "I know. It helps to work on your troubles here." "Yes it does," she said, "You are nice people. You don't get angry." In the waiting room she insisted that her mother finish the story she had been reading to her before the session started, and I observed a warmer attitude on the part of the mother as she complied.

In the following months Janie was in a very complicated situation. She was struggling to establish herself as the comforted, protected, cared-for child with her mother; she kept emphasizing that she, too, would be a good Mommy and talked at great length about having babies of her own. Her anger with her father, who was at that point often physically and emotionally not available to her, was also anxiety-provoking. She was deeply troubled about not having a penis, and fought violently with her brother. Any movement toward the oedipal position elicited anxiety and she returned to oscillating between oral and anal gratifications. Fantasies of fathers who were bad, dangerous to their children, even to the point of eating them, and mothers who were reliable and protective emerged. These were revealed in the "Mrs. Owl Game" which had been in process for weeks in our work, and continued for some months after the following session, taken from the ninth month of treatment.

She told me to get busy, "Don't waste time. Get them ready," referring to the owl and alligator puppets, as well as the large wooden troll she had added. I had to be an active participant because as she had told me many times, "This is very hard work and I'm only a little girl." As soon as the puppets were placed on the table she took command. I was Mr. Alligator and she Mrs. Owl. "You are Mr. Alligator. You are the bad one." Meanwhile she, as Mrs. Owl, was cuddling the tiny cardboard baby owls and feeding them. A cardboard Mr. Owl I had made previously at her direction was thrown off the table. "Mrs. Owl is dead. Mrs. Owl didn't like her husband. He was arguing with her. He was a very bigger man and he said he was bigger and they agreed." She looked at the cardboard Mr. Owl on the floor remarking, "Mrs. Owl said 'I'll throw you in the river,' and she did." She directed me to have Mr. Alligator kidnap the babies while Mrs. Owl was asleep. It had previously been established that Mr. Alligator represented all fathers. Mrs. Owl wakes up, looks for her babies, and cries, "Oh my babies! Where are my babies?" Much distressed, she enlists the aid of Mrs. Troll to find them. They grab Mr. Alligator, "You are very wicked." She then turned to me and said, "He has eaten the babies. They are in his stomach." She shakes them out, takes them home, gives them nursing bottles, saying "Don't worry. Go to sleep. I will take care of you." Mr. Alligator returns and the kidnap and rescue situation is repeated many times. I commented,

"It's safer to make Mr. Alligator the bad Daddy." She nodded and said, "I like my Daddy." "But you are angry with him." Nods, "He works too much. He is cranky." "And you are afraid that he can do bad things," I suggested. "Mommy yells at him, too." I said, "And you and Mommy get angry with Daddy." Nods her agreement. "And when Mommy loves you and takes care of you, you are not afraid," I said. "Yes. I love my Mommy," and then she grabbed Mr. Alligator and bit him. "He is the bad one. Now he has to go to the hospital." But then she bandaged him very tenderly saying, "Now you rest and you'll get better." Finishing the session, she ordered me to write down what we had said, "and we'll do it more tomorrow." It should be noted that she was aware of acting out her own wishes and feelings in the role of Mrs. Owl. In fact, a few days before, as I started to make a comment, she had said, "Don't talk now! I'm not in this today."

Although this child skillfully depicted the activities of the home and fantasies emerged freely in her sessions, the paucity of communication with her parents posed particular problems in the analytic work. For instance, in the first session which I reported, primal scene material was revealed, but it was not until some months later that I learned from the mother that the child had witnessed the primal scene shortly before this particular session. The parents had been greatly distressed over the fact that she had walked into the bedroom while they were having intercourse, but were uncertain about the child's reaction. In my work with Janie, interpretations of the anxiety which the night activities of the parents evoked in her had been rejected flatly, and it was not until almost a year after the first emergence of this material that she was able to undo the repression of the event and verbalize her excitement, the fear of being injured by both parents, and her other distortions of the situation.

In general, I felt that the analysis proceeded more slowly, and perhaps more cautiously on my part, because I had so little knowledge of the realities of this young child's life situation. Because the mother did not report information regarding the daily life activities in the home, I was working under a handicap in not hearing from her comments which children make to their parents about the analysis. Frequently, having acquaintance with the reactions and remarks of a child outside of the analysis is helpful in understanding the significance of particular situations as they arise in the analysis, and even some basic aspects of the analysis. However, the parents' support of the child's dedication to treatment and the child's recognition and acceptance of my function as her analyst, as distinguished from her feelings and thoughts about me as a helper and a friend, enabled the analysis to progress.

Summary

The case of Janie demonstrates that a young child can be analyzed without active participation of the parents so long as they are convinced of the need for analysis. In spite of my doubts about the feasibility of analyzing such a young child under the circumstances, the analysis proceeded and she made real progress (actually the child expressed clearly in some sessions that her mother did not provide proper "mothering"). Janie's ability to recognize the need for help and her immediate involvement with me, as well as her talent for communication, which was perhaps also influenced by her feeling for me, may have made the analysis possible. At this time, Janie's sleep problem has disappeared, she is able to be friendly with children, boys as well as girls, although she still finds it easier to have the children come to her house. There has been a considerable diminution of her tantrums; they are much less violent. She has even managed to elicit tenderness from her mother.

JOHN B. MCDEVITT, M.D.

A Separation Problem in a Three-Year-Old Girl

THE ROLE OF THE MOTHER in the analysis of the child and the mother's relationship to the child analyst have long been an area of concern in the psychoanalysis of children (Burlingham, 1951). The problem becomes more complex when the child, because of its inability to separate from the mother, insists frequently on the mother's being present in the office. Since the primary intention of this paper is to present clinical material and to discuss the advantages and disadvantages of the mother's presence for the treatment, more detailed and general considerations of the developmental and theoretical aspects of the child's infantile neurosis will not be dealt with at this time.

ILLNESS

Becky was an attractive, bright, verbal child, three years and two months old when the analysis was begun. During the previous three months, beginning shortly after the parents had been away for two weekends, she had become in-

From the Yale University Child Study Center, and the Masters Children's Center.

I would like to express my appreciation to Drs. Eleanor Galenson, Elisabeth R. Geleerd, and Margaret S. Mahler for their helpful suggestions and critical comments.

creasingly unhappy, developed a marked fear of separation from her mother, as well as a fear of being bitten by a man with a mustache. She was quite advanced for her age, both physically and intellectually, particularly with regard to her ability to comprehend what was said to her and to communicate verbally. This was in marked contrast with her need to cling to her mother, her demandingness, her sad and anxious expression, her poor sleeping, her continued use of the bottle, and her occasional baby talk. Her fear (expressed verbally, in dreams, and in anxious clinging) that her mother might leave her and not come back disturbed her to a far greater extent than did her fear of being bitten. The threat of a brief separation from her mother was a frequent occurrence, whereas seeing a man with a mustache occurred only rarely. Becky reacted to any threat of separation from her mother by clinging and crying inconsolably and by insisting that her mother remain with her. Her mother, realizing Becky's terror, was sympathetic and concerned, and did not leave her except when it was absolutely necessary. At bedtime, Becky demanded that she be allowed to sleep with or near her mother, or that her mother maintain a constant vigil by her bedside. She awoke frequently during the night and went to her parents' bed.

Becky had enjoyed a close relationship with her father. He was quite attached to her, often caring for her and playing with her, and was vaguely aware of sexual feelings toward her. For more than a year prior to the onset of her illness, she had frequently seen him bathe and use the toilet, and had expressed interest and curiosity. However, shortly before the onset of her illness, a definite change occurred in their relationship. At this time, Becky would become frightened when he expressed anger, or when he rode her on his back or teasingly tickled her in the ribs (experiences she had previously enjoyed with excitement). She could no longer play a game she had formerly played with him, in which she placed a pill in his mouth.

The parents' trips were precipitating events at this stage in Becky's development, when her father's behavior had become too stimulating and too frightening. The heightened oedipal wishes and penis envy were experienced as dangerous, and the intensity of her conflicts resulted in symptom formation and regressive behavior.

Becky's phobic illness was characteristic for a child of her age, who is in the phallic and early oedipal phase. The oedipal attachment to her father was frightening, both because her fantasy of the sexual relationship with him was a sadistic one, in which she imagined herself being attacked and hurt, and because it brought her into rivalry with her ambivalently loved mother and led to death wishes against the mother.

As a consequence of her phallic and oedipal conflicts, along with her sibling rivalry with a sister two years and four months younger (less so with an older stepsister), there was a partial regression to the oral-sadistic and the anal-sadistic phases, expressed in her infantile behavior and symptom formation.

The analysis revealed that the fear of being bitten by a man who wore a mustache expressed Becky's fear of her father, with the pubic hair displaced upward. There were two sources for this fear. On the one hand, the wished-for but feared sexual attack by the father was experienced regressively as the fear of being bitten by him. On the other hand, the oral-sadistic impulses directed toward her father's penis, which stemmed from her intense penis envy, were projected and displaced, thus also contributing to her fear of being bitten by a man.

The intensity of the penis envy, the root of much of Becky's problem, resulted from: early disappointments in the mother-child relationship; oral and narcissistic fixations and subsequent regression; the frequent observation of the father's penis; and the wish to succeed as a rival to her father and her siblings for her mother's love, as well as the need to assume a masculine role, in defense against the feminine wishes that were so frightening to her.

Becky's terror of being bitten by a mustached man shifted after several months of treatment to a fear of being bitten by a witch. Fear of the witch, or the phallic mother, was the result of the projection and displacement of oral-sadistic impulses, directed, this time, against the mother. Finally, Becky's dread of being abandoned by her mother was one consequence of the death wishes she directed toward an ambivalently loved mother, along with the complementary need for her mother's protection against the man with a mustache, or the witch. The extent of the aggression directed toward the mother resulted, on the one hand, from the highly charged oedipal situation (as well as her resentment over the lack of a penis, and the attention paid to her siblings); on the other hand, it had its roots in the disturbed mother-child interaction that had been characteristic of the entire pre-oedipal phase.

In the interest of clarity, the use of the descriptive term "separation anxiety" will be limited to those phase-specific reactions of anxiety on separation from the mother during the first three years of life, at which time the child is learning to cope with, and to master by various means, the usual and routine experiences of separation from the mother. Although disturbances and a subsequent regression in this line of Becky's development were predisposing and contributing factors, the fear of being abandoned by her mother, which developed shortly before she was three years old, was a neurotic symptom, resulting primarily from the death wishes directed toward the mother. What was once a developmentally appropriate external danger (it was exaggerated, in Becky's case)—the fear of being left by her mother and of the consequent state of helplessness—had now become an internal danger—the dread of being abandoned as a result of her death wishes. However, Becky continued to experience the danger as if it were an external danger. Although it would be possible to make a distinction between these phase-specific reactions to separation by the use of the terms "developmental separation anxiety" and "neurotic separation anxiety," in the report on the clinical material, Becky's fear will simply be described, and the use of the term "separation anxiety" will be avoided. It should be stressed at this point that any reference to separation in this communication refers to the everyday separations that occur in the ordinary mother-child relationship.

History[1]

From birth onward, Becky had had a difficult relationship with her mother. According to the mother, they had gotten off to a bad start because, as an infant, Becky cried frequently, was tense, slept poorly, and was difficult to comfort. The mother, an intelligent, well-educated, shy young woman, had been torn between her wish to have a professional career and her duty to Becky. She was unprepared for and resented the demands her infant daughter made upon her. She felt unhappy and inadequate as a mother and, as Becky grew older, there ensued mutual provocation, conflict, and struggle between them. Often the mother eventually exploded in anger, at times hitting Becky; more often, she simply withdrew from the child, both emotionally and physically. Withdraw-

---

[1] For the purposes of this presentation, the family and developmental history have been considerably abbreviated.

ing was her characteristic manner of handling her anger. She
would turn away from Becky, often going into another room,
and would become unavailable and unresponsive to her.

During the first six months of her life, Becky showed a
marked startle reaction to the slightest noise. She had frequent bouts of abdominal pain, which would cause her to cry
for ten to fifteen minutes; she would frequently wake in tears
and could not be comforted. She never seemed satisfied or
able to relax, so that both mother and child were tense and
uncomfortable, in effect maintaining a vicious cycle.

At about eight months, prolonged infantile separation anxiety appeared. From then on Becky was sober-faced, hesitant,
and cautious in her approach to adults and children. She became a sensitive and anxious child, closely tied to her mother
in a highly ambivalent relationship, with much more than
the usual (although a variable) amount of separation anxiety.
By contrast, there was never any difficulty in the mother's
relationship with her younger daughter, who was an easy
child to care for and showed no subsequent difficulties in her
early development.

In the middle of her second year, following a trip to Eu-
rope with her parents, during which time she was left with
baby-sitters on several occasions, and coinciding with the
mother's pregnancy, Becky's separation anxiety, which had
by now subsided somewhat, again became acute. She developed a severe separation and sleep disturbance which
lasted for several months. The mother did not feel well during the early months of her pregnancy; she was dissatisfied
with her relationship with Becky, and became somewhat
withdrawn and depressed. Becky would alternately cling to
and run away provocatively from her mother. In the park,
she would either stay by her mother's side, or else would provoke her attention by hitting other children, eating sand, or

running out to the street. This need to tease and provoke the mother (in order to get her attention and to express anger) and the mother's reaction (of anger, hitting, and withdrawal), along with an even earlier struggle with the mother over eating, were early forerunners and one determinant of Becky's subsequent sadomasochistic impression of the primal scene, and contributed to a sexualization both of danger situations (to be attacked, to be deserted) and of the reaction of anxiety to these danger situations.

During this time, almost in despair, the mother turned the care of the child over to a maid. The pediatrician advised that the bottle, which Becky had just given up, be returned to her at night; that the parents should let her cry at night, no matter how long the crying lasted; and that the mother should go out during the day, leaving Becky with the maid, no matter how unhappy Becky was. All of this was painful to the mother and, in retrospect, she wondered how she could have followed this advice. Gradually, the sleep and separation problems subsided but never completely went away.

It seems reasonable to assume that Becky reacted to these changes, the mother's withdrawal and the introduction of the maid, especially at this time in her life, with an increase in her aggressive feelings toward her mother and by feeling both unloved and uncertain of her mother's love, with a consequent doubt regarding her mother's emotional availability and a lowering of her beginning self-esteem and self-assurance. These reactions, in turn, would tend to increase her symbiotic tie to her mother, and to diminish her trend toward individuation and object constancy.

Both parents had always had difficulty with the everyday experience of leaving Becky. The mother, in order to avoid her own guilt as well as Becky's crying, would leave when Becky was asleep or "when her back was turned," thus avoiding the pain of separation. The father's overconcern about his daughter's welfare reached its height when they parted. At such times, he would repeatedly warn Becky and her mother of the many dangers that might befall the child, such as a car jumping the curb and hitting her. Thus the parents' ambivalence was at its peak at the time of the everyday experiences of separation from Becky. Not only, by their attitude and behavior, did they increase her feeling that separation was dangerous, but, more important, they were unable to help Becky to face directly and to cope with the usual separation experiences. Both parents had unresolved separation problems, which were mobilized anew by the act of separating from Becky and by Becky's separation anxiety. Their attitude and behavior with regard to separation repeated both the attitudes and behavior of their own parents and their own experiences with separation during their childhood. The mother had had many fears as a child, and the father had suffered from a severe phobia prior to the onset of Becky's illness. During latency, he had had the fear that his parents would leave him and would never come back.

During her third year, prior to the onset of her illness, Becky's development proceeded more satisfactorily, probably as a result of her attachment to the maid, of some lessening of the conflict with her mother, and of her precocious, in part defensive, intellectual advance. Although she was still quite shy, the separation anxiety had become less severe.

The following information will complete this brief report of the developmental history. From the age of nine months on, there had been a mild struggle between Becky and her mother because of Becky's finicky eating habits. She received a bottle at night until she was three and a half years old. When she was tired or anxious, as well as at bedtime, she would suck the thumb of her right hand, at the same time fingering a diaper (which was a constant companion) with the other hand. The mother could recall no difficulty with bowel training, which was begun when Becky was a little over two years old and successfully completed within a few months. Becky continued to wet the bed at night until she was four and a half years old. Occasional masturbation was first noticed when she was two years old. The parents had no reason to believe that Becky had at any time witnessed their sexual relations. Following a brief negative reaction to the birth of her sister, Becky had been quite considerate of her, up to the point when she began treatment, at which time her marked jealousy became apparent.

TREATMENT

The purpose of this section of the paper is to give a picture of the first ten months of Becky's treatment and to indicate some of the changes which occurred in her during this time; to discuss the reasons for the mother's frequent presence in the office, and to illustrate some of the effects of the mother's presence on the analysis; and to present, in some detail, three analytic hours.

Becky's analysis was complicated by the fact that she was frequently unable to separate from her mother. She would either have to go to the waiting room several times during the hour, or would insist that the mother remain with her for part or all of the hour. As the treatment progressed, she was able to spend more time in the office without her mother, but the situation could change quite abruptly, depending upon events that occurred either outside or within the analysis.

For example, she would cling to her mother if they had had a fight, if she was overly anxious, if she was ill, or if there had been an actual or threatened separation. At such times, she could not let her mother go and became excessively pleasant and overly considerate toward her. By contrast, she would either ignore me or else attack me or my possessions by messing, throwing, breaking, or hitting. In attacking me, she could both safely express her anger without threatening the ambivalently loved mother and avoid the fear of retaliation of being left by her mother. Her anger was handled by displacement (onto the analyst who, as the result of projection, represented the "bad mother") and by reaction formation. At other times, when Becky felt relatively well, she was able to spend the whole hour without her mother—unless sufficient anxiety was aroused in the analysis, at which times she would again have to turn to her mother. When I represented the mother in play, once the aggression toward me became too intense, she would have to turn to her mother. Or, if the attachment to me, either as a substitute good mother or as the father, became too strong, she would have to return to her mother because of her conflict of loyalty. Or, finally, when her penis envy outweighed her affection, or her masochistic provocation became too frightening, she would once again have to turn back to her mother.

The major themes at the beginning of Becky's analysis, and throughout it, were the jealousy toward the younger sister, the penis envy, the fear of the man, the close ambivalent tie to the mother, and the frequent provocative behavior. She soon became aware of the intense jealousy she felt toward her sister, and began to fight with her at home. Her penis envy was expressed in concern about cuts on the girl doll, which she covered with many Band-Aids, and by a wish to bite off the leg of the male doll and to tear off his penis. On several occasions, she became terrified on seeing a male patient leave the office; she mistakenly thought that he had a mustache and told me that she was glad that neither I nor her father had a mustache. The oedipal theme was soon apparent in her play. After a number of occasions of playing house, or caring for the doll children and fixing dinner for me as the home-coming father, during one hour Becky wanted to go to bed with me on the couch. However, she insisted suddenly that her mother join her in the office, expressing the already familiar fear that her mother would leave her. Once her mother was present, Becky ignored me in favor of exclusive play with her mother.

Whenever Becky behaved provocatively, by messing, or throwing, or jumping on the couch and threatening in a teasing manner to knock the picture off the wall, it was often difficult to know to what extent her behavior was the expression of anger and to what extent it expressed a wish for me to respond to what she was doing, to stop her physically. If I represented the "bad mother," the anger was predominant; if I represented the father, teasing was uppermost.

The mother's presence, on a number of occasions, provided me with additional knowledge and a better understanding of events prior to Becky's illness. During one hour, Becky was playing house and running the toy vacuum cleaner. I made an accompanying buzzing noise, which frightened her so that she ran to her mother in the waiting room. I then learned from the mother that a similar buzzing noise had been made by the father while tickling Becky in the ribs, and that, shortly before the onset of her illness, she had rejected this game completely. When we returned to the office, she indicated that she wanted me to tickle her, but she was afraid. It might be noted here that, during this period of the analysis, on occasion Becky would openly masturbate in the office.

A similar incident occurred when she was playing doctor. She hesitated to look into my throat, fearing that I would bite her. After moving closer to her mother for protection and listening to my explanation of the reason for her fear, she was able to examine my throat. I explained to Becky, as I had done previously, that it was she who wanted to bite me and that, in turn, she was afraid that I would bite her. She was pleased with her accomplishment. During the course of this session, I learned from the mother that Becky had formerly played a related game with her father. Before swallowing a pill, he would drop it from his mouth into her hand, and she would then place it in his mouth. She had begun to withdraw her hand prior to the onset of her illness; soon after, she would not play the game at all.

After several months of treatment, Becky's fear of a man with a mustache had almost disappeared, and she could tolerate more easily brief separations from her mother. At this time Becky was enrolled in nursery school, where she had the occasion to see the small boys urinate. However, she was able to stay for only a brief time, because of her extreme anxiety, which caused her to cling to her mother. As a result of this brief nursery school experience, there was now a marked increase in her penis envy, in her enuresis, in her anger toward her mother, and in her separation problem. Insisting that she had a penis, she would stand up in order to urinate. Otherwise, in her manner and play, she behaved like a little girl, and showed no other tendency to imitate or identify with boys. In the analysis, she wanted to cut off the male doll's penis and to put it on herself, and to cut off and bite off my finger. The increase in her enuresis was caused by the heightened penis envy and the accompanying anger toward her mother. Invariably, like a barometer, whenever anything occurred to stir up Becky's penis envy, her enuresis became worse. (Additional, although less important, determinants of the enuresis at other times were sexual excitement and

envy of her younger sister.) The fear of being left by her
mother had returned in full force, and Becky constantly demanded her mother's presence. The main reasons for the increased separation problem were her intense anger toward
her mother for not having provided her with a penis and for
having planned to leave her at nursery school.[2] Becky was preoccupied with her anger toward her mother, and again
handled it by displacing the anger onto me. Repeatedly she
would punish me, deprive me, and leave me in play, while
in a very transparent manner she was overly nice to her
mother, assuring her that she felt no anger toward her, only
love. It was during this time, after seeing *The Wizard of Oz,*
that Becky developed the fear of a witch.

By the eighth month of the analysis, the fear of the witch,
the penis envy, and the fear of her mother's leaving her had
diminished considerably. Becky no longer needed to insist
that she possessed a penis, nor was she any longer as castrating
toward me in her play. There were times when she was glad
to be a girl, and would brag about a bracelet or a pair of red
shoes. This change in attitude had come about gradually. For
the first time, she was able to state clearly, without confusion
or dissatisfaction, that she was a girl, that she was happy to
be a girl, and that she realized that she did not have a penis
but instead a clitoris. She now began to express a wish to have
a baby. On one occasion, when she was playing mother to a
baby doll, she asked if she might take the doll home with her.
She explained that she had told her Mommy that she wanted
to have a baby, but her Mommy had said that it would be
many years before she would be able to. She said that she did
not want to wait that long and asked could she please take the

---

[2] Although it was not clearly discernible in the analytic material, it is also
possible that Becky's concern over having "lost" her penis might have increased
her concern over losing her mother.

baby home with her. She was happy when I allowed her to do so. During this time, she talked of wanting to go to school, no longer competed with her younger sister by behaving like an infant, and was able to permit her parents to go out in the evenings. However, the situation would frequently change— often abruptly—with periods of progress followed by periods of regression, in a back-and-forth manner.

We might illustrate some of the above by reporting in more detail the following analytic session:

In several previous hours Becky had sucked her thumb and in-sisted that her mother remain with her (the parents had been out for several nights in succession; following one such night, Becky had awakened at 1 a.m. and could not go back to sleep until 4 a.m.). Today, in contrast, Becky was very alert, alive, and some-what elated. When I went to the waiting room, she did not want me to look at her, her candy, or her toy bird. However, she soon became friendly, led me into the office, offered me candy, showed me the bird's hurt mouth, and the number of teeth she, Becky, now had. She then went to the bathroom to make "peepee," in-viting me to accompany her and to stand beside her. I politely refused the invitation.

When she returned, she chose to play with the "Visible Man" (a plastic toy man with the internal organs visible). This play led to a discussion of the man's penis. While she was playing, I reminded her of how she used to see her father's penis when she went to the bathroom with him. Without hesitation, she told me that she still sometimes saw his penis when he was lying in bed. At first she indicated, using her hands, that it was ten to twelve inches long, but then gradually brought her hands closer together to indicate that it was only several inches long. She then said that he did not want her (or her mother) to look at it; he was afraid, she said, that someone might take it away from him. Becky went on to describe the plan of the witch in *The Wizard of Oz*, to cap-ture Dorothy's dog. She thought the witch should not have done that. I responded by saying, "Do you remember how often you wanted to bite and take the boy doll's penis away from him and to have it for yourself, and how you were once afraid that a man might bite you? Maybe when you went to the bathroom with your father, you wanted to take his penis, too, but now you are thinking that you should not want to do that."[3] This interpretation must have aroused some anxiety because Becky then went out to have a brief talk with her mother about the witch. On returning, she excitedly described a television program in which a boy and a girl take a bubble bath together. I pointed out to her the excitement she experienced when she described the boy and girl looking at each other and said, "When I came into the waiting room today, as on so many other days, you didn't want me to look at you or your toys, but later you showed me your toy bird, your mouth, and even wanted me to stand by you when you went 'peepee.' Didn't you like the way you looked, or were you afraid? And did you then change your mind?" Instead of answering me directly, Becky asked me to write my name and then wrote her name. Following this, she asked me if she could take home with her a hollow toy plastic egg to put the doll baby in so that it could grow. On leaving, she told her mother that the baby's name was Johnny (both the name of her analyst and the name of a boy friend whom she envied).

In this hour, along with the abundant primal scene material, we see Becky's wish to have a baby by the analyst, alongside the wish to be a boy and to own a penis. Because of the trend of the material in previous sessions, I selected on this occasion to stress Becky's wish to take her father's penis and her fear of his retaliation, knowing that the other material could be dealt with as it came up again in its proper context. As Becky's analysis proceeded, and as more abundant material—both from the side of the drives and of the ego—became available in the sessions, the essential analytic task was to select what was appropriate to discuss with Becky at any given time.

[3] In recording the analytic hours, no verbatim records of interpretations were made. In this and subsequent quotes I have attempted, for the purposes of this presentation, to approximate as closely as possible what was actually said.

In the hour just reported, we saw not only the fear of father's retaliation for the wish to take his penis, but also the fear of mother's retaliation for the same wish—the plan of the witch (mother) to take Dorothy's (Becky's) dog. Thus, the seemingly different strivings—to take father's penis, to take father, to get a baby from father—were so closely related and indistinguishable that they were all equally punishable by mother.

In a subsequent hour, Becky playfully stuck an apple under her skirt, at first in front and then in back, and said that she had an "apple baby, an apple 'boomy' and an apple penis." Thus, in her play, according to the primary process, penis, feces, and baby were equated. Although there had been a slow shift from the insistence that she had a penis to the acceptance that she had a clitoris and to the wish to have a baby, it was striking, during this phase of the analysis, how the two wishes —the one for a baby, the other for a penis—existed side by side and would come up alternately in the material. Similarly, Becky continued to act at times as if she had a penis—that is, the presence and the absence of the penis were also able to exist side by side and to come up alternately in the material.

During another hour, after playfully attaching a penis to herself. Becky licked the boy doll's buttocks, announced that she was going to have a baby, and went to the bathroom to make "boomy." In play, she then laid an egg, which was supposed to be her baby. Upon questioning, she declared that the baby's father was her father, and that her mother "didn't think that was so good," expressing in this manner her positive oedipal wishes.

As the intensity of her penis envy waned, and Becky's wish for a baby increased, she became more affectionate toward me, and was often able to spend the whole hour without her mother. She brought increasing amounts of oedipal material to the sessions, with a clear sadomasochistic coloring. In her play, she loved me and became engaged to her father and to me; she wanted to have a baby by me, whom she could spank. After an incident of being spanked by her father for sticking her finger in her sister's eye, Becky tried to provoke me by asking that I spank her "hard." On still another occasion, stimulated by a jealous reaction to a woman patient, Becky's picture of the primal scene evolved. She imagined it as consisting of undressing, kissing, spanking, wetting, biting, etc., sometimes with the sexual roles reversed.

However, as each new topic came up in the analysis, the ambivalent feelings toward the mother had to be dealt with anew. Thus, Becky could not always stay with me for a whole hour, because she did not seem to know what to do about her mother. She was compelled at times to invite her mother into the office, where she treated her with excessive kindness. When playing house, she often imagined two mothers (herself and a doll representing her mother), in order that her mother should not be excluded. Although Becky enjoyed winning when she played simple games with me, in playing with her mother she seemed uncertain who should go first, or who should win. In addition, at times she reversed roles with her mother in play—Becky acting the mother, and treating the mother as if she were the child.

In order to explain to Becky the fact of her competitiveness and her ambivalence toward her mother, I told her that she did not know whether to hit her mother or to hug her, to win the game or to lose it, to take the first or the second turn, to be the mother or the child. Becky's mother was helpful at such times in her assurances to Becky that she understood her competitiveness and her anger.

Another way in which Becky handled her many problems (the masochistic fear of the father, the penis envy, and the ambivalence toward the mother) was to reverse the sexual roles in complicated ways. During one hour she threw the boy doll to the fish (to be eaten), then shot him with a gun; she loved the girl doll and then me; finally she stuck her finger in my eye. Suddenly she became afraid that a witch might punch her mother in the eye, and she ran to the waiting room to check on her mother's safety and to leave a gun for her protection. Spreading her legs apart, she demonstrated how she intended to attach a penis to herself, advising her mother to do the same.

In this sequence, we see evidence of the negative oedipal strivings which mobilized the wish to possess a penis. The strong sadistic component expressed the identification with the male as the aggressor, the envy of the man and the anger with him, and the sexual aggression directed toward the mother. However, it was her concern for her mother that led Becky to advise her to obtain a penis for protection. Although it is phase-specific, the negative oedipal complex is exaggerated in Becky's case, because of the intensity of her penis envy and her fear of the feminine role. Along with my interpretations, in this instance too, the mother was helpful in explaining to Becky that she herself was not afraid of being a girl, that she liked being a girl, and that she hoped Becky would also.

There was a somewhat similar emphasis in theme during another hour, which proceeded as follows:

As soon as Becky arrived in the office, she resumed her play at a fishing game which had occupied us for many previous sessions. The essential theme of the game was that we had to be very careful, while fishing, not to get into the water, because if we did the fish would bite us. After briefly cuddling with the boy doll, she called the boy doll the girl, and vice versa; then, in anger, she attacked the boy doll's penis, punched him in the eye, and threw him in the water, wanting to do the same to me. While cuddling with the girl doll, she suddenly decided to go to her mother in the waiting room. For a moment she nuzzled up to her mother, then, intending to say that she wanted her mother to come into the office, she said instead that she wanted her mother to die. Her clear awareness of the slip permitted me to say, "Becky, I know that little girls frequently get so angry with their Mommies that they want them to die. You are angry with Mommy and want her to die because you are unhappy and angry that you are a girl and do not have a penis; you blame Mommy because you think she did not give you a penis." Becky listened, but without response, and she did not react when her mother told her that she, too, understood how Becky felt, and that it was all right for Becky to be angry with her. Becky's first words were to demand that her mother come into the office.

Here she spent the bulk of the remaining time in overbearing and annoying care of her mother. While this was going on, I tried to tell her, "Becky, you are being so nice to Mommy because you are afraid that your anger will cause Mommy to die. But you need not worry, your angry thoughts and feelings can not cause Mommy to die." Nevertheless, Becky persisted in being preoccupied with excessive care of her mother, which clearly expressed her underlying anger. Becky would not permit her mother to read a magazine she had brought with her from the waiting room. Instead, she repeatedly offered her mother other things to read, suggested that she might be more comfortable in another position, and in general was most annoying. At no time did she indicate that she wanted her mother to read to her. Finally, I said to Becky, "You are trying to be so nice to Mommy and to prove to her that you are not angry with her, but everything you do is annoying and makes her uncomfortable. You get in her way and you give her other things to read, even though she is quite happy with what she is reading. You must still be quite angry with Mommy." While "taking care of" her mother, Becky stumbled several times and almost fell, indicating her need to punish herself.

Becky's anger disappeared and she became more relaxed and cheerful toward the end of the hour. She was able to let her mother return to the waiting room. She then took a children's book and pretended to read to me a long, garbled and confused story about Peter Rabbit and Peter Pan, about Peter Rabbit throwing something at Peter Pan and so chasing him away, and Peter Rabbit crying when he saw his mother in the window.

In the hour described above, drawing on both the content and the context in which it occurred, I tried to help Becky understand her anger toward her mother, as a result of her penis envy. I also attempted to reassure her, as did her mother, that she need not be so frightened of her angry feelings, that they were not dangerous. And, finally, I pointed out to Becky that because of her fears she had to handle her anger by the use of the mechanism of reaction formation.

In contrast to the hour above is one that occurred somewhat later in Becky's treatment, during a period when she felt better, was in less conflict with her mother, and could accept the feminine role more easily:

When I entered the waiting room, I found that Becky had torn up a magazine because she was jealous of a female patient who had just left. She sat on her mother's lap, thumb in mouth, and wanted her mother to carry her into the office. She told me that she had been swimming. When I told Becky that the dolls would like to hear about her swim, she immediately came into the office, with no further mention of her mother.

With the help of the dolls, Becky was able to speak of how she hated the "stupid lady" who had just left. She said that we had spanked each other, and that the lady had spanked me on the head (Becky's primal scene fantasy). Abruptly Becky decided to stick her right index finger into her right eye, asking me then to repeat the action. While talking with her about her wish for me to stick my finger into her eye, I reminded her of her recent desire to have me spank her. However, in the process of talking, I moved my right arm, and suddenly Becky became frightened. She covered her eye and drew back from me. "Do you remember," I took the opportunity to ask, "how frightened you became, just before you got your fear of the man with the mustache, when your father wanted to tickle you with his finger? And do you remember how before that you liked to have your father tickle you?" Becky then wanted to be tickled. I asked her whether she remembered having told me recently that she used her finger to tickle her genital. She agreed that she did, with a brief demonstration, and immediately had to go to the bathroom to make "boomy." This need reminded us both of the fact that she had recently mentioned a desire for a baby, and then had gone to the bathroom. When she returned, I said to her, "Becky, you seem to want me to put something like my finger into your vagina so that you can have a baby, but wanting me to do that frightens you, just as being tickled by your father frightened you, and just as men with mustaches frightened you." (By now Becky knew, at least intellectually, about impregnation and childbirth. She had been given explanations by her mother and me in connection with the pregnant "Visible Woman." This figure makes visible all female internal organs, including the uterus containing the fetus.) As we continued talking, Becky corrected me on one aspect of her sexual views. In referring to making "peepee" and "boomy," and to putting her finger in her vagina, she informed me that it felt best of all to put her finger in her "boomy" hole (thus referring to her cloacal fantasy).

At this point, Becky shifted back to her identification with the male. She decided to pretend that she was a boy named Johnny, and that the boy doll would represent herself. "You know, Becky," I told her, "I think you want to play that you are a boy because you are so frightened to be a girl and to have a baby. You are afraid that you will be hurt." Becky agreed with this, saying that she wanted to be a boy and have a penis, but that she also wanted to have a baby. She showed the boy doll that she had a large Daddy penis by inscribing an oval shape with her hand. The boy doll answered Becky by saying, "I don't think you really have a penis, but it looks like you want both a Daddy penis and a baby, and you want to get both of them from your Daddy."

This led to a discussion about where babies come from. At first, in all sincerity, Becky informed me that babies were bought in the hospital, then brought home. I answered her by saying, "We've talked so many times about where babies come from, and Mary (the maid) is so big now that you must know that her baby is inside her. I think that you are afraid to remember how babies get started and how they are born." Becky then recalled that the baby grows in the mother and comes out through the vagina. From this we considered the Daddy's role, including the fact that the Daddy places the seed in the mother.

Throughout our talk Becky played that she was the boy, Johnny, while building a small structure out of dominoes. At the end of the hour she asked her mother to come in and see it, and only at that point did I learn from her mother that the previous night Becky had hit her sister and had in turn been hit by her father.

During the month preceding this hour, Becky brought an increasingly large amount of primal scene material to the analytic sessions. In her play, she was attached to me and to her father. She repeatedly expressed the wish to have a baby. She wanted to see and to touch the penis and to expose herself. She touched her genitalia frequently, and the mother reported that she had observed Becky examine her vagina and had heard her speak of putting objects in the vagina, including a penis. Becky told me that porcupines could shoot you with "things" that burned like a match. As I questioned her, she asked me to put my finger on her knee and at the same time spread her legs apart. At home she mothered her sister and liked to get into bed with her father. She seemed to understand my explanation that she felt guilty and was afraid of her mother because she wanted to be father's wife and to have a baby by him. She told me that she was no longer afraid that her mother would leave her.

At times Becky was very friendly when she was with me. On some of these occasions she would gently fondle the boy doll's penis (similar to the way in which she would sometimes fondle her father's leg). More often she attempted by various means to provoke me into physically restraining, spanking, or attacking her. At these time she was more likely to attack the boy doll's penis aggressively. This difference

in her behavior depended on her mood, particularly on the
intensity of her aggressive feelings (seemingly irrespective of
the reason for these feelings, e.g., disappointments, frustrations, penis envy, sibling rivalry, etc.) and, more particularly,
on the amount of aggression currently present in her sadomasochistic primal scene fantasies. Just as she frequently
provoked me, she occasionally provoked her father, as she
did on the night prior to the hour reported on above. Thus,
the primal scene fantasy which she continually expressed in
the analysis occasionally broke through in her behavior at
home with her father. Having actually been hit by him further excited her and led to a more direct expression of the
wish to be sexually attacked by me in the hour, as it had on
a previous occasion when Becky, following a spanking by her
father, had asked me to spank her "hard." In this session I
attempted to make clear to Becky the connections between
the oedipal (and primal scene) fantasies and wishes; the fear
of these wishes (to have me stick my finger in her, to be
tickled by her father, and to be attacked by a man with a mustache); and her defensive handling of these fears by pretending to be a boy (one of her reasons, a defensive one, for her
wish to be a boy), as well as by temporarily forgetting facts
that she knew about impregnation and childbirth. In order
to help her understand her relationship with her father, it
was of particular importance to take up with Becky repeatedly her reactions to frequent observations of her father's penis.

During the remaining month of the ten months of clinical
material reported on in this paper, the themes of the hour
just referred to reappeared in many sessions. The mother
reported that Becky asked fewer questions about witches and
instead asked numerous questions about traffic—about cars
bumping into each other, about the noise, about the angry
drivers (again expressing her primal scene fantasies). During

her hours in the office, she not only stuck her finger in her eye, but also put the boy doll's penis first in her eye, and then in her mouth, complaining that it burned. I learned from the mother that this incident recaptured an experience of many months before, when Becky's father had put iodine on her cut finger. Despite the fact that Becky had become more aware of her fears and their meaning, she often continued, defensively, to reverse the sexual roles by threatening to put a burning medicine on the boy doll's penis and change into a frightening witch. Doing so not only would protect her, by way of identification with the aggressor, from her own anger projected onto the phallic mother, but would also, as we have seen, protect her from the fantasied sexual attack which was part of her primal scene fantasy.

At home, during the months of the analysis reported on, Becky continued to be in constant conflict with her mother. The reaction formation and the displacement of her anger occurred only during the analytic sessions. At other times her anger toward her mother was openly expressed in provocative behavior, which resulted in many scenes. The mother was conscientious and well-intentioned but, as a consequence of her ambivalence and guilt, she was not able to be firm and consistent in her handling of Becky. She would permit the situation to develop to a point where she would either explode in anger, fighting with Becky on a childish level, or else withdraw both physically and emotionally, going into another room and ignoring Becky. Although she was sympathetic to Becky's fears and the separation problem, she found Becky's clinging and demanding behavior difficult to cope with. As I shall indicate below, my observations of Becky and her mother together confirmed the mother's report, gave me an increased understanding of their relationship, and enabled me to offer some help to the mother.

With her father, Becky was more reasonable and well-be-haved: she only occasionally provoked him or expressed anger toward him, but she was more likely to feel hurt and to with-draw in tears when he scolded her or punished her. When she was feeling better and was in less conflict with her mother, Becky could express her preference for her father. She then relegated mother and sister to the back seat of the car, so that she could ride beside her father. The oedipal and castrative wishes, so openly expressed in the analysis, seem not to have been acted on at home, or, if so, in an occasional, more subtle and playful manner. The father followed the advice given him not to allow Becky to see him naked, but there is reason to believe that his seductive and exhibitionistic behavior con-tinued, even though unconsciously, in more subtle ways. In spite of the fact that the clinical material was replete with references to the primal scene, there was no indication from the parents' reports that Becky had at any time observed their sexual relations. Although I attempted on a number of oc-casions to inquire of Becky what she might have seen, again I could obtain no material relating to actual primal scene ob-servations.

Away from home, Becky was a shy, demanding, and jealous girl, difficult to please or to satisfy. She was ill at ease on meet-ing adults; in the park, she found it almost impossible to play with other children. Although she was intrigued with boys from an early age, she could seldom bring herself to play with a boy friend whom she both admired and envied.

At the end of the first ten months of the treatment, Becky's fears of being bitten by a man or by a witch had disappeared, she was more tolerant of the usual separations from her mother, she had reluctantly accepted the fact that she was a girl and did not have a penis, and she had taken the matura-tional step forward of developing the wish for a baby, which was expressed simultaneously with the wish for a penis. Although she continued to be apprehensive about her oedipal and primal scene fantasies, she was able to express them more openly. The most difficult problem for her to deal with continued to be her anger toward her mother. As we have seen, although she constantly expressed this anger at home in her behavior, from the onset of her treatment she had to protect herself from the conscious awareness of her anger by displacing it, by reaction formation, by clinging to her mother, etc. Each new development in the analysis which mobilized or threatened to make conscious her anger was followed by heightened defensive activity. It was several more months, following an enjoyable summer vacation, before Becky was able for the first time to openly and directly say to me that she was angry with her mother. Even then, as we began our work again, she had to retreat partially from this position. (I doubt if the issue was ever fully resolved in the analysis. Possibly, in a situation such as this, it cannot be, because of the young child's continued, almost complete, dependence on the mother.)

As would be expected, the themes already presented occupied the remaining one and one half years of Becky's analysis. By then she had improved considerably; she was free of symptoms, although she remained prone to a reactivation of the separation problem when under stress. Certain character traits which were primarily related to her penis envy persisted, such as envy, jealousy, and a tendency to be dissatisfied with herself or her efforts. She handled these feelings by projection ("You are the stupid one!"), by identification with the aggressor, and to some extent by denial. On entering latency, as well as for reality reasons, she became less tolerant of the analytic work and developed a strong need to be "grown up" and to "work out her problems by herself." Although a sign of growing up, this need also expressed her masculine identification.

The most difficult hurdle for her to overcome prior to the termination of treatment was attending nursery school when she was four and one half years old. Her mother had to remain with her for months, both in nursery school and in the analysis. The child's need to cling to her mother at this stage in the analysis almost disrupted the analytic work. Subsequently, Becky slowly managed to make a fairly good adjustment to school, to classmates, and friends. At home she became much easier to get along with. Following the acute phase of her illness, she was able once again to engage in active and constructive imaginative play at home—e.g., with dolls—as she had been able to do prior to the onset of her neurosis. In the analysis, her play was sometimes similar to that of a child playing in nursery school. Although some elements of resistance were evident in this play, it seemed for the most part to represent a step forward. Most important, she became less closely tied to her mother and could turn her energies and interests to satisfying relationships with other adults and children.

DISCUSSION

As a rule, young children with a separation problem are able, after a brief period, to continue their analysis without the frequent presence of the mother in the office. Because of her marked inability to separate from her mother, this was not possible for Becky. Before proceeding to consider the influence of the mother's frequent presence on this analysis, let us briefly examine the reasons for the particular severity of Becky's separation problem.

At the time of the onset of her illness, just before she was three, Becky's inability to separate from her mother was a neurotic symptom, the result primarily of the ambivalent tie to the mother during the early oedipal phase. Her wish was to dispense with both mother and sisters and thus to have father to herself; she wanted to have a sadomasochistic relationship with father, to get both a penis and a baby from him. At the same time, she had the fear that, as a result of her death wishes directed toward her mother, her mother would leave her and would never come back. She also needed her mother's presence to protect her from the man with the mustache and the witch.

We must, however, consider other interrelated factors that predisposed and contributed to the severity of the separation problem. First, as we have seen, Becky had had a highly ambivalent relationship with her mother from the earliest months of life. The extent of the aggression directed toward the mother, and the sexualization of danger situations and of anxiety, both originating in this disturbed mother-child interaction, intensified the conflicts of the phallic-oedipal phase and thus contributed to symptom formation. Second, also as a consequence of the disturbed mother-child relationship, Becky had found it difficult to loosen the symbiotic ties to her mother and to reach the level of object constancy. Third, because of the parents' attitude and behavior at the time of the usual separation experiences, Becky was deprived of the opportunity to learn that separation need not be dangerous. At the same time, Becky was not helped by her parents in the task of mastering separation and separation anxiety. She had had an excessive amount of separation anxiety during her first and second years. She had not acquired adequate means for dealing with the usual separation experiences. These means would include those aspects of ego development which make separation possible. In particular, one would think of the neutralization of aggression, which furthers the develop-

ment of object constancy, and of the development of basic
trust and confident expectation that the love object is not lost
when not actually present. Thus, Becky arrived at the phallic-
oedipal phase predisposed not only to conflict and symptom
formation, but also to the development—in part, the reactivation—of the particular symptom of intense anxiety with the
threat of separation from her mother. The long history of
excessive separation anxiety had "sensitized" Becky to the
experience of separation. Marked fear of object loss had persisted, ready to be involved in the conflicts of the phallic-oedipal phase. The intensity of this symptom was therefore the
consequence both of experiences in the oedipal phase, such
as the father's seductive behavior, as well as the predisposing
and contributing factors stemming from the disturbances in
her preoedipal development.

Although, in reporting the clinical material, we have de-
cribed the various mechanisms that were used by Becky in
her efforts to manage her conflicts, it might be worthwhile at
this point to summarize them. Regression was a significant
factor, both in her symptom formation and in her infantile
behavior. On the side of the drives, we have seen a partial regression to the oral-sadistic and anal-sadistic phases and a defensive heightening of the negative oedipal wishes. Regarding certain aspects of ego functioning pertaining to object relations, there was a reinstinctualization and regression of
those secondary autonomous ego functions involved in the
maintenance of object constancy and in the mastery of separation experiences and separation anxiety. In dealing with her
oral-sadistic impulses, Becky utilized the mechanisms of projection and displacement, with the resultant fear of a man
with a mustache and of a witch. Becky had the fear that her
mother would abandon her both because she feared retaliation for the wish that her mother would disappear, and as a

consequence of projecting the same wish onto the mother. Later, when she pretended that she was the witch, we saw her use of the mechanism of identification with the aggressor. When she reached early latency, these mechanisms—projection and identification with the aggressor—although no longer responsible for symptom formation, assumed an important role in her character structure, as did repression and to some extent denial. Finally, Becky utilized the mechanisms of reaction formation and displacement in order to deal with the heightened intensity of her aggression toward her mother, as well as the threat of becoming aware of this aggression during her analytic sessions.

Because of her severe anxiety over threatened separation, Becky had to have her mother present frequently during her analysis. The effect of the mother's actual presence on the analysis can now be considered. In the first phase of the analysis, the mother's presence in the office offered me the opportunity to observe the dynamics of the separation problem in terms of what situations either intensified or diminished Becky's need to be with her mother. However, beyond a certain point, and because of the frequency and repetitiveness with which it occurred, the mother's presence became a hindrance to analytic work, in that it could be used by Becky as a way of handling her ambivalent feelings toward her mother by action rather than by understanding. At times her need to cling to her mother and exclude me were so strong that very little could be accomplished in the way of explanation or interpretation.

Although these disadvantages, from the point of view of the total analysis, outweighed the advantages, there were definite advantages in having Becky's mother present *at times* during the analytic sessions, similar to those described by Schwarz (1950). She spoke of the mother's presence as a reassurance to the child, as well as a sign of approval of the analytic procedure. Problems of clashing loyalties, of guilt about confiding secrets, and of two sets of standards could be eliminated when the mother participated in the analysis. And, from the point of view of the analyst, a better opportunity was provided to gain information about the child and to study the emotional interplay between mother and child. Finally, from the mother's point of view, it made for greater understanding of the child's problems, thus bringing about a synthesis of therapy and education. In contrast to the analyst's infrequent contact with the child, the mother has to deal with the child and her problems twenty-four hours a day. In the treatment of a three-year-old girl, Kolansky (1960) found it helpful to invite the mother into the playroom whenever he considered it therapeutically appropriate; he had concluded that the mother's presence would give full support to the treatment in the child's eyes and help the mother to handle some of her conflicts with her child more appropriately.

As a result of my experience in working with Becky, as well as with other young children, I am in agreement as to the advantages described above, provided that the analyst can choose when it is therapeutically advisable for the mother to be present, and if her presence is not primarily determined by the child's symptoms. In this analysis, not only did I have a close-up view of the separation problem in the mother-child relationship, but, as I have described in the case material, I was afforded access to material concerning events prior to Becky's illness—material which might not otherwise have been available to me. It seems likely that in the treatment of a young child some information may become accessible only when there is ample opportunity to observe mother and child together. As a result of the mother's presence, I gained knowledge and a better understanding of such events as the father's

tickling, the pill game, and the burning effect of the iodine—
all of which proved helpful in Becky's treatment.

In addition, I was able to observe the mother-child relationship directly, not only from the child's point of view, but
from the mother's as well. Particularly valuable were the
mother's expressions of ambivalence, which became apparent
in the difficulty she had in being firm with Becky and in her
own problem of separating from her daughter. With this
knowledge, I was better able to help the mother understand
her relationship to Becky as well as Becky's illness and behavior (to help her understand whether Becky's difficult behavior in any instance resulted from fear or anger, or the need
to provoke, and the reasons for each of these). Even though
the mother had been analyzed, these discussions helped her
to handle Becky in a more appropriate manner, rather than
to remain involved in a continuous struggle with her. An example of such an occasion, in which the mother was helped
regarding the separation problem, was the following:

Because of her own guilt, the mother found it easier to
leave Becky when she was asleep or otherwise occupied
("when her back was turned"), thus avoiding the pain of the
separation scene. During one of Becky's early analytic hours,
the mother stood at the office door, asking Becky if she might
go into the waiting room. Although Becky did not want her
to go, she did not answer directly; instead, turning her back
on her mother, she walked into the playroom. Her mother
picked up the cue and left; a few minutes later, Becky
screamed when she realized what had happened. This incident made it possible for me to advise the mother more mean-
ingfully as to ways in which separation could be handled, and
to point out to both Becky and her mother their common
avoidance of conscious awareness of the act of separation.

And, as a final advantage, Becky's mother was able on many

occasions, with my advice, to help Becky in her treatment. She repeatedly had the opportunity, and used it, to assure Becky that she understood her anger and that Becky need not fear lest her mother abandon her in retaliation. A young child's reality testing is so poorly developed that such statements on the mother's part undoubtedly had more impact than any that the analyst might make to the same effect. The young child is so close to the mother that many statements or interpretations made by the therapist gain their full significance only when the child, verbally or otherwise, obtains confirmation from the mother. We are most aware of this fact when we discuss with the child such matters as impregnation, childbirth, and masturbation, at which times we try to obtain the mother's cooperation. Further, the mother was at various times able to enter into, and share, Becky's concerns. For example, she told Becky that, although she understood Becky's penis envy and the child's feeling that she had to protect herself by having a penis, she herself was definitely not frightened and, in fact, preferred Becky to be a girl, just as she preferred to be a girl herself.

I also agree with Schwarz (1950) that the problems that should be dealt with in the mother's presence, and the length of time for which she should be included in the treatment, can be determined only by the specific situation. In Becky's analysis, I limited myself for the most part, in the presence of the mother, to dealing with the conflicts between Becky and her mother. The attachment to the father, the primal scene material, and to a large extent the hostility toward the mother resulting from the oedipal situation—these were dealt with when the mother was not in the room. It was, however, only because of the intensity of Becky's separation problem that the mother in this treatment was present much more often and for longer periods than would be normally advisable therapeutically.

In such a situation, one not only analyzes the child, but to some extent influences the mother-child relationship as well. Insofar as the treatment situation involves the mother, it contains many of the elements described by Jacobs (1949) on the education of mothers, by Bonnard (1950) on the mother as a therapist, and by Furman (1957) on the treatment of under-fives by way of their parents. Fortunately, Becky's mother was an intelligent, sensitive woman, sincerely concerned about her child and well able to use the knowledge and advice given her. There was no indication of its misuse, and no indication that Becky reacted adversely to what was said to the mother, or by the mother, in her presence.

SUMMARY

Clinical material has been presented from the first ten months of the analysis of a three-year-old girl. The focus of the presentation has been on the major symptom—the separation problem—particularly as it affected the analytic treatment. Because of the severity of this symptom, the mother often had to be present in the office during the analysis. Up to a point, and if the occasions are chosen therapeutically, the mother's presence offers important advantages. Beyond this point, and if the occasions are dictated primarily by the child's symptoms, as was frequently the case in Becky's analysis, the mother's presence acts as a hindrance to the analysis.

REFERENCES

Bonnard, A. (1950), The Mother as a Therapist, in a Case of Obsessional Neurosis. *The Psychoanalytic Study of the Child,* 5:391-408. New York: International Universities Press.

Burlingham, D. (1951), Present Trends in Handling the Mother-Child Relationship During the Therapeutic Process. *The Psychoanalytic Study of the Child*, 6:31-37. New York: International Universities Press.

Furman, E. (1957), Treatment of Under-Fives by Way of Their Parents. *The Psychoanalytic Study of the Child*, 12:250-262. New York: International Universities Press.

Jacobs, L. (1949), Methods Used in the Education of Mothers. *The Psychoanalytic Study of the Child*, 34:409-422. New York: International Universities Press.

Kolansky, H. (1960), Treatment of a Three-Year-Old Girl's Severe Infantile Neurosis. *The Psychoanalytic Study of the Child*, 15:261-285. New York: International Universities Press.

Schwarz, H. (1950), The Mother in the Consulting Room. *The Psychoanalytic Study of the Child*, 5:343-357. New York: International Universities Press.

ROBERT A. FURMAN, M.D.

A Technical Problem: The Child Who Has Difficulty in Controlling His Behavior in Analytic Sessions

ANY CHILD WHO is frequently unable to control his behavior in his analytic sessions presents his analyst with a most difficult technical problem. Early latency children most often present this difficulty, although they have no exclusive claim to it. I would like to report a segment from the analysis of such a child. I hope that the clinical material the patient brought and my approaches to this material may be of interest to others who are dealing or have dealt with this problem.

The case I have chosen is one I described earlier (1964), the six-year-old boy, Billy, whose mother died soon after the start of his analysis. I had undertaken his analysis reasonably certain that the mother's health would not be a factor in the treatment, but two weeks after we began, she had a recurrence of a previously operated breast cancer. Her disease then ran an extremely rapid course, and she died about four months after his first session.

I am indebted to my wife, Mrs. Erna Furman, for her assistance in bringing clarity to this paper, clarity of concepts as well as of expression.

From the Department of Psychiatry, Western Reserve University School of Medicine, Cleveland, Ohio.

In the previous paper I tried to outline the technical problems that arose in the wake of this tragedy and how they were managed. I also tried to describe the unfolding of the boy's mourning as it could be observed in the four months after his mother's death. In this report I shall describe the next eight months of the analysis, again to focus on a technical problem, this time his difficulty in controlling his behavior in the analytic sessions. This second eight months' work will, in addition, essentially complete the description of his mourning reaction.

I chose this particular case for two reasons. First, not only is Billy an unfortunately good example of a child who was often unable to control his behavior in his analytic sessions, but also, in this particular instance, I gradually changed my approach to this problem, and I think I know why I did. Second, although the more complete account of the mourning reaction which should emerge here is not the primary focus of interest, it seemed appropriate to utilize this opportunity of augmenting the description given in the earlier paper.

Before describing the clinical material I wish to stress that this paper does not deal with the resolution of Billy's difficulty in controlling his behavior. He was "out of control" just as frequently at the end of the period described here as he was at its beginning. My purpose is to describe our coming to grips with this problem.

CLINICAL MATERIAL

Billy was six years, three months old when the parents came to me seeking an analysis. Their main complaint was his persistent enuresis. Billy was referred by Miss Marion Barnes who had worked with the mother for about two years within the framework of the University Hospitals Therapeutic Nursery School, now the Hanna Perkins School. Miss

Barnes's main concern had been Billy's femininity, increasingly manifest in his gestures, choice of toys, friends, gifts, and games. The parents rationalized and minimized this symptom. Their second concern was Billy's provocative teasing of his brothers who were five and seven years older.

The very earliest work with Billy led me to believe that, unknown to everyone, he had seen the mother's amputation site. This Billy confirmed in his anxiety the day he learned of his mother's re-hospitalization: "She letted me see it once. It was all wrinkled." But I could not discuss this further with Billy at that time for three reasons: (1) it had erupted almost as a slip at a time of great stress; (2) in these early months, he did not give another direct opportunity to discuss it; and (3) his parents could not have tolerated his bringing up this topic at that time.

It was shortly after learning of the return of his mother's sickness that Billy set the tone for the analytic work. Totally uncontrolled behavior, which had just begun to characterize his sessions in the first two weeks, immediately became quite accentuated. In play, one day, he told me about two animals who were fighting a forest fire. The fire got out of control and they had to go to someone for help. With that help the fire was brought back under control. Billy had then himself gotten out of control. This enabled me to tell him he was asking for my help in managing his lack of control, and that I would try to do this by helping him understand his feelings. His response had been to tell me he had nightmares about fires and to begin a series of girls' games.

It seems pertinent to add here what I knew historically about his behavior. He had not had any unusual difficulty in controlling his behavior in the nursery school and kindergarten. He frequently exhibited an excited hyperactivity that he controlled or suppressed when the teachers spoke firmly

to him. There was no report of such behavior at home, initially. He brought the inability to control his behavior into his
sessions during the first two weeks, almost in proportion to
his ability to master his initial anxiety about the analysis. In
this way his behavior over the first two weeks was not unlike
that of many children for whom difficulty with control is a
dominant symptom. Only much later was I able to verify that
this was true for Billy too.

Initially, his uncontrolled behavior had a very angry
quality. He would do destructive things such as marking up
the walls, defacing the calendar, breaking crayons, using up
paper, paper clips, paste, scotch tape, without being able to do
anything constructive. This activity was accompanied by a
staccatolike speech that jumped from topic to topic with little
continuity and was interspersed by verbal attacks on me: "You
BM—you stinky." He would spit at me when he was really
enraged.

Our first understanding of this anger was that it was a reaction to the tremendous worry he felt about his mother and a
reaction to the tremendous sadness of missing her—initially
in her depressed withdrawal and later in her final hospitalization. Perhaps one example of this work might suffice. He told
me one day, after he had visited his mother in the hospital,
how much better she was, alluded to a little girl whose mother
had died, and then got angrily out of control. I told him that
I knew why he was so angry, that it made him angry to be so
worried that his mother hadn't really seemed better to him.
I suggested it was better to face his worry rather than let it
drive him out of control. With this type of work his teasing
outside the hour subsided and he was able to achieve partial
control within the hour.

In the weeks just before his mother's death, he was quietly
and wistfully preoccupied with many pretend games, for ex-

ample, about trips the family would take together. I felt he was not denying his mother's status but rather was wishing it were different. It seemed he used this time to prepare himself for the impending loss.

Immediately after his mother's death, we had six weeks to work before the summer holiday intervened. In this period Billy was angry at every reference he could find to a family with a mother: classmates and their parents, a former teacher who had just had a baby, and, of course, my family. In the hour, he mixed his toys with the other children's by way of saying that he wished we were all one family here, he no different from the others. He again did not deny his mother's death but rather was constantly busy saying it made him angry that his mother was dead. In retrospect, I felt that he had spent these six weeks gradually accepting the dreadful reality that his mother had died.[1]

In the first six weeks after the vacation, Billy brought his mourning reaction to the hour. It seemed as if he often tried to ward off the unpleasant feelings associated with the mourning by losing control of his behavior in the rather angry way I have described above.

But successful analysis of these episodes of anger always brought us back to a feeling of sadness which we called "the mommy missing feeling." This sadness came in relation to every instance where a nearly seven-year-old first grader would ordinarily feel his mother's presence: starting school, coming home from school, the first accomplishments in school, coming to his hour, going home from his hour, times of progress in his hour, buying clothes, getting haircuts, receiving presents, getting presents for others.

[1] In discussion of the earlier paper, Dr. Justin Krent pointed out that the summer separation from me may have been an important factor in the delayed onset of Billy's mourning.

What had been striking to me had been the absence throughout of any denial of his mother's death. It began to appear just at the end of this six weeks' period after the summer vacation, at the end of the period that I reported previously. His denial came initially in school, e.g., obtaining passes for both mother and father for a PTA meeting, when he knew that his teacher had been informed of his mother's death.

This, in essence, completes a brief recapitulation of the first eight months of his analysis that had been described previously. In reporting now on the next eight months of work, I shall be following him from the fall, four months after his mother's death, until the late spring of the following year, when his father announced his intention of remarrying. Chronologically, this period begins just two months before his seventh birthday and covers the first half of his eighth year.

The external events that deserve special mention concern Billy's father. During the first part of this period the father's mourning was at its height and times of withdrawal were impossible to avoid.[2] In the latter part of the period the father made a number of out of town trips, at first for business reasons, later because of his courtship. I felt I could detect little response to the vacillations in the father's moods, but the responses to the actual separations were definite and usually analyzable.

The denial of his mother's death referred to above began to show itself in the analysis in a number of ways of which I will describe two. The first of these concerned Billy's wish to take a walk with me during his hour. When this had first occurred, shortly after his mother's death, we had been able

[2] Dr. M. Katan has suggested that Billy's denial may have been related also to his father's withdrawal. I believe this may well have been a contributing factor.

to understand it as meaning he had been thinking about the mother's death and was preoccupied with some aspect of it. During this later period of work, however, he became anxiously insistent about his wish to take walks during his hour and the old understanding of it had no meaning to him. Finally, he was able to tell me he wanted to walk in the hope that he might see his mother somewhere on the street, something possible, of course, only if she were not dead.

The second way his denial manifested itself came in relation to those he saw as substitutes for his mother. He developed an intense need to be special with these substitutes, special with me, with his father, with his teacher. In the hour, this manifested itself in his wish to come with me on weekends, leaving his mark in the office on any papers of mine he could reach, attacking other patients' things. I first approached this as a sign of his intense longing for his mother, his need to have a substitute for her to bring him at least a temporary respite from his feelings of missing her. This interpretation was not without benefit, and the need to be so special seemed to abate briefly. But then it returned with the same anxious insistence that had characterized the need to walk. It subsided only when I next interpreted the need to be so special with those he felt were substituting for his mother as one way of pretending he was not without a mother, that his mother really was not dead. In response to this interpretation, he verbally probed who was I like, a mother substitute, a grandfather, or a doctor? He identified with his mother, getting some of her hysterical symptoms at times when she would have had them, a headache at the kindergarten reunion party, for example. But then he returned to being furious at me and all the other inadequate substitutes.

His anxiety about this anger was quite intense. He had to leave the hours early after telling me of his anger toward his

teacher, his wish that a bomb might fall on me. As we
explored this anxiety, he told me he could never really be
Billy again until his mother returned, because it had been
Billy's anger that had killed her. After this, he told me he
was worried that his "tinkler" was broken and this explained
why he "pishied" his bed. He brought a broken toy from
home that could not hold water. He used it to demonstrate
his point and to explain that it got broken somehow because
of his excited feelings. Understanding the relationship between his enuresis and his excitement took many days. It was
particularly significant because he stayed with this theme before, during, and after his birthday with its associated intense
missing of his mother. For the first time, some direct analytic
work on his original symptom was not blotted out because
of his mourning reaction.

Around the time of his birthday, he exhibited an old finger-
sucking symptom in his analytic sessions. He also told me of
his wish to kiss me and be kissed by me. He felt he was missing being kissed by mother, but being kissed by her as a baby
is kissed. When I wondered if he might suck his fingers and
wet his bed to go back to the time of being a baby when his
mother was still alive and he didn't have all his present worries, he replied, "That's important." He had two dry nights
immediately after this interpretation.

About a month after I had felt this change within the hour
regarding his mourning, namely, the time when it no longer
seemed to obliterate any other work, he told his father, "Is
it all right that I don't think of mother all the time? I used to
[think of her] even when I was playing!" For the remainder
of the time covered by this report the mourning gradually
occupied less and less of the analysis. By a few months after
his birthday the feelings we had called the "mommy missing"
ones, the defenses against them, and their derivatives were

central less than half of the time. By the end of the eight months covered by this report, they were central less than a third of the time, and had definitely become episodic. The episodes of mourning would appear in any of three situations: (1) around specific events where mother's memory had not previously been decathected—learning to read with no mother to share this, the first snow, times of analytic progress, her birthday, Mother's Day; (2) in response to acute precipitating events in reality such as his teacher's saying, "I'll get sick if you're bad," two boys teasing him because his mother was dead, his father's telling of talking to "Mom," a business client he has always called by this name; (3) after times of analytic progress in which he had recovered memories of earlier episodes with his mother, both pleasant and unpleasant ones, or in which he had re-experienced certain feelings about her in the transference. Perhaps the details of a few sessions might illustrate a part of this process in operation. They will also convey some of the flavor of this analysis.

Billy arrived on a Friday afternoon in mid-November eating a candy bar. His greeting was a perfunctory "Hi," and he took off his coat and let it just fall to the floor. As I started to make a comment about his coat, he crumbled the candy bar so that its cracker crumbs scattered to the floor. He ignored a comment of mine that he was showing me it had been a rough day for him today. He began deliberately and obviously grinding the crumbs on the floor with his heel, and started to get excited in the process. I said, "Hold it. We'd better get that cleaned up before you get so out of control we'll never find out what this is all about."

He seemed relieved, but as he started to brush the crumbs together, he scattered them more. I said I guessed he needed my help, and with me working beside him, he managed to clean them up. I took the opportunity in this interlude to say I thought we knew that when he messed it meant he was angry. I said it was better for us to understand why he was angry than to lose the feeling in his excitement.

The task finished, he went to the toy cars and began crashing them, saying a bad guy was causing all the trouble. He then went on to the airplanes, with a Nazi plane fighting an American one, with Billy in the Nazi one. I said little during this play, just inquiring for details until the pitch began to rise. I said I thought he was angry with me, maybe because it was Friday, and I added how much better it would be if he could tell me his anger, as he recently had been able to do with father, than to act and show it to me as I presumed he used to do with mother.

He then related a war story about his father which he had often told me before, one which is essentially true. His father and his friend were in a building. It was bombed. His father got out but his friend did not and was killed. I said he was afraid if he got angry with me, even though I was a friend, he might want me dead.

He went back to the cars crashing, saying the bad guy had caused it all. He said I wasn't his friend, as he liked father better than he did me. He then impulsively picked up his coat and left, there being about ten minutes left of the hour.

The following Monday he arrived looking sad and anxious. He wanted to take a walk. It was a nice fall day and as he was feelingful, I said, "O.K., because maybe it will help us understand what you're feeling today and what was so rough Friday." As we started out, I reminded him that as long as he used the walk to help with his feelings and our understanding of them, it was fine. Otherwise we would return to the office. He set as a goal for us the top of a nearby hill, but after we had walked silently half-way there, he said, "Let's go back." He was obviously disappointed and sad. He stopped to examine some stones and worried they'd be taken away. I knew from what he had told me the previous week that there had been a discussion at home about a stone for mother's grave. I said I knew now he'd been looking for mommy. Was it the feeling of missing her or the worry over an angry feeling of his? He didn't answer me and did not talk until we saw a dead cricket on the sidewalk. He said he was worried the cricket was cold, and he began getting anxious. I replied that I knew he was worried about mother being cold in the earth only when he had been pretending she was not dead, that she still had feelings.

Back in the office he sang a song about the holidays and said he never would cry here about mother. I asked, "Why not cry here? You can at home." He at once got out of control, throwing his coat, shouting his song to drown out anything I might say. He tore a picture off the wall which he had drawn earlier and said, "I broke it, I broke it." I asked if the upset was about the wetting, losing sight of his flight from his tears. He sang a wild song about wanting to be dead. The hour ended here.

The next day, using a play about school as his vehicle, he told me that on the previous Thursday two boys had teased him about his mother being dead. They had told him, "Your mother is dead, kid. If she weren't, I'd kill her." He told me how scared he had been, how glad he was that he had told his brother, who got very angry about the boys. He said it made him angry and sad, too. He became quite sad, but then stopped the play, switching to another theme in which he asked indirectly if I was angry with him, did I like him. This led again to his fear that his anger had killed his mother.

These three sessions provide an example of what I have referred to above as an episodic occurrence of Billy's mourning reaction, this one precipitated by the actions of the boys at school. The defensive maneuvers Billy used to try to avoid experiencing his sadness and his anxiety in his analytic hour are typical. Also typical is the lost confusion I felt as a result of the angry, uncontrolled behavior that characterized the first session and the latter part of the second one. And, finally, there is the slow groping through his defenses until we could reach his sadness.

As the mourning reaction receded from its central position in the analytic work, his difficulty with controlling his behavior did not change, and I had to assume a new attitude toward this problem. Heretofore, we had treated it as an unwelcome state he wished to eradicate, something we had been trying to achieve by understanding the feelings behind it. We had, in effect, considered the out-of-control times as a manifestation of anxiety and then had searched for the feelings behind the anxiety, the feelings he feared would overwhelm him. This approach had been possible because we both had been keenly aware of what these feelings were a response to—first his mother's illness, then her death. But by the time the mourning reaction had become less central, we no longer had the advantage of knowing in advance what the stimulus was for the feelings that were arousing Billy's anxiety. We no longer had the relatively simple task of uncovering the dreaded affect that was a response to a succession of known stimuli. Our only clue was the out-of-control behavior itself. Why did his anxiety manifest itself in this way? Did not this behavior serve other purposes besides expressing anxiety? We had no alternative but to analyze the behavior itself.

I now pointed out Billy's lack of control to him as a specific problem we had to master. I stressed two points to him: (1) we would never be able to understand why he "pishied" his bed unless we could talk about it, and we could not do this when he was not in control; (2) if we were able to understand why he could not control his behavior in his sessions with me, then we would be a long way toward understanding why he could not be in control in his bed at night. I was trying in this way to put his inability to control his behavior in the center of the analysis, as a symptom we had to analyze, and to say that we could no longer treat this inability as a sign of his anxiety which we could just acknowledge and bypass as we looked for its source.

In beginning the analysis of his inability to control himself as a symptom, there was sufficient material for me to know that, initially, he would not be able to tolerate interpretations of its superego and libidinal aspects. He would tolerate only those interpretations which related to its defensive or ego side, and perhaps also to his aggression. One example of the material that prepared me in this way was in the analysis of his reponse to my practical approach to his times of not being able to control himself during his analytic hours.

I had told him that I would always let him try to control himself and would not intervene unless he was in danger of hurting himself, the office, or me. I had said that I knew if I allowed him to hurt himself when he was with me, he would not believe I really wanted to help him. I had also said that if I allowed him to hurt the office or me he would always be afraid of his feelings when he was with me. In these instances I explained that I would take over and bring control to him until he could reassert his own. He also knew that when he was able to mark up the walls, damage something, or spill things on the floor, that the damage would be repaired before he left, with my assistance if necessary.

These ground rules had, of course, led to my having to hold him upon occasion, to which he sometimes responded with great excitement. From these episodes we learned of earlier times, when he would cuddle with his father, being "made comfortable." When I interpreted his wish to be held by father, or by me in the transference, as a wish to recapture pleasant cuddling times with mother either just for pleasure or else to deny her death and hence his guilt, or when I interpreted that in cuddling he had been doing with father as he had seen mother do, then his out-of-control behavior would increase, or would begin if the interpretation had been made at a quiet time. These interpretations were of the libidinal aspect of his symptom or, in reference to his guilt, of its superego aspect. But if I interpreted his wish to be excited in order to avoid an unpleasant feeling, such as worry, anger, sadness, an interpretation of the defensive use of the symptom, then it would help him regain control. Likewise, if I interpreted his out-of-control behavior as an exhibition of his distress or as an attempt to avoid the painful awareness that verbalization might bring ("showing rather than telling"), such an interpretation of the defensive aspect of the symptom would also be helpful.

I felt later that I could understand his sensitivity to interpretations of the superego side of the out-of-control behavior. As will be shown below, he tended to employ identification with the aggressor, a defense we are used to associating, from Anna Freud's work, with an early stage of superego development. I think that some aspects of his inability to control his behavior originated when his superego had been immature. Work on this aspect of the symptom must await further working through of his identification with the aggressor.

My thinking about his difficulty with interpretations of the libidinal aspect of his symptom requires that I describe yet another technically difficult aspect of this analysis. Billy always evidenced a very short attention span, particularly if I was saying anything to him or doing anything with him. He very obviously would have to stop listening to me, hide in the closet or get out of control after even a few sentences. More and more, I got the feeling that he was afraid that I would somehow overwhelm him, and not just with aggression as when he identified with the aggressor. His constant use of the defense of turning passive into active seemed also to indicate many prior experiences of feeling overwhelmed with excitement, experiences whose exact nature eluded me at the time. Interpretations that involved more than a sentence or two usually could be offered to him only over the span of a few sessions.

The work on the relationship between his excitement and his enuresis that I have described above, and which we worked on around the time of his November birthday, dropped from focus as we prepared for separations over Thanksgiving, early December, and Christmas. His response was to tell me of his great preference for his father over me, that he would tell only father his feelings and that he hated me and my family. He was very angry with me, projected this anger onto me, was terrified of me, and then attacked me or wanted to flee from me. The more we worked on this identification with the aggressor, the more he messed, left for bowel movements during the hour, called me a BM. But he was able to verbalize his longing for his father when he was away on a business trip, and to give him a present on his return. Then he wanted me to be his father, to give me a present, saying Daddy would then be like his mother. I told him I thought now we could understand what had been going on when he had been so angry with me, preferring father so much, talking about BM's. I said I thought he was repeating with father and me an old time with mother and Mary, a maid who had trained him only to leave the family shortly after his training was finished. When he thought about my leaving, it must have reminded him of Mary's leaving to be with her family. He had been showing in his anger to me how angry he had been with Mary. He had been showing in his preference for his father his old yearning for mother at the time of his training. His response to this was to tell me he told everyone he came to Art class each day because the analysis was such a BM place. I said I was sure then that I had been getting the old feelings about Mary. He left to have a bowel movement.

He brought me no Christmas present. He forgot because he had been afraid I would forget him. When I said, "As you felt first mother and then Mary had forgotten you," he replied, "You BM." I said I guessed that he must have felt like a flushed away BM when he had felt forgotten by them.

After Christmas, his difficulty in controlling his behavior during the hour became particularly intense, and he expressed more excitement. I emphasized again his preference for pleasurable excitement over unpleasurable sadness. Once, after being sad at bedtime rather than excited, he had a dry night. He said what made him sad was that even if he wanted me to think of him all weekend as he did of me, I didn't. He later said it was just like that with Mommy, although he thought of her often, he knew she never could think of him.

His excitement at this time seemed clearly to be feminine in nature. "Let's play house, you be the daddy and I'll be the sister." "I use my tinkler as a BM hole at night when I'm excited." When I was to be away, he jumped excitedly to sit in my chair to pretend he was me. Despite such an example with which to show his identification with me as a defense against missing me, any interpretation of his identification with mother in his excited loss of control as a defense against missing her only exaggerated it. When he was dry after shouting a wish to kill me at the end of a Friday hour, I tried a different tack. I told him I thought he became Mommy so as to pretend she was not dead, so there would be no trouble with angry feelings with her. He replied he "pishied" his bed because he was angry at me for scaring him, but would hear no more from me on this.

He swung back to being afraid of me, seeing me as the angry doctor who cut things off people. There were stories of boys kidnapped by men who cut them up. There was a "Mr. Chopper" (a pair of scissors) in his plays who cut up the other characters. He broke the pencils and crayons in half. Two things seemed clear: his fear I would do to him as mother's doctor had done to her and his projection of any anger onto me, particularly about separations.[3] He explained that he became frightened of me sometimes and lost control so that I would hold him (now rarely necessary) because that was exciting.

[3] Billy himself had never experienced any surgical procedures.

At this point, I insisted to the father that the amputation be discussed with Billy. Originally, the boys had been told only that a lump had been removed from the side of mother's chest. I feared if Billy now alluded to the amputation at home, the father would not pick it up; if Billy brought it up directly, the father, if unprepared, might have to deny it. When I discussed it with the father, he felt more comfortable, bringing it up directly with all three boys at the same time. This he did in terms of setting the record straight, saying they all had always managed well whenever they had all the facts. Billy's immediate response was guilt for having seen and a fear of his brothers' anger for what he sensed correctly as his role in their needing to be told. He felt guilty about murderous wishes toward father before telling me that his anger had made mother angry, and her anger had caused her lump and thus her death. His excited inability to control his behavior then reached a crescendo in which he started to undress in the hour. I said he was showing me rather than telling me his worry because he had been shown the amputation rather than told about it originally. His response was striking in that he immediately regained his control and composure. I knew that my interpretation had a simple accuracy that was most difficult to achieve in this phase of his analysis.

In the period immediately following the father's discussion, Billy's hours included evidence of his attempts to work through some of the material the discussion had provoked. In addition, his sessions were characterized by a bit more control. But despite the relative increase in his control and the addition of a known stimulus to his material, the hours were difficult to follow for many days. One session in mid-February was typical of this phase. It was a Monday after a weekend in which his father had been out of town from Sunday morn-

ing until Monday noontime. When Billy came to his afternoon hour, he had not yet seen his father since his return.

Billy announced on entering the office that he was going to call
his father. I kept my hand on the phone, reminding him he could
call only in a real emergency. He angrily insisted he had to call.
Finally, the reason emerged: he wanted to know if father had
brought him back a present from his trip, a knife he had asked
for. As I continued to block his wish to call, he said the knife was
to cut up his father. I said he needed a present to make sure father was not angry, not angry back at Billy who was so angry that
father had left. Billy then left for the bathroom. His excited
laughter just prior to his return to the office indicated some
trouble there. He soon told me he had spilled the liquid soap,
something he called "naughty." He said he had cleaned it up. I
said I thought he had arrived feeling naughty and had wanted to
do something naughty, to try to explain away the feeling. He ignored this and again demanded that I allow him to use the telephone. He struggled angrily to pick up the telephone. I said I
thought he wanted the "present" of the phone call from me to
make sure I too was not angry with him.

He stopped abruptly to try to get me to play a guessing game,
called "You take one away and guess what's missing." He took
the top off a clown doll and substituted a candy wrapper. Then
he wanted to hide the clown for me to guess where it was hidden.
Before I could guess or really begin to think about the material,
he had the top of the clown doll in his mouth and stopped the
game. He then sat quietly in the chair in the corner sucking his
fingers. Just before the hour ended at this point, I had the chance
to say he was showing me he still had worries about the amputation.

When the material began to crystallize, Billy was again trying to deny liking me, to provoke me, saying he preferred
father to me. But he became anxious about Daddy when he
was away and had an anxiety attack when the hired man instead of father appeared for him after the hour one day. I

said he acted as if liking me would somehow kill his father. I pointed out how this problem with me came about in relation to father's being away, and wondered if he had turned to Dad in the past at times when mother had been away. His answer was "You mean when she played golf all day?" He then was able to be angry with father on the telephone about a separation and could control his behavior during the hour when I interpreted his trying not to like me, trying to get me not to like him; his trying not to repeat an angry turning away from the absent love object, mother in the past, father in the present.[4]

The anger then turned on me, especially at the separation at the end of the hour. He was frightened of this feeling, leaving early to avoid it, apologizing whenever its expression was unavoidable. He said, "I pishied my bed to be angry at you. The warm pishie is to kill you, maybe." This material brought no dry beds, but did help him to maintain control in the hour for a bit.

The anger toward me in the hour then took a definite new turn; it became primarily oral. He shouted, screamed, and spat. His only apparent means of controlling these impulses were to fill his mouth with food (eating cookies he brought for that purpose) or with his fingers, which he would suck vigorously. The anger was related to two brief separations from me. He became anxious after the outbursts. He was afraid that he might cry, "Let's get out of here before I cry like a baby would," and he feared retaliation, being killed by cars, lightning, fires. All I could show him here was that since we had understood his fear of preferring me over father

---

[4] The further Billy's analysis progressed, the more I became aware of the unusual number of separations from his mother he had endured. Two very major ones, at four and a half, the time of his mother's initial hospitalization, and at five, the time his parents took an extended vacation alone, had not yet come to the fore in the analytic work. They did subsequently.

now, as he had preferred father over mother long ago, all his anger toward me about leaving him had been expressed by his mouth, and not in words as by a seven-year-old. Was this an old, early anger toward mother which he had warded off in switching to and preferring father?

References to his masturbation that had come very indirectly before with the frequent use of words like devil, bad, fire, now came a bit more directly. He worried about being consumed in fires that were out of control. In a circus game, he enacted a tightrope walker, and fell in such a way that he would have injured his genitals had he been using a real rope. I told him that he was worried about many feelings on being left: worried that his excitement as well as his sadness and anger might get out of control.

He often became a teacher in play, with me the schoolboy. His questions were clear: how do caterpillars become Monarchs? How do seeds make flowers? I said that he had questions about babies and how they were made which he was frightened to ask me. When he finally did ask, he was too out of control to discuss it. All I could do was point out again his defense of turning passive into active, reversing the roles by becoming the teacher when he was anxious, this time about sexual information.

He then told of an out-of-control plane that needed fixing so there would be no more destruction. He said he had a hidden secret he could not tell me because I would be so angry. He hid behind the foot of the couch, both hands presumably on his genitals, saying "tickle, tickle." He agreed when I said he was worried about tickling his penis and was afraid if he told me about it I would do to him as mother's doctor had done to her. I included the latter part of the interpretation because there were many current references to me as a "detaching devil." The next day he avoided the material but tried to play a game of checkers with me, the first real age-appropriate latency activity I had seen in his analysis.

There followed a confused week that included Mother's Day on which he tore up an American flag because, he claimed, he was so angry he had no mother. This seemed important in helping to understand his war games, the Americans standing for mother, the Germans for those who had harmed her. But he returned to a whole consecutive week of profitable analysis. On the first day in his play with the toys he had what he called a beautiful American plane destroyed by a sneaky little German plane. The German plane was not Billy he said, not his brothers, but I was close. It was father! I told him his fear that he killed mother must hide his fear that father had killed her. The next day he told me a dangerous secret, "I like you." The third day he was afraid of tornadoes. I said I thought he was telling me he was afraid his father would kill him if he knew Billy's secret feelings for me, just as he must have been afraid before that father would kill him if he had known of Billy's secret feelings for mother. He replied, "That's a fact!" The fourth day he was the tornado, apparently feeling safer being the dangerous father than worrying about what father might do to him. He regressed to BM words and bathroom trips. The fifth day he went to urinate after I had a chance to review the week's work. On his return, he showed me his nipple. I said that was the source of so much of his fear of me, his fear that daddy would have me cut something off, his penis, as he must have thought daddy had cut off or had someone else cut off mother's breast —and all this because of Billy's secret love for his mother, an old feeling for her which came back now in the analysis with me.

The next week he was struggling to ward off phallic excitement by anal and oral regressions ("I use BM words so

I won't get so excited") and could tolerate little talk about excitement. But he brought a dream which, among other things, indicated his awareness of his father's as yet undiscussed remarriage plans. "Boxer [his dog] has a leg cut off by a train and dies. Father gets me a new Boxer but the old one opens his eyes and has a new leg." His associations were all to running away from me, and I said the dream told us why. He was still so afraid that as mother lost a breast and Boxer (in the dream) a leg, so he could lose his penis because of his excited wishes. How much he wished there had never been an operation. After this interpretation he was dry twice on the weekend, and on Monday attributed it to "getting this doctor business straight and about mother."

DISCUSSION

In discussing the analytic work I would like first to make a few observations about Billy's mourning. In the year and a half's work that has transpired since the end of the period I report here, (this analysis is still ongoing) there has been nothing to make me think that the great majority of Billy's mourning work was not completed in the period described here. This means that his mourning task completely dominated his mental life until five months after his mother's death, but was in large part completed within a year.

Elsewhere, in reporting this case, I have stressed what seemed to me a significant sequence observed during the first year or so of his analysis. There was the period of preparation for his loss prior to his mother's death, the period of acceptance of the loss in the six-week period from her death until the summer holiday, the period of intense sadness described in the six weeks after the summer holiday, the time of the most intense decathexis of the inner representation of his mother, then the time of the denial and its relation to his aggression and guilt, and finally the more prolonged period of the less intense, more episodic decathexis and sadness described here.

I have also stressed elsewhere the restriction of his denial to the time of coping with his guilt over his aggression. It was easier for this boy to accept his loss in the outside world, to begin and accomplish a great deal of the painful decathexis of the inner representation of his love object, than it was to acknowledge and deal with his guilt over his aggression. It may be of interest, incidentally, to report that no one outside his immediate family made any observations of his depression or his mourning. His mourning was a private task of which his father was aware, that Billy worked on with me, but that he otherwise kept successfully very much to himself.

In discussing Billy's difficulty in controlling his behavior there are certain points that I would like to emphasize. The first concerns the practical aspects of the management of the out-of-control child. What seems important here is that there must be a realistic explanation given to the child of the reasons for whatever steps are taken to deal with this behavior, and then an analysis of the child's response to these steps. I have tried to illustrate this in the instance of holding him. I do not mean to suggest that measures employed with this boy would be applicable to all other children with this difficulty. They might well be contraindicated, as the measures taken will vary according to what the analyst knows and feels about each child's problem. My emphasis is purely on the importance of explanation to the child and on analysis of his response.

Second, it seems important to approach the child's loss of control as one would approach any other symptom. This includes the tedious, difficult task of helping the child see the **disadvantages** to him of his symptom, trying to make the

symptom ego-alien. I have described the beginning of this
work with Billy. I feel I was a bit slow to approach his inability to control himself as a symptom because I was reluctant to accept the fact that, after all we had been through with
the death of his mother, his uncontrolled behavior was a
symptom that was going to be with us for a long time. It is
often easier, in theory, to accept that whatever the patient
brings is meat for the analysis, particularly if what he brings
is a lack of control that seems to interfere with the analysis.

The third point that I would like to emphasize is the approach to Billy's symptom through the analysis of its defensive aspects. I have tried to show what happened when I did
not do this, as well as why I think his reaction at these times
was so acute. This does not mean that the transference was
ignored. I have reported some of the analysis of the transference that emerged in this period as well as some of the constructions that were possible from this work. But these evolved
from the analysis of the defenses.

I was not unaware of Billy's identification with his mother
in what must have come across to him as out-of-control times
of hers. I was not unaware that, in his inability to control himself with me, he was repeating in the transference times when
he had not controlled himself when with his mother, although I could at that time get no historical confirmation of
this. I was not unaware that, in his great excitement with me,
he was also repeating times of great excitement with his
father. I just kept hoping that subsequent material would
clear the way to what I felt to be these basic aspects of his inability to control his behavior. Ultimately, it was possible to
analyze the identification with his mother and to analyze the
excitement in the transference toward me as the mother and
as the father. This later analytic work may well be the subject of another paper, exploring the internal conditions that

had to be established to permit this work. But at the point described in this paper, the understanding of these aspects of Billy's difficulty with control was of value primarily in giving me the picture of his earlier relationships, particularly with his mother. It had been a most difficult relationship long before the traumas of her illness, surgery, and death.

The fourth point about this segment of the analytic work that I would like to emphasize is that, despite all the technical difficulties that have been described, the analysis was moving ahead. Short of a year after losing his mother, Billy had accomplished the major part of his mourning and had made a move to bringing his masturbatory problem into his analysis. His behavior outside the hour, while not as ideal as reported to me, revealed a growing ability for age-appropriate behavior in his relationships with his peers, in his schoolwork, and in assuming responsibility for himself, e.g., with his clothes and personal care.

Perhaps the out-of-control child may sometimes be like the silent child. It always seems as if they bring so little material, participate so sparingly, until one realizes, after a given period of time, they may have brought as much significant material as any apparently more cooperative, fully verbal child.

SUMMARY

This paper reports a segment of the analysis of a latency child. It is presented with two goals in mind: (1) to complete the description of the major part of this boy's mourning for his mother, a reaction described in an earlier paper (1964); (2) to bring material that could serve as a basis for considering a technical problem in the analyses of some children, children who are unable to control their behavior in analytic sessions.

REFERENCES

Freud, A. (1937), *The Ego and the Mechanisms of Defense.* New York: International Universities Press, 1946.

Furman, R. A. (1964), Death of a Six-Year-Old's Mother During His Analysis. *The Psychoanalytic Study of the Child,* 19:377-397. New York: International Universities Press.

MARJORIE P. SPRINCE

The Psychoanalytic Handling of
Pseudo Stupidity and Grossly Abnormal Behavior
in a Highly Intelligent Boy

THIS PAPER SETS OUT to examine aspects of the analytic
treatment of a thirteen-year-old boy whose behavior at first
sight presented a picture akin to borderline psychosis. His
response to analytic interpretations during the two years of
treatment, however, confirms the fact that gross pathological
behavior can, in certain cases, be reached by interpretation
of the defenses, the affects, and the transference. In such
cases the clinical picture may be misleading and the disturbance less ominous than it appears at the outset.

While the basis for Ivan's disturbance will be seen to have
had its origin in very early childhood, probably at the oral
and anal levels, the "selection" of the symptom of pseudo
stupidity itself appears to have taken place somewhat later, so
that the structure of the neurosis only became firmly established around the solution of the oedipal phase. This is con-

This case was treated by the author at the Hampstead Child-Therapy Clinic.
The Clinic is maintained with the aid of grants by the Field Foundation, Inc.,
New York; The Anna Freud Foundation, New York; The Grant Foundation,
Inc., New York; The Estate of Flora Haas, New York; The Walter E. Meyer
Research Institute of Law, Inc., New Haven, Connecticut; The National Insti-
tute of Mental Health, Bethesda, Maryland; The Old Dominion Foundation,
New York; The Psychoanalytic Research and Development Fund, Inc., New
York; The Taconic Foundation, Inc., New York.

firmed by the fact that it was possible to bring about marked changes in Ivan's symptomatology by oedipal interpretations within the transference. In addition, analysis of the defenses and the lifting of repression re-established a connection between conscious and unconscious processes (Geleerd, 1963), bringing about the insight and relief necessary to establish a firm working alliance.

At the time of his referral, Ivan was described as lazy, slovenly, living in a state of social isolation, and lacking all spontaneity. He was greedy and always hungry. His extreme apathy, backwardness at school, and inability to make friends had been noticed by his teachers and other adults. It was said that he could not follow simple instructions such as those involved in running an errand, and he would lose himself in daydreams and return with the job unachieved. If asked to switch off a gasfire, he would absentmindedly turn the tap of an unlit fire, thereby turning on the gas without igniting it. In general, he appeared to follow instructions according to the letter of the law without any real sign of comprehension. He would sit without heat for hours at a time, appearing to experience no discomfort from the cold. His behavior was uncivil and inconsiderate, particularly to the young housekeeper who had run the home since a few months after his mother's death, to whom he would barely speak. Although painfully backward at school, he at times showed sudden sparks of ability, so that his teachers considered him disgustingly lazy and, in one case, asked for his removal from school. Ivan had no hobbies, but he filled his leisure time studiously attending all sorts of classes which he did not enjoy but which he hoped would "improve" him. He spent the remaining time in daydreams, inventing gadgets and systems, or reading books of self-instruction, usually on methods of thinking. He had no friends but practiced conversational gambits in the hope that he might make and keep one. Ivan was a boy with obsessional symptoms and the function of his systems and ruminations was to ensure that his mind was in complete mastery over his emotions. At times he thought of himself as a computer.

Magaret Mahler (1942) sets out the accepted psychoanalytic genesis of intellectual inhibition. She describes how erotization of the intellectual functions of the ego may cause the abandoning of these functions so as to avoid conflict. She emphasizes how intellectual restriction is often used to disguise aggression, as well as offering an opportunity to display castration and thus escape threatened castration and loss of the love object. In her paper, she adds to these another essential function of pathological stupidity—that of restoring or maintaining a secret libidinous rapport within the family.

All of these features will be seen to have played a part in Ivan's symptoms. It was on the basis of this understanding that we were gradually able to unravel the unconscious motives behind his behavior. Of those features described by Margaret Mahler (1942), the wish to disguise aggression and to display castration, thereby escaping real castration and loss of another love object (his mother had died when he was nine) was most prominent in Ivan's material. This feature should, however, be linked with another with which we are already familiar in the context of school phobias, and to which Margaret Mahler also draws our attention, specifically in terms of the early mother-child relationship. This is the part played by the patient's background in unconsciously providing specific stimulus for the defect, which may fulfill an unconscious need in the parents' pathology (Johnson and Szurak, 1952).[1] Ivan's material illustrates how he construed warnings, accusations, questionings, and even helpful sug-

[1] See also Hellman (1954).

gestions, as directives not to move forward developmentally. Above all, comments upon his stupid behavior were experienced as demands that he continue to play a particular role, that of family dullard and scapegoat.

BACKGROUND AND HISTORY

Ivan was the oldest child and only son of a family with three children. Knowledge of his developmental history has depended almost entirely upon analytic reconstruction. However, it was reported that at the age of four, when his sister was born, he gave an almost "mongoloid" impression and would wet and soil in the middle of a carpet, and bite and pinch. Shortly after the birth of his youngest sister, when he was six, his mother developed a serious illness which necessitated frequent hospitalizations and from which she eventually died when Ivan was nine. She was replaced by a young housekeeper who soon became a substitute mother to the children and who was expected by them to, one day, become their legal stepmother. The relationship between housekeeper and father was an ambivalent one. There were frequent arguments, mainly over Ivan whose behavior often resulted in her threatening to leave the family. Her attitude to Ivan was one of dislike, since she had hoped for affection and felt that he did not appreciate what she did for him and the family. In addition, she may have felt that her difficult relationship with him jeopardized her prospects of marriage.

The father, who came from a Welsh mining village and a strict chapel background, had worked his way "to the top." He was a politician, with an immense driving force—a man who appeared to know everything and everyone and who felt himself to be always right. He ceaselessly compared his own achievements with those of his luckless son. He had little faith in therapy since he could not control it himself, and demanded concrete evidence of improvement from the treatment by daily interrogations. He controlled school and out-of-school activities to the extent of insisting upon overhearing his son's telephone conversations to assess his social improvement. If Ivan arrived home with news of any success he would be told that it was not his achievements that were important but his failures, so that something could be done about them.

Ivan was small for his age. His nails were long and uncut. He had a roundish face with a permanent, quite expressionless grin. At times this grin would change to an open and friendly smile, while at other times it could only be described as sly and suggestive. When anxious, he would blush or laugh uproariously, and often his laughter was inappropriate and embarrassing. He spoke quickly and with pressure, using stilted speech and pompous sentences which appeared to have been rehearsed. At times his thoughts tended toward concretization, as when he remarked that I seemed to "counteract certain things" because there was an alcove in one part of the treatment room while the wall jutted out in another part. Two of his predominant defenses—intellectualisation and the need to isolate mind and body—were reflected in his use of odd and inappropriate scientific expressions for affects. Thus, describing an acquaintance with emotional difficulties similar to his own, he said "he has virtually the same properties as myself." While speaking of his teachers' anger, he remarked "my researches have enabled me to neutralize it."

It is important in Ivan's history that he had many physical defects similar to those found in deprived children—a mild stammer, a malformed bite for which he used a dental plate, and the use of spectacles. His gait was rigid, and his movements often clumsy. Contrasting with his continuous flow of speech, Ivan frequently lost himself in fantasies while making strenuous efforts to remain in contact. In treatment, a characteristic feature was his manner of compliantly taking over my attitudes, words, and opinions and reproducing them mechanically, as if they were his own. There was a strong fixation to orality and, at this level, his assessment of reality was often shaky. For example, he would believe that the housekeeper's anger with him at any particular time was reflected in the supper she chose for the entire family, and he would speculate upon the cause and speak of his disappointment or hopes, ceaselessly.

The indications are that, in both oral and anal matters, rigidity and force were a family pattern, so that intake and expulsion soon became areas of conflict. No information about habit training was available, and direct anal material during the period under discussion was sparse. Marked fixation and regression to anality is, however, evident in Ivan's symptomatology (obsessional symptoms, ruminations, problems over cleanliness, tendency to hoard, excessive ambivalance, etc.) It will be seen, too, that sadomasochistic features form an integral part of the transference relationship.

TREATMENT MATERIAL

Relationship to His "Two Mothers"

The peculiar behavior reported to us soon became evident in his sessions—he picked his nose and examined the mucous unashamedly, or played with the scurf droppings from his hair as if they were sand. He would arrive late for his sessions or, on other occasions, arrive at unexpected times, when he would try the doors leading from the waiting room into my room and then be found rummaging unashamedly through my desk or cupboards to "memorize the contents and train his mind." If other patients were in the waiting room, he would ignore them and force his way into the house to read my books and attempt to examine the kitchen furniture or bathroom gadgets. In the coldest weather, he would turn off all the heating and open the windows without consulting me. During the hour, he would sit tearing pieces of material off the chairs while demanding food and drink. I did not comply with his demands for supplies, preferring to make him aware of the nature of his needs and interested in their meaning.

Ivan's apparent lack of shame at his odd behaviour contrasted markedly with his distress at being a social misfit. While he had grave doubts about the efficacy of treatment, he felt it was worthwhile to give it a try if there was any possibility of becoming like other boys. He described his plight by means of a joke at his own expense—he was, he said, like an Army recruit who said to his Sergeant Major "the whole Army is out of step sir, only I am not."

I am limiting myself in this paper to discussion and illustration of areas in which gross pseudo stupid behavior responded to analytic interpretation. It must be borne in mind that material which is significant to the full understanding of this case has often to be omitted, and that the facts did not always emerge in the order in which they are presented.

The early sessions of Ivan's treatment were taken up in dealing with his defenses and affects. His late arrival for his sessions, his doubts about the efficacy of treatment, his demands for alteration of appointments, and his curiosity about my person and possessions were analysed in connection with his hopes and fears about the help he might get. Ivan then described how he used the part of his session which he missed by coming late in examining the interiors of refrigerators, vacuum cleaners, cocktail cabinets, etc., in a nearby department store. We understood that he was seeking for understanding and answers to his problems without becoming dependent upon me. Ivan said that he had once been dependent upon his own mother and had lost her. For many months to follow, Ivan would assure himself that he could manage without me, saying, "I'm not so much in treatment that I can't survive without it."

In the very first sessions his fear of disloyalty to his dead mother had been taken up. His visits to shops and his preoccupations with kitchen activities were understood as associated with memories of their times together. It was in the early period of treatment, too, that Ivan's overwhelming compulsion to examine the internal workings of my household gadgets (which was, of course, denied him) revealed itself as a need to understand the human body and discover what could go wrong with its mechanisms. Ivan's intellectual functioning was completely restricted to daydreams and fantasy inventions which concerned sexual curiosity interwoven with attempts to understand the cause of his mother's death. His inventions, which appeared to outside observers as completely stupid, fell into three groups. The first group concerned inventions which affected the whole world in that they ensured that if natural resources failed, supplies would never run dry. The second group of inventions concerned gadgets ensuring complete self-sufficiency, such as bags containing all the requirements for living, or a packaway vehicle. The largest group of inventions concerned gadgets to do with perpetual motion, such as dynamos that would never run down and lamps that would never run out.

It was at this point that the transference began to take shape and reflected Ivan's preoccupation with his "two mothers"—his dead mother and the housekeeper who he believed would some day be his legal stepmother (myself in the transference). The rows about him between Ivan's father and the housekeeper heightened his feelings of omnipotence on the one hand, and on the other increased his fears that he might again be abandoned. This situation may have lent additional force to the conflict of loyalty which he experienced at home and which would have been displaced onto the treatment relationship and endangered it, had it not been dealt with as soon as possible.

The session described below took place within the ninth week of treatment, and enabled Ivan to verbalize some of the conflicts surrounding his mother's death and his relationship to the housekeeper and to me.

Ivan had insisted as he did at the beginning of every hour that I must speak first. He now told me that his idea was that I must set him in motion as if he were a pendulum. He would then be able to go on like an automaton. I said that he meant that he could "go on" regardless of the fact that the power that had started the motion was withdrawn. I spoke of his fear that he might lose me before I had fed him with enough treatment supplies to enable him to manage alone. I added that perhaps his need to stuff himself with food and knowledge was a way of taking in and keeping people and things so that they could be safe inside him and could not disappear, or be damaged. Ivan replied that after his mother's death he had eaten ten slices of bread for every meal and drunk many glasses of milk. He added that everyone knows that you can live on milk alone. I said that he had perhaps tried to go on feeding and caring for himself as his mother had done for him when he was little, and as he hoped that I would do for him now. The point was that he feared that I would leave him before he was ready to manage alone.

Following this discussion, Ivan again referred to his own mother saying, "the world has gone too far to bring her back." I said that as time went on situations and people changed, that he had grown and the mother of his memory belonged to a different period. Ivan asked if I believed in a machine based on H. G. Wells' Time Machine which, he said, was a matter of fourth dimension. Such a machine would enable him to go back to the period when his mother was well and to remain at that time until a cure for her particular illness was found. He could then push time forward again so that his mother would be alive today. The crux of the problem was that if she were alive there would be no place for one of the two mothers—his own or the substitute. "There is not room for two inside, so I have to keep one outside."

It should be noted that although the interpretations of oral material were prominent in this session, they were linked with the present and with his mother's death, and not with conflicts in the oral phase. In fact, I did not know at this period about Ivan's historical developmental conflicts.

This session brought considerable relief to Ivan, since it made sense of fantasies which he considered mad, and relieved to some extent his guilt about the growing relationship with me. A real treatment alliance began to develop from this point.

The Conflict Surrounding Aggression

An important aspect of Ivan's fantasy life was magical and omnipotent thinking. It was difficult for Ivan to abandon his conviction that he was powerful enough to restore his mother to life, since with this belief went the fear that he might also have been powerful enough to have played a part in causing her death, and might therefore cause other deaths.

Ivan's belief that his mother had died (left him) because of his angry feelings and behavior gradually became evident, although the genesis of his extreme aggression did not become clear for many months. This was because he could not face his conviction that his mother had been both disappointed in, and ashamed of him. Later memories associated with her attempts to arrange treatment for his physical defects led to intense castration fear and pointed to his anger at being badly made—anger which he projected onto his objects. His fear that treatment would not help him to control this anger and that he would omnipotently damage me and lose me is the material I wish to illustrate next.

In the ninth week of treatment I had sympathized with Ivan's fear of being disloyal to his mother and of becoming fond of me and then being hurt for a second time. During this session, Ivan was tearing the material of the armchair in which he sat, and he commented that he might be doing this to show me how annoying he really can be and to see if I would be angry with him. During the subsequent week, the tearing increased and Ivan said, "In two years there won't be a chair left unless you remove it." I said that he wanted to show me that he was so ill, that he needed at least two years treatment, and that I must assure him that I would not abandon him before then. Ivan responded by provoking me in every possible way. He made as if to break the typewriter case, he took out and unwound the typewriter ribbon, he almost broke a small statue standing on the mantel shelf, and he emptied the drawers of my desk. I said that it looked as if he were doing one of his pieces of research to see if I would abandon him because of his destructiveness. At this point, he unscrewed the legs of the table while he told me of a happening at school in which two boys had been kept "in bounds" as a punishment. I remarked that perhaps he was testing out whether I would let him do any amount of damage or whether there was a point at which I would set limits. I added that he might also be trying to discover whether I believed he could control his destructive actions or whether I thought he had to be controlled by being kept "in bounds" before he did irreversible harm.

This led to a discussion which was overdetermined, having its roots both in his castration fears and in his problems surrounding aggression. One feature was his conviction of inborn brain damage, which would imply that he could not be expected to master his impulses. The fact that I did not remove the furniture or use force, but interpreted his motives, acted as an immense reassurance.

Ivan asked, "Can psychiatry cure things that have grown in one or that one is born with?" He was, he explained, thinking of a boy born without fingers. I said that the boy he was describing may have felt different from other boys because he lacked something.

To this Ivan replied that *he* (Ivan) lacked the wish to resist doing forbidden things. He went on to say that he knew that he
could master destructive impulses, the worrying thing was that he
did not always want to. I acknowledged this fact which to him
confirmed inborn madness, and his fear that I might not want to
treat a boy who gets so very angry. I thought, however, that he
might have many good reasons for feeling so angry and that anger
itself was a normal response to certain situations. I said that some
children are really born with less than the normal amount of
brain and that these children cannot be helped by our sort of
treatment. I explained that if I had removed furniture or used
force, Ivan might have assumed that he was such a person and
that I did not believe that he would ever be able to master his
anger alone. Ivan said, "At home I get hit." I answered that punishment and treatment did not go together because analysis was a
sort of working partnership. Since neither punishment nor force
was likely to further our work, I wondered whether we could find
ways of limiting his destructive behavior so that we could talk
about it and understand its meaning. Ivan wondered whether doing something with his hands would help—he might try tearing
a piece of cloth especially brought here for the purpose—but he
said, with a grin, "this mightn't work, since it would not make
you angry, would it?"

The next day Ivan started on making a rug and said, "I am using all my mind doing this so that there is not any mind left to do
destructive things." I said that he had to use so much of his mind
fighting against his angry, destructive urges that there was not
much left for work or anything else. I added that this, and the
fact that he came regularly to his sessions, showed me that there
was a side of him that very much wanted to deal with the problem of his angry feelings. Ivan said that he supposed there was a
difference between being angry and doing angry actions. I replied that angry feelings like unchanneled electricity could be
frightening until their nature was understood. Electricity could
be dangerous but, if one understood it, it could be harnessed and
then became a valuable source of energy.

Following this Ivan was able to verbalize some of his aggression toward me. He discussed with me his need to believe

that science could bring his mother back, and he suggested that with such a belief he could also avoid the danger of other deaths and separations: "If you have only one real parent left, you can't risk his life by being angry."

One day Ivan asked how it would help him to know that his mother could never return. He went on to describe how angry he felt with me for making him doubt the possibility. He wanted to say to me, "Go and drown yourself because you have taken something from me," but he didn't dare. I said that the childish part of him that believed in magic feared that even his angry thoughts might be powerful enough to come true and damage me. Perhaps, in the same way, he felt that he had been partly to blame for his mother's death and must therefore bring her back. In my experience, understanding daydreams enabled one to distinguish between magical ideas and reality. If one had to live in a world of make-believe, one was not able to concentrate on work or be free to make friends.

The Oedipal Conflict

The fact that Ivan had reached the oedipal phase and battled unsuccessfully with his oedipal conflict emerged in the transference. In his fantasy, sitting and talking to me was equivalent to a sexual relationship. This could be understood in the context of his intense fear of sitting alone with the housekeeper or even speaking to her. I was the lady psychiatrist with the sexual "claptrap" who was treating him not for his own good, but for my personal pleasure, and onto whom he projected his oedipal wishes. The verbatim material of one week is condensed here to illustrate how some of his pseudo stupidity had its origin in the oedipal conflict and in his need to demonstrate to his father that he was a silly child and no real rival to him.

Ivan recollected what the boys at school had told him about school leavers. All school leavers had to have sexual intercourse with the headmaster's wife. He had been worried about this but had worked out that it could not be true because she would have had hundreds of children. He went on to ask whether each sexual intercourse resulted in the conception of a child. I said that he was showing me how confused he was and how difficult it was to get reliable information. I answered his questions factually and then went on to speak of the implication of the "headmaster's wife" story from the point of view of the transference. Ivan said, "If you tried any such thing on me I would run off." This remark was accompanied by his usual suggestive and sly laugh which now could be seen in its appropriate context. He went on to tell me of how he was tempted to listen and look at forbidden things at school, and he added that there was no difference between things that are bad at school and things that are bad in treatment.

Initially, I dealt with Ivan's projections of his own sexual impulses and desires onto me, by taking a realistic attitude. I reminded him of my past refusal to gratify his "hungers" in reality, during treatment. We recollected that I had refused to give him food when he demanded it because I had explained that in treatment we didn't *do* things, but we *spoke* about the feelings until we understood them. I said that, in spite of this, at times he feared that treatment did not aim at helping him to gain control, but permitted him to think and talk about things which he believed to be bad, might in fact unleash forces that he would never be able to control again. We discussed that, in order to gain control of oneself, one needs to understand how one works, just as a driver must understand the mechanics of a car before driving it safely.

Although this discussion was relatively coherent, Ivan's behavior was at its most confused during this week. He reported how he had accidentally handed a new suit together with a bundle of old clothes to the old clothes man and how this had been discovered too late for the suit to be recovered. Numerous other incidents were reported. At the same time, Ivan suggested that his preoccupation with sexual matters was a sign of abnormality. I said that at the moment it was true that Ivan was excessively preoccupied with sexual matters and that he seemed to fear that sexual thoughts and acts might not only be a sign of madness but might cause madness. I agreed that there are many things equally as important and interesting in life as sexual matters, but I said that he could not enjoy these things and put sexual matters into their proper place until his confusion about the facts of life had been cleared up.

Toward the end of the week Ivan spoke of the fact that his stupidity was the cause of arguments between his father and the housekeeper and how he feared that he might one day cause her to leave. It struck him that he was really getting very fond of the housekeeper, but that he could not let her know of his feelings. As he spoke, Ivan picked up a pencil and, with rhythmic continuity, pushed it up and down through a hole in the chair. When I commented upon this he said that it reminded him of school and that it was the boys' way of indicating sexual intercourse. I said that boys are sometimes frightened of their feelings toward their mothers because they consider them grown-up feelings which they should not have. In Ivan's case, it might be all the more complicated since his housekeeper was not his real mother. Ivan said that he could tell me one thing—boys at school never spoke of having sexual intercourse with their mother. I agreed, but wondered whether the stories of the headmaster's wife might not show that boys could imagine such things more easily with someone they substituted for their mother. Ivan said, "One could never have such feelings for one's own mother anyway."

During this week the same material was brought in different forms, such as Ivan's persistent attempts to get into my room and rummage in my desk and drawers. I said that I thought he had to do these things to demonstrate his right to come into my room as a husband comes into his wife's room. Equally, I thought his provocative behaviour was a way of testing me out and forcing me to be strong, to prove that I would not give in to his wishes. During this week and for the last occasion Ivan suddenly turned off the central heating in my room without asking me, thus condemning me to sit in the cold. We discussed his need to "turn off his own heat" to demonstrate to himself that he was master of his impulses. Ivan said, "I did it at home last night and Ann (the housekeeper) thought I was crazy." He went on to tell me that his father had been out for the evening and Ann had invited him to watch television with her. He added, "I always do something stupid at such times" and then, in a whisper, he went on, "A fool cannot be blamed for his actions."

This material from the first four months of treatment brought about a marked change in Ivan's behavior at school and in his ability to make friends, but above all in his behaviour in the sessions. He would now arrive punctually, wait in the waiting room until fetched, and could even tolerate meeting another patient—something that had been quite impossible initially. It should be noted that the improvement took place on the basis of interpretations of oedipal material in the transference and related to the housekeeper. These interpretations were not taken back to his own mother. It was only very much later in the treatment that the original oedipal material emerged. This material, which cannot be fully given here, supports Margaret Mahler's additional explanation for the choice of pseudo stupidity as a symptom, in terms of the need for a libidinous rapport in the family. There is evidence that Ivan used stupidity to provide a cover for participation in his parents' sexual life. As will be seen, Ivan has recollections of sharing his parents' bedroom until the age of four, and often his father's bed.

Ivan's idea of sexual intercourse was that of an aggressive attack against which the helpless woman cannot protect herself. His mother's death was linked in his mind with a fantasy of her suffering in sexual intercourse with his father, and with his own wishes toward her. This colored his fear of his own masculine urges, so that he could not allow himself to grow up and be responsible for a similar catastrophe. Thus tender feelings and sexuality had to be isolated. He retreated from the oedipal conflict by regressing to an oral level in which he demonstrated to myself and everyone else that his relationships with women were based entirely on their need-satisfying function.

The fact that Ivan had reached the oedipal level and regressed from the phallic phase as a result of conflict has an important diagnostic significance. It differentiates him from the borderline adolescent who, in fact, never reaches the oedipal level, and from the psychotic who loses the complex entirely (Rosenfeld and Sprince, 1963).

Masturbation and Castration

Ivan introduced his intense anxiety about masturbation and castration early in his analysis. The following session is from the eleventh week of treatment.

Ivan's destructiveness now included tearing pieces of cane from a table from which he made catapults for use in the session. Each shot was accompanied by a leering laugh. To my question about whether this reminded him of anything, he told me how he had played with the padlock hook on another boy's desk until it had loosened and he feared it would fall off. Examining my propelling pencil, he remarked that he was investigating it through and through, but that he was not likely to break it. He suddenly remembered how his real mother had called him "bats" for not learning well, and that she had often been disappointed in him. She had told him of a teacher who had helped a boy who could not concentrate. He thought he had always been fidgety and had a need to break things, and that his mother had been irritated by this. I said that this told us how his learning difficulties and stupidity may have started before his mother's death, and that perhaps he thought his fidgety need to touch and break things had something to do with it. Ivan said that he could give me a hint— all boys at school need treatment and two boys he was thinking of needed it especially. Almost unthinkingly, he took up two colored pencils and rubbed them together alongside each other. I remarked that he was perhaps showing me something that went on at school, because telling me was so difficult, and yet the need to talk about it was very great. Ivan answered with raucous laughter. I said that laughter of that sort did not really fit in with a serious conversation, and perhaps he had to laugh out of relief or embarrassment. I added that the cane can be broken off and cannot be put back, and that I knew of boys who thought that parts of their bodies could break off in the same way. Ivan thought of an arm or leg and said, "When I tell you the next stage, you will probably think of another part of the body to which this can happen," and then, a moment later, "I have just seen what you mean."

This session was followed by a period of considerable resistance and working through, which lasted for six weeks. The cane breaking and fidgety behavior, however, diminished considerably, and the inappropriate laughter disappeared for good. The "next stage" developed in the sixteenth week and gave, I think, a hint of his homosexual problem.

Ivan told me that in his opinion boys' schools are dangerous— they have, he explained, a very high "standard of sex" because there are no girls and that makes boys oversexed. If there are girls about, you can train yourself to think about them. He made as if to tear off some cane and was surprised at the recurrence of this behavior. I said that perhaps he wanted to tell me, "the next stage." Ivan then told of two boys who made catapults of elastic with which they used to shoot pellets at each other's penises. He did not participate in the game but was terrified that one of the masters would come in and discover it. He became extremely incoherent, rubbing his piece of cane rhythmically with his hand. Suddenly he remembered a girl on holiday who had spoken about keeping a man's bed warm. He thought that what really interested him was what the boys did in bed in the evenings after the games; he believed they took pictures of nude girls to bed. I said that boys and girls, like grown-up men and women, get excited feelings in their genitals which make them want to touch themselves to increase these feelings. Sometimes boys or girls who did not understand about this did these things with each other to share the responsibility. Also, they felt that they were not so odd or bad if others wanted to do the same things. Ivan replied that girls don't have that sort of feeling, but boys, or at least men, "flog themselves out on girls when they marry." Until they marry, boys don't have feelings any more than he does. He added that his grandmother had said that he would end up as a criminal in Borstal.

For many weeks there followed numerous descriptions of mutual sex play and suggestive signs made to the boys by unmarried masters. A story of a man whose penis shrivelled up and who was found to be pregnant when he died hinted at passive feminine indentification.

Ivan's extreme occupation with compulsive systems and his need to fill up every available minute of his time with "improving activities" indicates the extent of his masturbation conflict and his castration anxiety (mainly displaced to the brain). Fenichel (1945) points out that such compulsive systems are also a defense against murderous and incestuous thoughts. In the first months of treatment, Ivan's masturbation conflict was dramatized by his attempt to "turn off the heat" and develop control and mastery while, at the same time, indicating through provocative and destructive behavior that he was not only unable to control his sexual and aggressive impulses, but was unwilling to do so. Ivan was convinced that whatever demands were made of him *no one* at home or at school believed that he could fulfill these demands. His insistence that this implied a birth injury was in part to direct attention away from his belief that any brain damage was self-inflicted as a result of masturbation.

Ivan also believed that boys with inferior or damaged brains had stronger sexual impulses because they had less brain control. Ivan denied ever having masturbated himself, but he had seen boys at school doing so. He had many fantasies of depletion and loss of energy. While discussing masturbation, he spoke incessantly of food, explaining that man can survive without sexual activity but not without nourishment. Gradually, early recollections of mutual sex games with a girl cousin were produced, and these memories, of a time before his mother's death, were associated with his refusal to allow his father to tell him the facts of life. The father's offer had implied to Ivan that he had guessed about the relationship and would punish him (castrate him). These memories caused Ivan to revise his conviction that he had never mas-turbated, and the head-scratching ceased with recollections of "ants in the pants" sensations. The fact that, at some period in his life, Ivan had been interested in a girl made him feel that he could not be so abnormal, but he added,"I was more mature then than I am now. Immaturity becomes more noticeable as you get older, so I am in danger of de-creasing rapidly and getting younger every day."

A less intolerant attitude toward his own sexuality fol-lowed; Ivan speculated continuously upon finding a girl friend and demanded formuli for conversation that would enable him to attract and keep one. His interest in girls was more a duty than a pleasure at this stage, and I doubt if it reflected a true adolescent search for a new object. His aim was to ward off masturbation and underlying homosexual fantasies and wishes, of which hints could be observed in the foregoing session.

Ivan's Relationship to His Father

By the time Ivan had been in treatment for a year, he was no longer destructive in his sessions or compelled to act out his fantasies in daily life. He was identified fully with the aims of treatment and, for the first time in his life, had friends by whom he felt accepted. His stupid behavior had diminished at school and in his sessions, but was still in evidence at home. His form master described him as quite popular, just about average in most subjects and capable of working for a profession.

The material concerning Ivan's relationship with his father only became clear at this point. It is, I believe, the most decisive factor in his pathology. It is of particular interest to us working with children since we are accustomed to giving the father a less important role in influencing early development. Hellman (1954) makes the point that to keep the child passive and stupid was often a necessity for mothers. She adds that the mother who exercises such overwhelming power over a child is felt to be not only a loving and safe mother, but also a dangerous castrating mother. For boys of such mothers, the move to phallic and genital levels is doomed to failure. In this case it will be seen that all of Hellman's remarks could be said to hold good for Ivan's relationship to his father. Ivan's intense attachment to his mother—an attachment which he could not allow even death to break—will be discussed more fully later. It must, however, be borne in mind in the discussion of Ivan's preoedipal relationship to his father.

Ivan had always insisted that he and his father were of one mind—they felt the same about everything. His one aim was to be like his father and to reach the summit as his father had done. His manner of compliantly taking over my words and attitudes and repeating them as if they were his own (to which I referred in the early part of this paper) reflected his attempts to identify with his father by imitation, and indicated the strength of his passive wishes. This was further confirmed by the gratification he seemed to experience in being scolded.

Ivan never appeared to tire of praising his father's achievements and kindness and his one fear was of letting him down. Father's criticisms of Ivan's stupidity and lack of initiative were, he said, entirely justified. Everything he did had the conscious aim of evoking father's praise and regard. Gradually, however, we began to notice that not only did Ivan always succeed in doing the very things that would displease his father, but he felt pleased when father was belittled or caught out in front of others. His anger toward his father initially appeared in displaced form, such as when he spoke of a teacher at school. This teacher was said to be like father in that his unpredictable temper and sarcasm terrified Ivan. The teacher taught father's subjects—which meant the subjects that father was good at and at which, not unnaturally, Ivan was bad. This teacher, in a fit of anger, once screamed at Ivan, saying, "Can't you get a move on; you haven't got a bit of life in you." The monotonous voice and silly expressionless smile with which Ivan recounted this episode enabled us to recognize the dangers of "feeling alive" because that would mean feeling angry. Ivan's way of dealing with this teacher was to decide that he would make no real effort to work at his subject until, "like a bankrupt," he reached the very bottom of the class, and then he would be able to start again from scratch.

Very gradually, Ivan began to express resentment at his father's daily questioning and his controlling attitude. This anger mounted over the months and was accompanied by appropriate affect. Ivan consistently linked his fear of the extent of his anger and of doing irreversible damage to his father, with his mother's death.

Ivan's stupid behavior could now be understood at one level as a way of shaming his father and thus punishing him for his critical and controlling attitude without appearing responsible for the underlying aggression. Once again, he acted on the assumption that a fool cannot be responsible for his actions. This pseudo stupidity was of special significance since it was based on Ivan's conviction that his father viewed him as part of himself. This became clear when Ivan began to speak of father's attitude as implying that everything of Ivan's, whether thoughts, ideas, possessions, time, or success, belonged not to Ivan but to father. Far from wanting Ivan to show initiative, Ivan believed that his father was unable to tolerate any independent action or thought on the part of his son.

This belief can be traced to Ivan's preoedipal relationship to his father, to which I suggest he regressed after the mutual sex play with his child girl friend and his mother's death. It was a relationship characterised by bodily intimacy and the underlying wish to merge and be one with him. The following material emerged eighteen months after treatment commenced.

It was an icy-cold day in March and I found Ivan sitting in the waiting room doing his homework with the window open, the rain pouring in, and the fire switched off. Responding to my surprised look, Ivan said that the window in the waiting room was too small and he needed to keep cool so that his body had training in developing its own body heat. He assured me that as a result of keeping cool he now had enough body heat of his own and did not need to depend upon the fire. He went on to describe many ways in which he practised developing body heat and added that father always demanded that doors were kept closed so he supposed he was being "contrary." Father, he explained, was not a cold person, he is the sort of man who sweats and has a lot of body heat of his own.

Ivan recollected that at times, while his mother was still alive, he had shared his father's bed, and he remembered how his father had "passed his body heat on to him so that he had felt stifled and had tried to move away to make ventilation." They used to lie back to back like spoons, he thought. I wondered whether he had other memories of this time. Ivan recollected happy times when he lay on the top of his father's body as if he were the upper deck of a tram and was "waggled" from side to side. He thought father must have loved him specially to have him in bed with him and he commented, "We were very good friends then. All the criticisms came much later." I said that the games seemed to make Daddy and Ivan part of the same vehicle.

Ivan went on to explain that, although his father was a hot person it did not mean that he was hot sexually, otherwise he would have slept with his wife and not with his son. He ruminated, however, that his father must in fact have slept with his wife, otherwise he would not have had a son and two daughters. (There now followed many associations about the homosexual masters at school and references expressing fear of homosexuality, which I will omit.) Ivan went on to tell me of some trouble that had taken place at home. Not only was his father insisting that he join a special club, but he expected Ivan to pay the subscription fees from his pocket money. Ivan had protested, but father had brushed his protest aside saying that he knew what was best for his son and that he had been a member of a similar club. In an angry voice, Ivan complained that his father did not understand that they were two different people with different interests. I said that Ivan felt that father was treating him today just as he did when he was little—as if they were part of the same vehicle—that is to say, as if father and Ivan were one. To this Ivan agreed and added, "If we are one, then all our qualities must be shared. That means that I've got all the bad qualities and father's got all the good ones."

Ivan arrived at the next session in a highly excited state and, in incoherent manner, reported how he had recited Hotspur's speech to Henry IV while cleaning his teeth the night before. When he reached the words, "My liege, I would deny no prisoner," he had a feeling of madness—like "genius is mad." He knew that he was not a genius, but he felt super special. It had to do with his anger toward his father and his feeling that at times he really was like his father and as powerful. I said that when Ivan was little and shared his father's bed, he had sometimes felt suffocated and overwhelmed by father, but he had also felt part of him and very happy. It was as if he had a share in father's mental equipment and could hope to be clever and powerful like father. The problem was that being so close to father made him feel like a prisoner. As he grew up, the healthy part of him wanted to develop its own body heat, that is to say to exist independently of father. This wish to be independent made him feel that if he separated himself from father he would lose all right to his share of father's qualities. This was especially so because in his anger towards father he so often wished to see him humiliated and he believed that father must feel the same towards him.

Ivan's idea that father's perfection depended upon their "oneness" had many ramifications. While Ivan believed that their union enabled him to hope for a share in his father's mental equipment, a corollary to this idea was that attempts to loosen the tie would mean either depriving himself of the very means of existence or depriving father of his. Open acts of aggression and attempts to sever the tie meant to Ivan an attempt to take father's intelligence from him and keep it for himself—that is, to castrate father. This conviction that father would lose part of himself as a result of Ivan's independent development lent force to his belief that father needed him and was determined to maintain their union. In addition, if father was to be at the top, Ivan himself must remain at the bottom.

Ivan's pseudo stupidity was, at the deepest level, a response to his passive homosexual wishes. By his stupid behavior, he repeatedly reassured his father of the continuation of their union and of the fact that the inferior qualities of the union remained vested in himself.

Ivan's stupid behavior held out one positive hope, however. This was expressed in relation to the teacher. Ivan had devised a technique of stupidity and failure based upon the idea that only if he reached rock bottom (returned to infancy), could he hope to start again from the beginning and become independent. This example of an obsessional fantasy as a defence, which was in fact acted out at school, illustrates Ivan's attempts to "undo" the union with father and how he employed pseudo stupidity to achieve this aim.

Ivan's fantasy of going back to infancy and starting again gives us insight into the development of his preoedipal relationship to his father, since it points to a time when it was not the father, but the mother, who was the most significant person in his life. Our knowledge of Ivan's relationship to his mother depends almost entirely upon analytic reconstruction. She emerges as a shadowy and initially idealized figure, aspects of whom are reflected in Ivan's attitude to his father, his feelings about the housekeeper, and in his relationship to me in the transference.

We cannot be sure how Ivan's mother felt about him. He may have been one of those children who are in some way unloveable at birth, and whose inborn ego structure both disposes to neurosis and sets in motion a relationship between mother and child which perpetuates rejection. Or it may be that there was something lacking in this mother's capacity to love and care for her first child. Whatever the facts, we know that Ivan felt that he was a disappointment to his mother and that she did not want him. His relationship to her had a definite bearing upon his lack of self-esteem.

Ivan's very few actual memories of his mother were either concerned with treatment arrangements connected with his physical defects, recollections of her disapproving remarks about his clumsiness or stupidity, and some happier times when they went shopping together or when he played in the kitchen while mother cooked. From the transference, we established that he experienced his mother's efforts to arrange physical treatment for him as evidence that she wished to castrate him more than he already believed himself to be. Anger and hopelessness about this were displaced onto the therapeutic situation against which Ivan defended himself initially in every possible way, maintaining that I was trying to make him more ill than he was and that I would then abandon him for patients who were less stupid and whom I liked better (referring to his younger sisters). On the other hand, it was evident that the more helpless and damaged Ivan felt himself to be, the more hope he had that I would care for him, feed him, and prefer him to all others. The kitchen and shopping memories, his longing to be fed and cared for, his intense greed, and the invention of gadgets to ensure that supplies would never run dry, all point to a tendency to regard the object as primarily need-satisfying. In the transference, the ease with which Ivan regressed to oral and anal levels pointed to a disturbance at these developmental phases as well as to the likelihood of real frustration and gratification at those levels. We know from his material that Ivan experienced deprivation of food as a punishment. It is equally likely that his mother pressed food upon him by way of assuaging her guilt and compensating him for her disappointment in him—an attention that may have given him much pleasure.

At times the transference confirmed a fleeting tendency to even earlier regression. Ivan's wish to merge and be united with the object could be seen in the way he compliantly took over my ideas, but even more when he occasionally appeared quite unable to differentiate between my thoughts and his. At these phases, he was unable to leave his sessions at the end of the hour. Having eventually separated from me, he would telephone me soon after, intent on resuming a lengthy and uninterrupted discussion. Analytic reconstruction shows that Ivan's fear that his mother would abandon him preceded her illness and death and threatened him with loss of supplies and starvation. The extent of his continued dependence upon her and his need to defend against vulnerability to object loss were expressed in the transference when he insisted that he was "not so much in treatment that he couldn't *survive* without it." He dealt with this intense separation anxiety by complete denial and isolation of affect. He showed no concern during his mother's illness and hospitalization and is said not to have cried at her death, or to have spoken of her afterward.

The characteristic of this marked disturbance in the early

mother-child relationship is reflected in Ivan's idealised image of his mother as a need-satisfying figure, with whom he longed for union and without whom he was lost. But behind this longing are hidden feelings of intense resentment toward her for rejecting him (together with the accompanying guilt). It is important to bear in mind, at this point, that the father's destructive, controlling, and seductive behavior was already present during Ivan's early childhood and over the length of the mother's illness. It is even possible that Ivan displaced some of his father's attitude towards him onto his mother, or that he projected his father's later criticisms about him back into the past so that his memory of his dead mother was additionally colored by them.

The other factor that must be taken into consideration is that the mother's illness occurred at the height of Ivan's oedipus complex. His longing for a close oedipal relationship with her was fused with his earlier aggression toward her for rejecting him. This played a part in his fantasy about her death and became embodied in another fantasy—that of sexual intercourse as an aggressive and murderous attack. In addition to the normal expectation of oedipal retaliation from the father, the period of his mother's illness and ultimate death can be seen to have represented for Ivan a confirmation of his belief in the danger of heterosexuality, and the omnipotent power of his own aggression.

It is only when viewed in the light of Ivan's preoedipal tie to his mother, that the full significance and effect of the father's controlling, seductive, behavior and need for closeness to his son can be assessed. It is an open question whether Ivan could have withstood the father's pathological needs, even if his own needs had not already been influenced by this earlier relationship with his mother. Theoretical discussion of the possible implications of such preoedipal relationships is not within the scope of this paper. Its relevance to homosexual development has been discussed by Anna Freud (1965).[2]

The point that has to be made is that Ivan's acute separation anxiety arising from such a tie, together with other features of his relationship to his mother (such as the need to disguise aggression and display castration, thereby avoiding real castration), prepared the ground for the passive homosexual role which his father's pathology additionally favored.

SUMMARY

This paper sets out to demonstrate how gross pathological behavior can be reached and relieved by interpretation of the defenses and affects. My aim has been to illustrate how working from the surface inward and utilizing the transference to throw light upon conflicts as they appeared in the material, it was possible to bring about a full treatment alliance and, ultimately, considerable relief and improvement.

REFERENCES

Fenichel, I. (1945), *The Psychoanalytic Theory of Neurosis*. New York: Norton.

Freud, A. (1965), *Normality and Pathology in Childhood*. New York: International Universities Press.

Geleerd, E. R. (1963), Evaluation of Melanie Klein's "Narrative of a Child Analysis." *Internat. J. Psychoanal.*, 44:493-506.

Hellman, I. (1954), Some Observations on Mothers of Children with Intellectual Inhibitions. *The Psychoanalytic Study of the Child*, 9:259-273. New York: International Universities Press.

Johnson, A. M., & Szureck, S. A. (1952) The Genesis of Antisocial Acting Out in Children and Adults. *Psychoanal. Quart.*, 21:323-343.

[2] See also Sprince (1964).

Mahler-Schoenberger, M. (1942), Pseudoimbecility: A Magic Cap of Invisibility. *Psychoanal. Quart.*, 11:149-164.

Rosenfeld, S. K. & Sprince, M. P. (1963), An Attempt to Formulate The Meaning of the Concept "Borderline." *The Psychoanalytic Study of the Child,* 18:603-635. New York: International Universities Press.

Sprince, M. P. (1964), A Contribution to the Study of Homosexuality in Adolescence. *J. Child Psychol. & Psychiat.*, 5:103-117. London: Pergamon Press.

MARJORIE HARLEY

Transference Developments in a
Five-Year-Old Child

IN ACCORDANCE WITH THE OBJECTIVES of this assignment, I
shall present excerpts from a five-year-old girl's analysis with
a view toward conveying a modicum of the interplay between
child and analyst. Rather than attempting an over-all account
of the treatment, I have singled out such fragments from the
first year as relate to some of this girl's transference manifestations. First, I shall describe how transference initially displayed itself and how it could be utilized for defense interpretation aimed at arousing the child's beginning awareness
that her conflicts ultimately lay within herself, and thus at
facilitating the development of a therapeutic alliance. Second, I shall sketch her enactment, through the transference,
of certain aspects of her masturbation problem and its ramifications.

During the decade between the late Forties and Fifties the
old gradually faded into the new as an increasing number of
child analysts came to observe the unfolding of transference
in their young patients and to gain a growing sense of its va-
lidity as a therapeutic tool. By 1960, at a Panel on Resistances
in Child Analysis,[1] the fact that all four papers dealt with
transference aspects of resistance was impressive as a reflection
of our changed attitudes in respect to the child's capacity for
transference developments. Nonetheless, these papers showed

[1] Held before the American Psychoanalytic Association. For details, cf. Harley
(1961).

115

some divergence of opinion with regard to the character and relative significance of transference factors prior to pre-puberty. For this reason it may be useful to comment briefly on the nature of transference in children in order to provide a frame of reference for the clinical material to follow—even though by so doing I risk repeating what by now is fairly common knowledge.

1. Transference is not limited to the extension into the analytic situation of current reactions to the original love objects, but includes earlier libidinal and aggressive strivings reanimated by the analytic process and directed toward the analyst. That these, then, to greater or less extent, are re-directed to the original objects need not preclude their continuing and varying expression in the transference. They may show themselves simultaneously and in like fashion within the transference and home situations, or their different aspects may be divided between the two. The converse also holds: that is, when repressions are lifted by interpretations which pertain to the relationships with the original love objects, almost invariably there will follow manifestations of the revived experiences in the transference; and instances may occur in which even the young child permits himself to re-enact these earlier experiences with greater intensity in the transference than at home.

2. Transference neurosis, as defined in the sense that a neurotic symptom formation, arising from regressed conflicts activated by the analytic situation, is centered on the analyst or his surroundings, is sometimes observable, albeit in limited or circumscribed form, in certain phases of treatment even with young children.

3. There is the factor of the child's ability to form a thera-peutic alliance based on that element of his ego which is cap-able of keeping in touch with the reality of the analyst and

his role. The therapeutic alliance is to be distinguished from transference proper. In most cases it allows the child to withstand phases of negative transference and affords us a greater sense of freedom to interpret the positive transference resistances when this seems indicated (Frankl and Hellman, 1962).[2]

It is with these three points in mind that I shall proceed, highlighting only such features of the child's history as have direct relevance to this presentation.

Anne was her mother's first child. Two teen-age half-sisters from her father's first marriage played a minor role in this first year of analysis. I mention them only to complete the picture of the family constellation. The mother was extremely sensitive, capable of intense feelings, and eager to be a good mother to her children. The father, also a sensitive and feeling person, had a certain empathy for Anne's tendency to dissolve into tears or else to withdraw into the background in the face of competition with her younger sister.

Anne had been given no preparation for the advent of this sibling until the moment of the mother's departure for the hospital. Shortly after the sister's birth, Anne, then two years old, suddenly and possibly too abruptly "weaned herself," apparently in a combined effort to quell her hostile feelings and to placate her mother. Around this time the mother re-

[2] This capacity to form a therapeutic alliance and to differentiate between her perception of the reality of the analyst and her transference reactions was expressed with marvelous understanding by a six-year-old girl. In a neutral moment, she told me very earnestly that she had come to realize it was not I whom she did not like; actually I was "quite nice." It was the fact that I was an "appointment lady" and had this "lousy job" to do that made her have all kinds of upset feelings about me. A few moments later she volunteered that since I did have this "lousy job" she might as well tell me she was having trouble falling asleep. She was only telling me this, she explained, because she did not like to feel tired in school. The derivatives of primal scene fantasies which then followed led to her expression of negative transference feelings which could be approached in terms of her exclusion from the private quarters of my apartment.

newed toilet training which she had abandoned earlier after
a period in which the child rather consistently and strenuous-
ly opposed her attempts. Now again, and in contrast to her
recent compliance in the oral sphere, Anne put up a fierce
resistance. There soon followed a period of such severe withholding that suppositories were resorted to. When these
yielded no result, and upon the pediatrician's advice, an
enema was administered one morning by the father, while
the mother held the frantic child forcibly on the bathroom
floor. That same afternoon, the mother, goaded by this same
pediatrician's insistence that she take a strong stand in training, forced Anne to remain on the toilet seat for almost two
hours, alternately pleading with and screaming at the child
in angry frustration. The forced movement which Anne
finally produced resulted in an anal fissure. From that day
on, she was bowel-and bladder-trained, but became ever more
submissive and compliant. It was also after this crisis that she
evinced increased anxiety in the presence of dogs, and for
several months thereafter was afraid that a zebra in the toilet
would bite her.

Anne was brought to me when she was just five. The presenting complaints were her fear of dogs, which in the past
year had reached phobic proportions, and a lingering tendency toward bowel retention. My decision to recommend analysis rested not so much on these two symptoms as on the
child's resigned and depressed-like quality, and on my feeling
that her exaggerated need to comply with her mother's demands and to curb any aggressive strivings might well impede
the development of her own self-forces. A related consideration was that it might be expedient to initiate treatment before the onset of latency, lest this particular child then erect
defenses which would constrict certain areas of ego functioning and also render her less accessible to treatment.

The following is an abridged account of my two initial contacts with Anne prior to her analysis which was initiated two months later, that is, after the summer vacation. Her mother had told her that I was someone who would help her with her fear of dogs and had also explained that I had a dog but had promised to lock him up when she came. As I saw it, the child's ability to accept this promise on faith was an indication of a fundamentally positive element in the mother-child relationship.

In the first of these two hours Anne almost immediately expressed the wish to draw a picture. Before embarking on this project, however, she asked me, without any perceptible apprehension, if my dog was locked up, and I sensed this was her way of introducing her problem. I said, "Yes, he is," adding, "Your mommy told me about your trouble with dogs; I know this must be a very hard trouble." She nodded. I asked, "Is it that you're afraid maybe a dog might bite you?" She said, "No, that's the funny part." When I now said, "I guess it's just that a great big frightened feeling comes over you and you can't understand why," she responded with a relieved, "How did you know?" and turned to her picture. She then proceeded to scrawl a few lines and dots on paper. I asked, "What is the picture about?" and she explained that it was a version of a little boy who cried. She continued, in a rather sloppy and undirected fashion, to cover the entire paper with tears. I said: "So many tears, the little boy must be very unhappy." She agreed, and her resigned smile and gestures which followed were like those sometimes seen in a much older person who has adopted an attitude of resignation in the face of an inexorable fate. Now, feigning a gayer mood, she said: "It's rain, not tears, and it's fun to walk in the rain." I replied, "I can see, Anne, that you try very hard to turn unhappy things into happy things." To this she came up with the remark that when she was older she might not be afraid of dogs. But, she added, if she waited until then it might take a hundred years. I said, "It seems like such a very great big trouble you want me to help you with it." She nodded, and was reluctant to leave.

Next day Anne built a house of blocks. A little boy, she said, had come to the house, so the dog had to be locked up, but this did not make the dog angry. I suggested, "I think maybe you wonder if my dog is angry at being locked up; I know it would worry you if he really was." She responded by enacting another drama in which a large mommy (teddy bear), who was "really a bad witch underneath," hit her little girl (puppet) and the little girl hit her back. In this tussle the bear-mommy fell over. With a forced smile, as though endeavoring to maintain the game element, Anne announced, "She's dead," and indicated she wished to leave; she needed her mother. She changed her mind after I helped her establish the distinction between reality and fantasy by saying, "You know, Anne, children get all mixed up sometimes and forget that make-believe things like a child killing her witch mommy aren't real; then their games aren't fun any more, they get too scarey."

Now Anne invited me to sit down beside her to tell me, as she put it, something that was real—not make believe. Pointing to a scab on her nose, she said it was bad to rub scabs because one might hurt oneself, but that her parents had said it was all right to rub places where there were not any scabs. By her tone she asked for my confirmation that her parents were right. I gave this reassurance (which I think I need not have done) by first saying, "Yes, that's right," and then added, "Children like to rub places on their bodies because it feels so good, yet this worries them, too." She replied that she would see me in September and that she hoped then to have a hundred appointments!

In these two hours Anne presented those conflicts that comprised the major themes in the first year of her analysis: her castration complex as depicted through her identification with the little boy who was, however, a sorry little boy, helpless to control and direct the splashing of his tears; her enormous aggression against her mother; and her masturbation anxiety. Omens of future transference developments were perceptible in her fear of my dog's anger followed by the aggressive play with the witch-mother. In this initial contact, however, I would see her hostile wishes as still having been mainly directed toward the original object, and her need for the reassurance of her mother's presence as an indication of this. Doubtless, she also wanted to escape from a situation that had evoked such a dangerous fantasy.

As regards the implications for the therapeutic alliance, Anne's desire for help was conspicuous. Her immature ego, however, had as yet not had much opportunity to gain knowledge of the real role of the analyst, nor had it experienced the workings of the therapeutic process. At this initial point of contact between us, it is more likely that in this very eagerness for help, precursors of transference (Frankl and Hellman, 1962) may have begun to come into play, and that her id wish for an all-giving mother who would use her magical omnipotence toward curing her ills had possibly already been stirred into activity in relation to the person of the analyst. It was, in fact, in this direction that transference unfolded itself most strikingly in the first stages of the analysis. I should add that, on the night of the second visit, Anne for the first time in a year removed her underpants upon going to bed; but I should also add that, having slept without them all summer, she put them on again on the night before her first analytic hour.

Now for some of the transference developments in the analysis: undertones of ambivalent transference reactions were detectible in the first weeks of Anne's analysis. On the one hand, she was friendly, eager to come to appointments and, on the whole, reluctant to leave. In many ways she indicated her high hopes that I would right her ills, revealing these hopes mainly in the context of her castration complex. As she came to partially recognize that aspect of myself that would neither punish nor condemn, she seemed to find delight in engaging in what for her meant aggressive behavior, such as making little impish remarks and daring to get paint on herself and the floor.

At the same time, I felt that there lurked in the background apprehension lest I might retaliate, and I often had the feeling that so much as an unsmiling expression on my part would cause her to retreat into passivity and compliance. I also noted a marked tendency to construe certain of my activities, which to another child might be quite acceptable, as my exertion of pressure on her. For example, she would respond to any encouragement for further elaboration of her play themes with an "I don't know," or else the play would peter out. As I came to recognize this area of sensitivity and thus became more passive, she showed increasing freedom in fantasy elaboration through play.

At first her play revolved mainly around the dolls, and I was the audience. As in a dream condensation, she frequently appeared simultaneously to reflect herself through the boy, girl, and baby dolls. At other times the boy and baby were unquestionably her little sister whom she saw as more loved and more adequate than herself. The children were exaggeratedly good, and when I remarked they seemed to feel they *had* to be *so* good I was met with a strenuous denial. As I eventually began to interpret her defense of denial, two new themes appeared in her play.

The first followed my transference interpretation of her denial of painful affects evoked by her fear that I liked my other child patients better than her, and appeared to relate to the sister's birth and the subsequent events leading to her displacement of her conflicts onto the dog. In this play, the mother went to the hospital. Upon her return, she left the house again and was replaced by a dog who took over the maternal role. The second theme involved a baby who was forced to be good by a bad person; but the baby revolted and killed the bad person. Immediately, Anne defensively shifted the responsibility for the murder onto an unknown person and the baby now led an army of good people to find the murderer and punish *her*.

Not long after, Anne reported two dreams: one was "about a wolf who ate up children but it wasn't a wolf, it was a bad person dressed up as a wolf"; and the other was "about a bad lady hitting and hurting me." When I remarked that every dream had a secret in it and that it was fun sometimes to hunt for the secret, she came up with: "I know this secret already; I got the bad lady mixed up with my mommy giving me a love pat."

It was after her admission, through her dreams, of the dangerous aspects of her mother that Anne first showed her equation of tears with urine and their relation to her castration complex. As she put it, the people in her play had been hurt in their vaginas and could no longer hold their pee-pee; and in a later fantasy she revealed that the baby let her pee-pee out through her tears because this was less bad and messy. However, a good doctor (i.e., the analyst) effected a cure. She pretended the stuffed dog was dangerous because a bad mommy had climbed into him and also added, although uncertainly, that my dog was probably nice because he had a good mommy in him. She removed her underpants at night for the first time since starting her analysis, and the following transference development entered into the foreground.

In brief, I now became the one who would fulfill all her wishes and protect her. The intensity of this transference fantasy was revealed in the state of high exuberance the child portrayed for weeks, both within and outside the analytic situation, and in the seemingly fearless way in which, for a brief period, she expressed hostility toward her mother. She "flew" around the office clutching the string of a red balloon and explaining that a good mommy had given her the wings which a bad witch mother had taken from her, and in various

ways implied that I had made her a superior child. She had
early revealed that I was accomplishing all my wonders with
my magic wand, that one day I would give her the wand and
she would have no more troubles: they would just disappear
and, she underscored, she would not even need to understand
them with me! When she began to assimilate that it was
neither my function to grant such wishes, nor had I the power
to do so, the transference began to shift in the direction of
the negative as may be seen in a show Anne put on for me.
This was the show:

There was a little baby (doll), and her family thought her ugly
and stupid, and the bad mommy (doll) made her more ugly and
stupid. Then a nice soft (stuffed) pussy cat, who understood children, adopted the baby. And the baby became the smartest, most
wonderful and bravest baby in the whole wide world. But then
the baby found out the pussy cat hadn't made her wonderful;
there was a boy (doll) who was much more wonderful. And the
baby felt just terrible. Anne agreed emphatically with me that the
baby must have been very angry at the pussy cat for making her
feel so terrible.

It is evident that the pussy cat analyst had failed Anne in the
same way as had the mother. The boy, who intruded into the
picture and was more wonderful, referred to the intrusion of
her little sister upon whom, as later fantasies revealed, the
mother had bequeathed the penis which she had denied Anne
and which I, too, now denied her.

The next day Anne broke the toy dog's leg while he and the
baby doll were engaged in a competitive race. On a conscious
level, this mishap seemed to have been accidental. Obviously anxious, she ceased the play. When I said, "I think you're worried,
even a little frightened that I'll be angry," she nodded in the af-
firmative. When I added, "It's almost as if you feel you might have
hurt me when you broke something that belonged to me," she
said: "Let's pretend that the dog is a bad mommy—I mean that
the bad mommy killed the dog." She wanted to mend the dog's

leg, and I offered to get some scotch tape from another room. Now very frightened, she implored me not to go into the back of the apartment. I commented, "You know, Anne, I think you're afraid my dog will be angry today." She admitted this, emphasizing she could see *I* was not angry; then laughed and said, "I got you and your dog confused." I said very seriously, "I think you really did get my dog and me confused." But now she insisted I could never get angry. I was the *good* mommy.

This fragment of an hour shows how Anne defended herself against aggressive impulses toward me first by displacing and then by projecting them onto the bad mother. These defenses apparently did not suffice, and her fear of my retaliation was displaced onto my dog. Then, having almost admitted this displacement by her statement that she had confused me with my dog, she returned to her first defense, insisting that I was the good mother, that is, as opposed to the bad mother. I would note that after her brief outbreak of hostility in the early weeks of the analysis, the child's behavior toward her own mother continued to be largely positive and compliant, and the bad mother, in her conscious mind, was still a make-believe figure. This tendency to deny her negative feelings for me by splitting her ambivalence between the good and bad mother had to be dealt with repeatedly in the transference. The following example shows one of the ways in which I handled this problem, as well as the child's beginning acceptance of her ambivalence.

After having killed the bad mother in play, Anne vehemently threw a toy lamp against the wall, explaining it was a night light and then deciding it was a bad wolf. When I suggested a bad wolf bothered her at night, she volunteered she had had a dream, that the secret of the dream was Little Red Riding Hood, and offered her own version of this story which, she said, she preferred to the real one. In her account the bad mother dressed up as a wolf and was about to eat her child, but the good mother rushed in and saved her. It was clear that I was the good mother. I suggested she preferred her version because by making believe a child could have two mothers, she could also make believe that a child never had to get angry at the good mother whom she loved. Anne asked what kind of mother was in the real version. I said she was more like a real mother, not a make-believe one. The same good mother whom the child loved also sometimes seemed like a bad mother, and then maybe the child worried because she was angry at the mother she also loved. Anne exclaimed: "A half-and-half mother." She reflected and added: "And a half-and-half child."

Likewise, her externalization[3] of her aggression conflict through the aid of projection had to be continually interpreted. The next example shows the child's further insight into the aggressive forces which lay within herself.

In one hour, when her anal aggression against me was close to the surface and she had made innuendos to the effect that I was messy, Anne playfully threw a rubber ball against the wall. As it bounced back at her, she turned toward me accusingly and cringed as though it was I who had thrown it at her. I interpreted that maybe she had felt angry at me and feared her own anger would bounce right back at her just as the ball bounced from the wall. Later in this hour she painted a picture of a storm and whispered: "A big bad storm has come." When I whispered back: "Who made the storm?" she replied: "I did; it came from me."

The following episode, after approximately four months of analysis, shows the child's growing ability to accept the fact of her own hostile impulses and to express these in the transference.

I had had to vanish, in effect, for almost a month of appointments because of back trouble. In the hour just prior

---

[3] According to Anna Freud (1965), externalization is not a form of transference proper, but rather should be regarded as a subspecies of transference.

to this separation the material had reflected a medley of pre-oedipal and oedipal hostility against the mother. At the end of the session, Anne had revealed a masturbation fantasy, the gist of which was that when she made the bad mother vanish with her magic hand, she stayed up at night alone with her father while he played the piano. Shortly after I had told Anne on the telephone that I could not see her for a while because of a "sore back," she complained of a sore leg and limped almost continuously. In her choice of her leg as the focus for her ailment, the fact that the child had previously broken my toy dog's leg is, of course, pertinent.

Upon her return to analysis, and having first announced my absence had seemed not like a month but a million months, she denied she had missed me. Nor did she give any indication of her leg trouble. She expressed eagerness for me to win a table game and I pointed out that she wanted to be especially nice to me at this time. She neither confirmed nor denied this. Her only reference to my "sore back" was her remark that she did not like the straight chair on which I was sitting.

The next day she wanted me to be a cowboy in a table game and asked if cowboys were bad or good. I said there were probably bad ones and good ones; that the bad ones probably had a little good in them and the good ones a little bad in them—like everybody and like her, too. I reminded her how she had once so wisely told me that it was because people were good that they worried about being bad. She noted a picture on the game board of a little boy who had hurt his leg and commented that his bad leg was the result of his badness. I said: "Poor child; he got all mixed up and thought angry thoughts could come true as though bad thoughts were the same as doing bad things." Now she looked me straight in the eye and said: "I'd like to use bad magic thoughts—and if I did I could kill you and your dog—I could make you vanish." This, of course, led to my interpretation of her concern that her angry thoughts had caused me to have a sore back and to vanish; and that like the little boy with the hurt leg, she felt she should be hurt for what she felt was her badness.

After this session it was not I, but Anne's limp that vanished. When her parents remarked on this, she replied casually that she and Dr. Harley had found more thoughts and feelings in her that she had not known were there. I mention this as an indication that the child had formed a therapeutic alliance and was experiencing the real purpose of analysis.

Thus far I have focused on some of the ways in which I dealt with Anne's defensive manoeuvers in the transference. I shall devote the remaining pages to a simplified sketch of how she conveyed, through the transference, some aspects of her masturbation problem and led me back along the genetic pathway to certain of the pregenital components of her castration complex and oedipal conflict.

Anne's masturbation theme was introduced gradually. As she climbed onto the high shelves in the playroom, I suggested she was telling me she was tempted to do dangerous things that were fun, yet that she feared might result in her hurting herself. Then, as I related her fantasies of dangerous fires to the little fires of excitement she perhaps sometimes felt in herself, she stressed the magical powers of her hand as she turned on the light of my electric heater. Finally, I was able to approach her masturbation anxiety more directly. The following occurred in a session in which she had expressed, in her doll play, derivatives of her dilemma as to whether her castrated state was attributable to her own or her mother's actions.

Anne went to the table and invited me to sit down (in a manner reminiscent of her prelude in the second consultation hour to her expression of concern over scratching her scab). She picked up a pencil, rubbed the eraser end against the table, and asked: "Could it (i.e., the eraser) come off if I rub hard?" I said that the eraser *could* come off, that some things came off when rubbed hard, and some things did not. She rubbed the eraser on a book and said: "The book couldn't come apart if I rub this way." I said, "No, it couldn't," and repeated that some things came apart when one rubbed them, and some did not and that sometimes it was hard for children to know what would come apart and break, and what would not—sometimes they even thought things would or had come off when they could not or had not. That was the way things often were with children, and that made a big worry for them. She nodded gravely, and I added, "And when they do secret things, sometimes they worry very much and don't know if they've broken something or not."

Anne returned to the dollhouse and put the mommy and daddy dolls to bed. Turning to me rather impulsively, she asked: "If I wanted to come to see you in the night would you let me?" I said, "I think you wonder very much what I do in the night time and if I would be more interested in someone else in the night time than in you—or not want you to see what I do in the night time." Now she asked, "If I came would you lock your dog up in the night time?" answering the question herself, with: "No, you wouldn't lock him up at night. I know it!" I said, "You're think-ing perhaps in the night time my dog would be more important than you, and that if you came here in the night time, maybe I would be doing terribly exciting, dangerous things and maybe even terrible, dangerous things would happen to you, too." (The more correct interpretation, I believe, would have been that she wanted my protection from her own night-time excitement. Also, it is likely, within this context, that my dog had the meaning of the dangerous, punishing figure—analyst-mother probably—who would punish her for her masturbation.)

Anne now picked up the pencil and, as though telling a story, said, "And now the little girl goes to sleep alone in her little blue bed," as she put the pencil in the bed and covered it up with a blanket. She went on to say, "And she has to stay alone in her own little bed and so she rubs the eraser on the bed." The hour was already over, which she knew since the doorbell had rung, but I added, as I followed her out of the room, "and thinks dan-gerous, exciting, wonderful-terrible thoughts."

The next day Anne made straight for the dollhouse. I noted she had brought with her two rather beaten up stuffed animals:

a floppy dog and a little rabbit. She put all the people in the doll house to bed, announcing it was night time and that they were asleep. She then explained that the bunny stayed up all night. I said that then it could see and hear all kinds of things in the night time and also do things that no one else could know about. The bunny played around a bit, hopping and peering into the house and then got under a blanket on the floor. Anne volunteered he was not asleep but just liked to be covered up. I told the bunny that I understood why he wanted to get under the blanket and be all covered up that way; it gave him a safer, more private feeling, as if the blanket protected him a little. Anne answered by taking a removable seat off one of the chairs in the dollhouse and handing me this little chair to "fix." When I had done so she proceeded to take apart the seats from the remaining chairs of the set so that I would fix them all. Again, I said what I had said in essence several times before: that she liked so much to have me fix things for her and that she wanted to feel that I was a good fixer and could fix *anything* for her. Her immediate response was to take out all the dolls from the dollhouse, and to gather the toy horses and soldiers. These objects comprised the army that was out to kill all the bad things in the "whole wide world" and all "the bad children" who "broke their toys."

The leader of the army was the girl doll who obviously reflected Anne, herself. She placed the girl on a horse, explaining that the horse was a "power" horse. When I said I guessed that the little girl felt that by riding the "power" horse she would get some of his power, she heartily agreed. Then she hit on what to her was a wonderful idea: "The little girl will be Peter Pan, Peter Pan is the leader of the good army!" Now suddenly the bunny was a bad person whom they were all after. I expressed surprise and was a little incredulous that the little bunny was really *that* bad. She picked up the bunny, came over to me, and showed me a big hole on its bottom, explaining his "winding machine" was gone—he had pulled it out. Maybe next time she would bring the winding machine to her appointment, she said, and I could put it back. Before I could answer she confessed: "*I* really broke it a long, long time ago. I pulled it out. I was rubbing him 'down there' with my hand—he was so soft and furry—and then I felt something there and I pulled it out with my hand. But I'll bring it next time and you can fix it."

I said again that she worried so much when she broke anything. She had been telling me of the bad things she felt she did with her hand, and had told me also of the wonderful fire of excitement she could make with her hand, and she had wondered if the eraser would break if she rubbed it too hard, and she had broken the bunny by rubbing him "down there." I knew, and I thought she knew too, that she was worried lest she do something bad by rubbing herself "down there." It felt so good and yet it seemed bad and she was so afraid maybe she had broken herself "down there." "You're very, very wrong," she insisted. "You're not so smart—you're *stupid*. If you were smart you'd know I only worry because I don't like my hands to smell bad." I agreed that I was pretty sure she did worry about her hands smelling; children sometimes had the idea that they were dirty and messy "down there," so that when they put their hands there they felt they were doing something dirty and messy. But, I said, I still was almost sure she worried also because she was afraid she had hurt, or would hurt, herself "down there." "Absolutely not, I never had such an idea," she said vehemently, and turned to the Peter Pan army. Before actually doing any more with this play, however, she turned to me and asked me very gravely: "Do you believe in the Never-Never Land? Do you believe there really is a Never-Never-Land?" "Do *you?*" I asked. She answered quite factuallly that she did not, it was only make-believe, and added: "Now I told you, so you have to tell me, it's your turn." I answered directly, feeling it was only right to accept her on this direct level at that moment, and said: "I, too, know it's only make-believe, but it's still fun to make believe there's a Never-Never Land." "I think so, too," she agreed emphatically. "Maybe you'd like to make believe you could go to the Never-Never Land," I said. "Oh, yes," was her reply, "I'd *love* to go there." I said, "I read about it so long ago I can't remember all the nice things about it—remind me."

"Well," she said, "Peter Pan could kill all the bad things. He cut off Captain Hook's hand, but nothing could ever happen to *him* (i.e., Peter Pan). He couldn't get *his* hand cut off, and *he* could never get hurt, no matter what he did." "So," I said, "If you could be like Peter Pan in Never-Never Land, you'd never have to worry about having your hand cut off or getting hurt, or hurting yourself with your hand. Don't you think maybe just one teensy-weensy reason for wanting to be like Peter Pan is because of that worry?" She said nothing.

Anne arrived the following day carrying a Tiger mask. Having put on this mask, she made menacing motions toward me and threatened to bite off my hand. In this game she merely growled; it was I who had to do the talking under her direction. For some time this consisted of my saying how scared I was. Finally, I injected, "That scary tiger—I'm so afraid he'll think I'm a naughty child and bite off my hand." A little while later, I said: "He's such a scary tiger. I'm just a little child, and he seems so big and powerful. I wish I had a tiger mask and then I'd scare him and make him into the one who would get his naughty hand bitten off and I wouldn't have to be so afraid." At this Anne removed the mask, gave me a little smile, and said, "If you think I wore the mask because of last time, you're *wrong*." Actually she made this statement in such a way that it was apparent to both of us that this was her way of telling me that she was indeed wearing the mask because of the events of the previous session.

At first I carried along in the same playful vein that Anne had introduced, saying that maybe I was *all wrong* if I had such a thought. However, I added a bit more seriously, no matter how wrong I was, I thought she was a very clever child to have had such an idea; she had said it, not I. "It was only make-believe," she said; "I know that really wouldn't happen. I know you really aren't a tiger, and that you wouldn't bite my hand off. Besides, I don't think you were even angry. I was just showing you my make-believe thoughts." I indicated in an unspoken communication that I was not sure she was yet entirely convinced I was not angry.

Anne's masturbation conflict and concomitant fears which, in fantasies, she had enacted with her mother now apparently encompassed me also, and I was no longer a benign "fixer." Her understanding that behind her identification with the aggressor-analyst lay her fears of the consequences of her masturbation resulted in her reverting to her Peter Pan game, in which the negative transference prevailed as she enacted some of her aggressive masturbation fantasies.

I was Captain Hook who was for the most part tied and gagged so that I could neither leave my chair nor speak. I represented, in large measure, the phallic mother—to the point where several times Anne slipped and called me Mommy-Hook. She, in turn, was Peter Pan, who hated all mothers. She would steal my sword, indicating what a dangerous, vengeful monster I was, and at the same time deriding me because I was helpless in the face of her invulnerability. My missing hand was obviously a condensation of the missing genital, and the instrument through which the forbidden act of masturbation was performed. Her increasing emphasis on her hand and mine, and her repeated insistence that first I and then she burn our respective hands on the radiator, enabled me, in ungagged moments, to link her masturbation fantasies with the act.

Not long after, and outside play, Anne demonstrated her masturbation and her concomitant anxiety by pulling at the crotch of her tights and tearing them. Still holding the crotch with one hand, she put her other hand over one ear as though to ward off hearing my response, yet apprehensively awaiting it. I said I was not sure what worried her more: the worry of doing something she felt was naughty and that she feared might hurt her, or the worry that I would be angry and hurt her for her naughtiness. "I don't know myself" was her spontaneous reply. This appointment occurred on a Tuesday and a few days before her sister's birthday.

Anne arrived for her first hour following this birthday event with her stuffed dog, Jamie, about whom she had told me in past hours. Jamie predated her sister's birth and was her ally in her night-time struggles (i.e., her masturbation fantasies) with the bad witch. Evidently she had brought

Jamie to this hour both as a representation of her masturbation and as a source of protection. She pointed him at me in a menacing way; then, abruptly dropping him on the couch, she gaily told me about her sister's birthday party and the consolation presents she, herself, had received. Among these she named a game which was unfamiliar to me. When I innocently indicated my ignorance, I was met with an unexpected explosion. Tearfully, she stormed at me that I was stupid, "a stinker" and a "butter fingers," and finally left the office. By the time I had caught up with her, she had her hat and coat on and was departing through the front door. She eventually agreed to return to the office when I told her I could see how very much I had offended her by not giving her a consolation present. However, when I tried to pursue her unhappy and angry feelings, she hotly declared it was not my duty to talk about her feelings, that I had only *one* duty and that was to help her with her fear of dogs; and defiantly she held her *nose,* explaining in this way she could not hear me talk, and thereby again projecting onto me her attitude toward herself as messy and dirty. At the end of the hour she was willing to discuss her obvious fear that I would retaliate for the anger she had expressed toward me. That was as far as we got at this point.

The following day Anne said: "I'll bet you thought yesterday was awful." I said I knew it had been especially awful for her. Her reply was that when she was getting ready for her supper in the evening I was still seeing children, and she asked me to write down: "I showed a secret to Dr. Harley on Tuesday." Here I could tell her that she felt I had not given her a consolation present because I did not like her after she had shown me her secret. I made this interpretation at the close of the session and, as Anne was leaving, she paused reflectively and said, "You're a nice Dr. Harley but in our games

I'll have to make you into a mean person again; I don't know why but I will; maybe not forever but for a long time." This, so it seemed to me, was an apt formulation of the distinction between the analyst in her real role and as a transference figure.

For some time thereafter, Anne, in various ways, referred to her secret as marking herself as a dirty, messy child. Repeatedly, in this context, she would say: "Let's pretend I'm two—no, I don't want to." At the same time, she would hint at fantasies that I might have a baby and go to the hospital. Finally, she volunteered she could remember one thing which had happened when she was two, namely her sister's birth. I remarked that those must have been troubled days, that it was so hard for a child that young to understand and not to feel that her mommy liked the new baby more, or even had had another child because she did not like what her first child did. Now Anne requested that I remain alone in the adult room while she went into the playroom and then called me to show me the surprise she had prepared for me. She had scrubbed off all the paint which in past hours she had smeared on the easel. On the floor, in a neat little pile, were all the initials she had removed from the other children's drawers; but, on her own drawer, she had printed her full name. She asked what I thought of the surprise. In essence, I told her it showed me how much she longed to be the only child who was ever with me, and that maybe she hoped if she were such a clean, tidy, good child then she *could* be the only one.

Now there were three new happenings in the treatment. The first of these was that Anne reverted to her Peter Pan game, but this time she was Wendy and I was Wendy's mother. Like Peter Pan, she would fly away to Never-Never Land because she was so angry with me. And once, like Peter

Pan, she returned home only to find the windows barred because I had had another baby. Sometimes she would pronounce me dead, sometimes merely asleep, the states of sleep and death being somewhat fluid. In either case, she would exclaim vehemently: "I hate you; I hate mothers." Her stated reason for her hatred was that I regarded her as a messy child who had taken her blanket from her. Her substitution of the blanket for the wings and sword over which we had formerly vied had genetic significance in that it referred to a blanket which had served up to her third year as a kind of transitional object, and which she had had to abandon because her mother had had to cut away so many soiled parts almost none of it had remained intact. Now Anne aggressively wrested this blanket from me in tugs of war. Soon she introduced another theme into this Wendy play. She brought to her hour a pair of thongs which she had recently taken to wearing in bed at night. Explaining that these were her night-time fighting shoes, she lay on the floor and enacted further masturbation fantasies. Exclaiming that she could make thoughts with her magic hand, she told how, in her thoughts, she fought off the bad witch who tried to take her blanket and her wings, and now added, who wanted to take her balloon. I did not yet understand the meaning of this balloon.

The second happening was that, in the same hour in which she first assigned me the role of the depriving mother, who regarded her as dirty and who had replaced her with a more loved child, Anne became afraid to flush my toilet. This fear was confined to my toilet only—no other. At first she rationalized this fear on the basis that my toilet was especially noisy, but then admitted her fantasy that my dog would jump out of the toilet and bite her. Actually, this fear of the toilet, which, in one sense, was a repetition of her earlier fear that a zebra in the toilet would bite her, was confined to the analytic situation, lasted for a number of weeks, and seemed to fulfill the criteria for a circumscribed transference neurosis as defined at the outset of this paper.

The third happening was that, not long after the hour in which she had enacted her masturbation fantasies and had added the balloon theme, Anne momentarily stepped out of her game saying, "Let's pretend I'm two," and reported the following anecdote that comprised an adroit condensation of the various meanings she had attributed to the traumatic events she had experienced in relation to the enema and the forced movement. She had gone to the zoo with her mother, she said, and had had a beautiful, long, red balloon, but the elephant had broken it.[4] This part of her anecdote was, in fact, true. But then she added earnestly, "I think he squirted water in its hole with his long trunk until it burst." When I said, "How awful for you," she exclaimed, "how awful for the balloon; I'll bet I felt sorry for it." I agreed she seemed to understand so well what an awful feeling it must have been for the balloon to be filled up with water, fearing it might burst, and not being able to do anything about it. She went on to say, "But it was awful for me, too, not just the balloon, because it was mine and it got broken. It was mommy's fault."

To recapitulate some of the foregoing material, we have seen how, in the transference, Anne enacted some of her aggressive masturbation fantasies which, at this point, were directed mainly against the preoedipal mother. At first she expressed these by assuming the role of the invulnerable boy, Peter Pan, who triumphed over the phallic mother personified by the Captain Hook analyst. When these fantasies were linked to the act of masturbation, she demonstrated, again

[4] Cf. Anne's use of the *red balloon* in her flying game.

through the transference, those aspects of her masturbation which marked her as a dirty, messy, castrated child, and hence less loved than her sister. As repressions of pregenital experiences associated with her sister's birth were lifted, she revealed the fantasy that I might have a baby and then showed her wish to be my only child, with the hope of achieving this by being the opposite of messy and naughty. This behavior was followed by her reflection of herself through the child Wendy as a dirty girl, unloved and punished by me for her masturbation and concomitant aggressive fantasies. That these fantasies related to all three levels of libidinal development, i.e., oral, anal, and phallic, was neatly illustrated in her choice of the blanket as a focus for her struggles with me. Its original loss was linked with her loss of the bottle; its ultimate destruction had resulted from her having soiled it; and now it was also endowed with phallic significance.

After the emergence of the genetic material relating to her sister's birth and her anal trauma (as depicted through her elephant fantasy), Anne was first able to approach my dog, albeit gingerly, for her dog phobia was by no means dissolved. Although this step may in part have resulted from the child's unconscious obedience to her mother's wish that she overcome her phobia before the summer, it seemed also ascribable to the events within the analysis. It is significant that on the day she first told me of her wish for a direct encounter with my dog, she became quite aggressive in the transference, threatening to make a mess on my floor. When I told her I thought one reason she wanted to do these naughty things was to prove to herself she could do things she had wanted to do when she was very little, without being afraid something awful would happen, she instructed me to tell her, over over, that I was not angry at her for having such bad thoughts. She also asked whether my dog was toilet-trained, how I had achieved this, and whether I would punish a child if she hurt my dog, or whether the dog himself would bite the child in retaliation. In this hour Anne made it quite clear that the dog reflected her own oral and anal destructive impulses against the sister and mother, and that he also represented the mother-analyst who would retaliate and punish her for these impulsive strivings.

In subsequent transference developments, Anne further confirmed that she had organized not only pregenital but also phallic conflicts around her anal trauma and, in addition, revealed how this earlier experience ultimately had also taken on the meaning of an oedipal sexual attack. As she sat at my feet while I sewed, she expressed the fear that I would give her a shot in the vagina with my needle, and that as a consequence all her pee-pee and B.M. would come out to the extent that she would drown in the dirty water, or that I would drown in it. She also expressed in fantasy how, by giving her a shot in the vagina, I would prevent her from being able to pee-pee while standing up without splashing. I should note parenthetically that her anal-vaginal-urethral confusion, as well as her fantasy that the vagina was the site of a concealed penis, had been implied at various times in the analysis.

Later, when Anne was relieved of some of the pressures arising from her preoedipal aggressive conflicts with the mother, when she had been able to express some of her feelings of sadness in connection with what she felt had been the loss of her mother and to admit some of her longings for her, positive oedipal material assumed a more paramount position in the analysis. Now, in the transference, and still through the medium of my sewing needle, I was the father who was no longer the mother's agent but the shot-giver in his own right. Anne admitted her dread of growing up and getting married. Her transient transference neurosis, that is, her fear of my toilet flush, which initially had made its appearance within the context of oral, anal, and phallic conflicts in relation to the preoedipal mother, faded away as oedipal material entered into the foreground and we discussed night-time noises in relation to primal scene perils. In line with my changed role in the transference, my dog became the father-husband, and once again she could not tolerate his presence.

By extracting the foregoing excerpts from a child's analysis, I have sacrificed not only the continuity but also the proportions of the whole. For example, all of the analysis was not mediated as predominantly through the transference as I may have implied; and what I have referred to as the child's anal trauma was but one genetic event, albeit a significant one, in the complex mosaic of her experience, and one used by her to screen later disturbing happenings. I would also underscore that my arbitrary division of this paper into two parts, with the emphasis on defense analysis in the first part, may have carried with it the erroneous impression that defenses were not dealt with repeatedly throughout the entire course of the analysis. If, however, I have conveyed the capacity of a five-year-old for transference developments and if I have shown some of the ways in which these became an integral part of the therapeutic work, I shall have achieved the aim of this paper.[5]

[5] It is perhaps relevant to note that, commencing in the second year of her analysis, Anne transferred her dog phobia exclusively to my dog and, outside the analytic setting, was readily able to approach various types of dogs. Simultaneously, although relatively free with her mother and others, she became excessively submissive and compliant with me, and her consistent and insistent attempts to please me constituted a rigid transference resistance. This transference neurosis persisted for approximately fifteen months. A discussion of its content and dissolution, however, is the subject for another paper.

REFERENCES

Frankl, L. & Hellman, I (1962), Symposium on Child Analysis. II. The Ego's Participation in the Therapeutic Alliance. *Internat. J. Psychoanal.* 43:333-337.

Freud, A. (1965), *Normality and Pathology in Childhood.* New York: International Universities Press.

Harley, M (1961), Resistances in Child Analysis. Panel Report. *J. Amer. Psychoanal Assoc.* 9:548-561.

Erna Furman

The Latency Child as an Active Participant in the Analytic Work

IN THIS REPORT, it is my aim to describe and illustrate one aspect of the analysis of a latency girl, namely, her inability to participate actively in the analytic work. An outstanding feature of this inability was a lack of communication with the therapist in words, play, and activity. The patient's difficulty presented a technical problem which stimulated me to think again about the level of object relationship and maturity of ego functions a child must have reached in order to cooperate consciously in the process of an analysis and to work actively toward its aims. This, in turn, helped me to understand this patient's character structure to some degree.

Anna Freud (1944) discussed the technical difficulties inherent in child analysis and traced their origin to the immaturity of the child's personality structure as well as to the individual child's disturbance. Many authors have followed her in further contributions to this topic. The present paper again draws attention to the fact that, to the child patient at any age, the analytic work presents a very complicated task, challenging to most of his ego functions, and indeed to all areas of his personality.

This viewpoint has certain technical implications. In the case to be presented, the patient was initially at the age when an object-centered phallic type of relationship, and ego functions appropriate for that stage, should have been attained

142

long since. The therapist therefore took the first opportunity to set before the patient the aim of the analysis in terms of achieving an understanding and mastery of problems, and the means by which this aim could be achieved, namely, the cooperative analytic work of patient and therapist. The patient soon confirmed that she understood what was meant, at least in part. She could grasp the concept as is the case with most patients upwards of three or four years of age. From then on the aim was to analyze, step by step, how and why her disturbance prevented her from carrying out the task, the goal of which she desired basically and understood intellectually.

In following the patient's attitude to the treatment task, it was possible for the therapist to understand, to empathize with, and to analyze the varying ego levels as they became manifest. This in turn helped the therapist to gauge the content and timing of instinctual interpretations in the context of what the patient's ego could integrate. In this process, different levels of object relationship appeared, which could be related to the corresponding instinctual levels and could be used to help the patient reconstruct her earliest experiences.

Originally, the patient had been fixated primarily on the level of the need-fulfilling relationship and on that of the ambivalent anal-sadistic relationship (A. Freud, 1963). Her relationships were based on aspects of these levels or on various primitive, unintegrated identifications which she utilized. By tracing these early identifications and fixations dynamically and genetically, the patient's delayed maturation could be reinstated. It was found that, although the patient's difficulty in communicating apparently remained the same for years, its meaning changed from level to level, until she reached a phase when she could overtly alter her analytic behavior. At that point she could talk about her problems and could actively bring material in activities, play, and accounts of her daily life and thinking. She could then regard the therapist, at least in part, as a helper in a goal-directed task, and could make effective use of interpretations.

CASE REPORT

Reasons for Referral

Susan was referred at the age of seven and a half years by her parents after consultation with Dr. Anny Katan. The presenting symptoms were a great fear of doctors and dentists, which made it impossible for her to be examined even when her physical health was at stake. Susan also suffered acutely from night fears and nightmares, often insisting that her mother stay with her for long periods in the evening and during the night. Her relationship with her siblings was poor. She appeared to be plagued by hostility toward them, to which she gave frequent expression in physical attacks, biting, and cutting verbalization. The mother felt that Susan was working well below her capacity at school. Dr. Jane Kessler, psychologist, could not establish Susan's I.Q. because of Susan's disturbed attitude during the test, but felt that Susan's problems certainly interfered with her capacity to function intellectually. The school, by contrast, felt that Susan was a poorly endowed girl, working at a fair level. The parents, in the first interview with me, mentioned one further difficulty, i.e., that Susan tended to become excited with men, showed off provocatively, and invited them to indulge with her in games or tussles involving bodily contact. There were also some instances where Susan walked in the street in a way calculated to attract strange men's attention.

In spite of these rather prominent symptoms, the parents had, until recently, largely disregarded Susan's troubles. Their attention focused first on their eldest boy, Jeff, two and a half years Susan's senior, and then on their third child,

Barbie, Susan's junior by thirteen months. Both children had received psychiatric help for their difficulties. Perhaps it was mainly the physician's alarm at not being able to examine Susan during a serious illness which decided the parents to bring Susan to analysis. In addition to Jeff, Susan, and Barbie, there was also a younger boy, Greg, born when Susan was four and a half years old.

This case, in its first two years of analysis, was presented several times for discussion in Dr. Anny Katan's child-analytic seminars. At that time, Dr. Katan contributed to my understanding of the case with her stimulating and helpful comments. More recently, Dr. Katan read this paper. I am most grateful to her for several suggestions which I have included in the final form of this article.

From the Department of Psychiatry, Western Reserve University School of Medicine.

Family Background

During the first couple of months I learned more about Susan's family. They were quite well-to-do. The children were comfortably housed and were afforded excellent educational opportunities. The parents frequently needed to discharge social and business obligations, often at short notice, which took them away from home. The children then stayed with a numerous household staff, whose members often turned out to have personal or other troubles, had to be discharged, or left of their own accord. As people, the parents were extremely honest, conscientious, hard-working, very fond of their family, and well-intentioned. They were keenly aware of their responsibilities and concerned at their inability to live up to them at times. The mother particularly was beset by guilt feelings, always ready to blame herself in the past or present, and sometimes preferring to be guilty rather than to face certain emotional situations in her children which she could not influence. It was striking from the beginning that she, who was culturally and intellectually so accomplished and to whom these interests meant so much in her children,

was unable to handle them on an age-appropriate level in the
areas of ego and superego development. She persisted in caring for their bodily needs, bathing them, clothing them, restricting or encouraging their eating, rubbing their backs,
and allowing them very infantile forms of instinctual expression. Thus the mother praised Susan for her crude verbal outbursts toward her siblings, with the idea that verbalization
would help her. She hardly reprimanded the children's petty
stealing from one another and from the parents. She never expected self-control of them in the absence of an adult. She was
shocked to learn from me that much of Susan's hostile and
uncontrolled behavior was an attempt to secure punishment
and thereby to alleviate her guilt.

I knew that in the past Susan's mother had suffered from a
serious emotional disturbance which made it hard for her to
function as a mother. Treatment had helped her considerably.
During Susan's early years, however, the mother wavered dras-
tically between overexertion and sudden exhausted withdrawal, emotional and/or physical. At the time of Susan's
referral she managed much better generally, was calmer and
better able to cope as a mother. She gladly availed herself of
weekly interviews with me in the first years of Susan's analysis.
Later on, she was seen less frequently. These interviews were
geared to gaining observations of Susan's current life at home,
as well as of her past, and to influencing some of the mother's
handling of Susan and the other children.

The father was as unemotional and rigid as the mother was
emotive and labile. He found it impossible to establish a
meaningful relationship with under-fives and got closer to his
children only as they reached latency. He definitely preferred boys to girls. The latter, to him, were mainly love objects insofar as he could admire their pretty bodies or clothes,
engage with them in teasing and excited rough-housing. He

regarded Susan as dull and intellectually uninteresting, an impression shared by Susan's school. Whereas the mother would disregard messing and bad manners, the father's own disturbance made it impossible for him to tolerate the children around at mealtimes. It was only recently that the family had started to have one joint dinner weekly, at which father tended to be punitive of minor transgressions. Mealtimes were an extreme instance of a general drastic difference in parental handling. Father's rules and expectations of independence were as high as mother's were low. His business frequently absented him from home. In Susan's earlier years, he used to be away for most of the week; more recently, he went only on brief monthly trips. When at home, he did not always exert his influence but withdrew from the children and criticized his wife's involvement in their care. In spite of this, he was genuinely concerned about Susan, proved himself at times a perceptive observer of her, and could change some of his handling in time, with the help of Susan's improvement and his monthly interviews with me. I soon found that I had to see the parents separately, for the most part, because joint interviews only served to bring into focus their sadomasochistic relationship centered on opposite educational and emotional views of the children. Although not quite continuous, this pattern of interaction was prominent at home, too.

Early History

I knew little of Susan's early history during the first months. Susan was a normal baby, breast-fed for about four months, then easily transferred to the bottle. At one year, a month before Barbie's birth, a nurse, Emmy, came to take care of Susan. She was reputed to be a kind person, fond of Susan, and Susan fond of her, until Susan grew to be three to four years old and "could really talk back." At that time Emmy took over the care of the new baby, Greg. A year later Emmy was found asleep drunk and presently was discharged on a pretext. Susan hardly reacted to her leaving. The hardest years for Susan were between one and three. The family concentrated on the new baby, Barbie, and on the older Jeff. The father was frequently absent. The mother was in psychiatric treatment and was hospitalized several times for physical illnesses, including a miscarriage of which Susan was not told. The mother recalled some outstanding features of Susan's behavior during these years: terrible screaming and sobbing outbursts which overwhelmed the child and which nobody could control, a sleep disturbance, and a tendency to attract the attention of strangers in the street by parading in certain clothes in which Susan regarded herself as pretty, a forerunner of the symptom described at the time of referral. During that time Susan was subjected to rough, hostile treatment by her older brother. She herself was not aggressive. Once she shoved the baby's empty buggy into a pond, her only protest of rivalry. Somewhat later she became very provocative and teasing with men. During these early years there was one other important figure in Susan's life, the paternal grandmother, Maman, who lived nearby and ruled the family household with an ever-present iron hand. She was quite fond of Susan, admiring her for her "stoical perseverence," a description of Susan's early trait of tight-lipped affective rigidity. Maman died after a year's illness when Susan was about five and a half years old.

Susan had no serious illnesses until a pneumonia shortly before her referral for analysis. Her early milestones of walking, talking, and toilet-training were normal. But from the beginning Susan was unable to express herself in sublimated activities, in spite of mother's encouragement and the siblings' successes in this area. Susan's drawings at the age of four were rigid little patterns. She could use no medium to express her inner life. Nor was she interested in intellectual matters. She never asked questions, never investigated on her own. She did not even ask about the mother's pregnancy during Susan's fourth year. In these respects she was very different from her siblings and mother, who discussed sexual matters perhaps all too freely. Susan made a shy adjustment to nursery school, then to kindergarten. Although her earlier troubles persisted and her fears and night problem had even increased, Susan's lack of verbal demands, her intellectual and sublimatory failings, and her tendency to give up and withdraw, left her behind her vociferous outgoing siblings. She received less attention in every respect.

Patient's Initial Attitude to the Therapist and the Treatment

Session 1. When I saw Susan for the first time she appeared somewhat small but well proportioned and coordinated. Her fair coloring, blue eyes, and regular features made her potentially very pretty, but her face was hard and icy, her whole posture rigid. She had been prepared for treatment, and her mother was to stay in the waiting room during Susan's first hour. Susan stared at me sullenly and clung to her mother, the latter explaining that she would have to leave for part of the time. Susan refused to enter the adjoining office without her mother. She stood motionless in front of the open office door and glanced disdainfully at the toys and materials spread out there. She refused my invitation to use them with a decisive shrug of aversion. When the mother later prepared to leave, Susan screamed, sobbed, and clung violently while mother tried to disengage herself with embarrassment. I suggested that Susan leave with her mother.

Session 2. The next day Susan clung to her mother as tensely as before, sullen panic in her eyes, and again refused to enter the office alone. So I said, "I think you showed me one of your troubles yesterday, a trouble you can't manage. You must have wished you could do what was expected of you. It must be hard to have such a trouble. I don't think I can help you by forcing you to stay here alone, but I can help you by finding out, and understanding with you, what makes it so hard. From today on Mommy will stay as close as you need her until our work helps you to manage on your own." Susan entered the office behind her mother. (As it turned out, Susan's mother was to stay in the office for three weeks, reading, sewing, making an occasional remark.) Susan was hostile and silent. She did not move from her mother's side or touch any toys. She had, however, glanced with interest at my cat in the waiting room. On leaving she remarked provocatively, "Give me this cat or I'll take her home." I replied gently, "I shall not let you. Do you believe I don't care about her?"

Session 3. Susan fingered the tinkertoys and told me about her beloved cat, Pansy, who had been run over many months ago while the family was away on vacation. "And she was going to have kittens. I didn't hear she died till we got back." "I can understand better now why you feel that it's best to be close to someone you love, if such a terrible thing happened when you were gone. You might even fear that Mommy might not be safe when you are with me alone." Susan responded with a warm look, then started to move away from her mother and asked me to draw a horse for her.

For several days Susan's hours were spent with myself drawing horses and children for her in different positions, at her request. She refused to do anything beyond fingering some of the toys. Mostly she just stood and watched me draw.

Session 9. That day Susan asked me draw the four children in her family. She inscribed their names. Then, without any affect but with icy determination, she crossed out each one except herself. "That's that." "It isn't that," I replied. "Of course these children are only drawings, but it must be hard to have to feel this way." Susan acted unperturbed.

That night she woke screaming from a terrifying nightmare of bleeding, slaughtered animals. I heard this from the mother, who had to spend the rest of the night with Susan. Susan herself never referred to it by word or act, even when I brought it up. Her behavior was changed, though. She was as cold and sullen as at the

start and became increasingly controlling of me. Her sparse ut-
terances were abrupt commands to draw for her or to pass her a
toy for inspection or fleeting manipulation. Sometimes she
ordered me by gestures only.

Session 14. Susan again ordered several drawings. She looked
very annoyed when I refused to comply and repeated what I had
said the previous day, "I wonder why you have to boss me so
much." Several minutes later she played a little with a tea set and
water, spilling it messily. To this I responded by saying, "Perhaps
you need to control me so much because you fear that you might
not be able to control your feelings here. Then you would feel so
badly. It is not the purpose of our work to get you to feel out-of-
control, and I do not let children act out-of-control. I try to help
you to understand your feelings, and then you can master them
better." Susan helped with cleaning up. At the end of this session
she announced, "I can come on my own tomorrow," and turning
to her mother, "You can leave me here."

From these sessions it was not difficult to guess at some of
Susan's instinctual difficulties, e.g., her exciting hostile fantasies, her ambivalence to her mother and siblings, her experience of traumatic sexual events. Her phallic and oedipal
conflicts possibly made her react to my private home office as
she had to the doctor's surgery. There was also evidence of
the primitive severity of her superego, her mechanisms to
ward off the anxiety stemming from it, and its ineffectiveness
in helping her to control her behavior. I chose to direct myself to another area, namely, her "I need you" relationship
with her mother, partly because this was the problem Susan
had introduced so urgently in requesting mother's physical
presence, partly because this relationship represented her
most striking defense against anxiety, or so it seemed to me.

*Some Phases of the Analysis of the Patient's Inability to Par-
ticipate Age-Adequately in the Analytic Work*

During the first few months of her analysis I was mainly

impressed with the numerous unintegrated facets of Susan's personality. In her sessions she was for the most part cold, rigid and silent. On one occasion I caught a glimpse of her aggressive seductiveness when I watched her impish laugh, exhibitionistic use of her body, and sharp-tongued repartee with the old chauffeur who brought her. Her rare reports of events at home pointed to her frequent aggressive tussles with her siblings, exciting games with them, high-pitched shrieking and uncontrolled actions, especially when only the mother was in the house or both parents were absent. At times, too, I heard of gossip and petty stealing with the maids. At school she was the dull, conforming pupil. It was striking that Susan kept these facets strictly isolated, acting quite differently in each setting, and never stepping out of character. Being with different people simply brought forth a different self, to be dropped abruptly the moment she left them. It was impossible to know which was the real Susan.

The most hidden facet seemed the most genuine. In rare sessions, when Susan felt I cared for her either by understanding her or by providing primitive comforts, such as warmth on an icy day, she showed sudden moments of relaxation. Her body softened, a babylike vulnerable expression appeared on her face, and she looked very, very small. These seconds of infantility were in line with Susan's inability to look after herself at home. She did not sleep alone, never bathed alone, did not prepare her own clothes for the morning, often ate messily, did not take responsibility for her homework. Her sense of time was so poor that she could not tell time from clock or calendar. On occasions she did not comprehend time in terms of yesterday and tomorrow. Susan was not aware that this infantile dependency revealed itself also in one aspect of her relationship to me. After several weeks of treatment I had to miss one session with her. I prepared her several days ahead and explained I had to attend a meeting. Susan did not react. The night of my day's absence she hardly slept and woke up repeatedly from nightmares she could not describe. In the morning she had an overwhelming sobbing outburst, shaking all over. The mother described her uncontrolled crying spell as identical to the ones during her second year. When Susan returned to her session the following day, she was astonished that she had been expected to come back at all but could discuss nothing.

Had it not been for these few nonverbal and unintentionally communicated clues, it would have been impossible to guess at the beginning of Susan's infantile "I need you" relationship to me. In the sessions all her efforts were directed at self-control, elimination of affect, deep resistance to any communication with me, and attempts to prevent any information about her from reaching me. She was silent, sullen. Her activity consisted of making meaningless scribbles, sharpening pencils, and, for hours, writing her name over and over. It was not possible to understand the full meaning of this activity until years later. Occasional clues from her behavior made it clear that she viewed me as another servant hired by her parents. Later, more specifically, she saw me as her first nurse Emmy of long ago. This led me to make interpretations of her fear of liking me, her loyalty conflict, her dread that either I or she would be "fired" if she felt too close to me, and that she warded off her feelings for fear of a disappointing separation.

In retrospect, I understand better why Susan was unable to work with me. Her infantile, undeveloped self was superimposed by a variety of unintegrated early identifications, none of which could serve her toward true mastery. They led either to uncontrolled instinctual breakthroughs or to dullness and rigid lack of affects. The threat of succumbing to an intense

dependency and demandingness in her relationship to the
therapist increased her defenses to the point where she did
not want to have anything to do with me except see me. Yet
these very defenses, and the protection afforded her by that
relationship, were factors in bringing about a marked change
in overt pathology. Within a few months Susan's nightmares
ceased. She slept peacefully without her mother. Her fear of
doctors and dentists disappeared. She discontinued, for the
most part, her aggressive and excited interplays with her
siblings. She was almost a model child. She managed this at
the cost of total affect block. In the sessions she dried up al-
together and her face was an impenetrable mask. It soon became clear that Susan's restriction of feelings affected many
areas of her ego functioning. In order to avoid feelings, Susan
could not speak, or know anything, or even remember what
she had once learned. She could not show interest in what
happened around her or within her. This applied to her learning at school. She was quite disinterested in the subjects,
managed to pass tests by memorizing the material with mother's help the previous night, and then forgot it again. She
worked hard, learning the same things over and over.

    At this time my efforts were aimed only at showing Susan
that, while she was able to achieve marvelous control over
her symptoms and behavior, she was losing all of her feelings
and restricting herself intellectually more than ever. It was
a hard task. At home her father praised her for her "even
stoicism." Her mother was relieved at the decreased demands
on her. The school had always been opposed to the treatment.
On her birthday, Susan received a requested present from
me, without a single change of her facial expression, in complete silence. This masklike attitude characterized all her
birthday celebrations, even at home. I used this occasion to
tell Susan again, "I am so sorry for you. How poor you have

made yourself! You have even given up your chance to feel happy." Susan began to see the point. She engaged me in playing tic-tac-toe. Through her pattern of losing at games, we learned of her guilt as it showed in failing to succeed. One day she showed me her marked-up nails, saying defensively, "Barbie and I took Mommy's nail polish set, and we used it, and it spilled all over the carpet." "Does Mommy know?" "I don't know. I did not tell her and she didn't say anything." "Did you clean it up or get new polish?" "No, it was hard to come out." "How badly you must feel!" "I don't know," Susan replied in a flat sing-song, shrugging her shoulders. Then she withdrew from me. That day she remarked coldly to her pediatrician on the occasion of a house call to her brother, "Why don't you just kill him?" When this remark failed to bring punishment, she behaved so badly with the music teacher in front of her mother that a scolding finally resulted. I reviewed for Susan the chain of events, tracing what had happened to the guilt she had disowned consciously. Increasingly Susan became capable of experiencing feelings of guilt. Then other feelings could emerge, especially a little warmth, expressed mostly toward her mother and her teacher. Also, Susan acquired a new skill. In the sessions she learned how to tell time and became the only person in her family to be punctual and fully aware of time in short and long sequences. Her mother was notoriously unpunctual and vague about time. With this new skill, Susan took over responsibility for coming to her analysis. She notified the chauffeur, arranged changes, etc. It was her first active participation in the analysis.

The main trend of our work now concerned Susan's attitude toward separations. Except for her nightmare and sobbing episode during the first one-day separation from me, Susan reacted to analytic separations by never discussing them beforehand, never inquiring where I would be or what

I would do. But since she was silent and inactive for over 90 per cent of the time, her lack of interest was not striking. When away, she erased her mental image of me and, overtly, did not miss me. During her first summer vacation, after nine months of treatment, Susan even forgot the name of the street she lived on. On later occasions she would sometimes be listless, withdraw with her "sucky" (a rag comforter used since babyhood), and complain of minor bodily discomforts. After some fifteen months of treatment, Susan returned from a short vacation with the adamant demand, "Draw me a horse." From the evidence of sparse past material I could refuse this request, saying, "We could easily gain a horse, but might lose something much more precious—your feelings." Susan insisted very angrily, pushing paper and pencil at me, "You draw me one, right now, right now." "You are so very angry at me, there must be many things I did not do for you when I was away." Tears came to her eyes for the first time. This opened up the topic of Susan's feelings of longing and rejection. We found that she dealt with them by having mother and me do everything for her, by denying her feelings, and by restricting attempts at independent mastery.

During separations from her parents, Susan reacted with an angry rejection of herself. She would disparage and destroy all her handiwork. Her usual minimal interest in schoolwork would fall off. She would fail to comprehend and to complete assignments. She would also strikingly neglect her body, dressing in shabby, dirty clothes, insufficient to keep her warm. I told her that she was doing to herself as she felt the absent parents had intended to do to her: she felt they had left her because she was a bad, worthless child. At first Susan linked this mainly to her father's rejection of her. She, who had frequently felt herself akin to the various family cats, told me that her father disliked cats because they were dirty, smelly, spiteful, and dumb, in contrast to his beloved dogs and, as we established a little later, his beloved sons. In discussing the next brief vacation, Susan started out with a snappy, "I wish I had a longer vacation from you." Then she sadly told the story of "Captains Courageous." A boy nearly drowns during his search for a father. A kindly fisherman rescues him, becomes a second father to him, and then dies an untimely death. Susan asked me to take her with me and, failing that, insisted on exchanging telephone numbers. As a parting gift, she made a drawing of cats with a loving inscription.

Susan's mother left for a few days, on short notice, two days after the end of the brief analytic vacation. Susan was rather thrilled to have her father more involved in the daily family routine. She anticipated special treats such as a movie or a restaurant. These, however, did not materialize. The day of her mother's return, Susan saw a frightening movie about a visit to Mars. That night she became extremely anxious, expecting monsters to come out at her from different parts of her home. She eventually fell asleep, with her mother at her bedside, but woke repeatedly from nightmares.

This acute anxiety continued unabated for almost two weeks. Susan would become increasingly worried as evening approached and restricted herself to a corner in the living-room in an attempt to escape from the monsters. She could hardly eat or work. By nighttime she clung to her mother physically. Mother had to sit with Susan, curtains drawn, and closet door shut. Susan would frequently wake up terrified and, if she found mother gone, would get into the parents' bed or insist that mother return with her to her room. Any attempt to leave Susan alone at such times resulted in a screaming panic. I had occasion to hear such an anxiety attack in the background when the mother once called me at midnight for advice. Both parents, but especially the father, felt they had

had their share of disturbed nights and were arguing as to
whether Susan should be locked in her room. It had been my
policy with both Susan and her parents that the anxieties represented progress for Susan, and that she should be encouraged to face as much anxiety as she could stand. I did not feel,
however, that it would help her analysis if she were to be overwhelmed by anxiety after a heated family quarrel. The parents were glad of a reasoned suggestion and followed through,
the mother sitting up with Susan. Up to this point Susan had
mainly talked to me about the content of the movie, a horror
film in which all but one of a party were killed by Martian
monsters. She could barely fathom my idea that she would
not become so disturbed unless the movie had given a focal
point to her unconscious conflicts. After I had taken my stand
on the usefulness of anxiety versus panic, she was able to tell
me the worst fear which formed the content of her repetitive
nightmares: she dreams that she is asleep in her bed and
dreaming that a Martian lands in a space-craft in their back
yard. He gets out and walks up to her window. She thinks she
sees his head and shoulders. He looks in at her. She wakes up
from her dream-in-a-dream as well as in reality, but her fear
of his haunting gaze remains vivid although she is awake.
Susan had been very afraid to put the dream into words and
could not associate to it. But her anxiety at home lessened.
Instead, she became more anxious in her sessions, which until
then had been the only truly anxiety-free time for her. Soon
she thought she saw a Martian look into our office. At first,
she was terrified; then her affect began to change. She appeared to be looking for the Martian. She drew pictures of
monsters with a tinge of excited gusto. I pointed out her excitement and defenses against it, and how clearly they were
related to the treatment situation. That day a minor anxiety
attack at home followed a game of looking at baseball player

cards and guessing facts about them. From associations to this incident, Susan was able to identify the Martian as my husband, whom she had never seen. When she began to cover the office windows with richly colored drawings, we could understand her wish to have my husband look at her. His gazing was a reversal of Susan's wish to gaze at him. Eventually, she understood that this wish had been the unconscious aspect of her demand that I take her with me on my vacation. These partial insights relieved Susan sufficiently to reduce her night fears to an occasional brief difficulty. In time this, too, stopped. She refused to bring any further material and lapsed again into a sullen silence of many weeks.[3]

About three months later, prior to the summer vacation, I expressed my concern to Susan about her inability to show any interest in or to ask any questions about my vacation, especially in view of her panic during the previous short vacation. Susan replied by telling me a ghost story: A professor, a photographer, and an engineer determine to make a documented investigation of a haunted house. They form an elaborate plan of attracting and photographing the ghosts. It comes off. The next day the professor is found dead, his hair white. He had developed the photograph, died of horror at what it showed, and destroyed it somehow as he died. I interpreted that Susan had always acted as if she were like the professor, with one important difference, i.e., she had looked at the worst and survived it miraculously. She lived with averted eyes, fearing to look at anything lest it turn out to be the worst and destroy her. That night Susan telephoned me around midnight. She could not say what she wanted, nor did she know how she had gotten to the telephone. The mother told me that Susan had come screaming out of her room and

[3] Further interpretation of this transference reaction was not attempted because Susan's ego at this time was not yet capable of the necessary integration.

had awakened mother, saying repeatedly, "I have to tell Mrs.
Furman right now. I want to talk to her." She was acting in
the midst of a pavor nocturnus and awoke from it when she
heard my voice. She could recall nothing from her pavor nocturnus, but told me the next day that it was the eve of her
younger brother's birthday. She suddenly remembered his
first homecoming and his first bath. Susan was then four. We
established that one of the "worst things" she had thus seen
was his penis. Our discussion of this helped her to ask some
innocuous questions about my vacation. From the mother, I
learned at this time—but did not share the information with
Susan—that father had, for years, walked around naked on
principle and, to this day, slept in the nude. I heard, further,
that Susan had witnessed parental intercourse at least once
at about two and a half years, and around that time had also
probably seen the bathroom flooded with blood after mother's miscarriage, and possibly had seen the foetus and the
mother in pain. I did tell Susan, however, what mother had
now come to realize, namely, that some of Susan's nightmares
in the past had actually been pavor nocturnus. I sympathized
with how frightening it was to find oneself doing and saying
things one did not even know about. Susan was deeply impressed with and appreciative of the fact that I understood
this fear.

During that fall, Susan's parents planned a month's trip.
After some initial denial, Susan reacted to this with excited
curiosity evidenced in physical restlessness in her sessions and
in tentative questions—all regarding animals—about sexual
differences and the father's role in conception. Once the parents had left, Susan lost all interest. She did not look at their
many letters, cards, and souvenirs. She refused to think where
they were, on the basis that "I know they aren't doing anything interesting anyway." I learned from her later, however,

that just prior to the trip she had drawn upon herself the attention of an adolescent boy, a visitor to neighbors, and had once ridden in the car with him. During the first two weeks of the parents' absence, Susan received several clandestine telephone calls from this boy. She even ran to answer the telephone in a private room when the boy promised to tell her something she would want to know. It was when the boy went back on this promise and hung up that Susan became anxious and guilty, as though suddenly left alone with her excitement. She admitted to me seriously that she had become frightened at her own lack of control in the whole matter. She could understand it in terms of an acting-out of her earlier sexual curiosity about her parents' trip.

I described in some detail these three bursts of "material" during the latter part of the second and beginning of the third year of Susan's analysis because they represent the only consecutive verbal and actively brought material during that period. The sequences also illustrate the discrepancy between the intensity of the instinctual and affective forces and the relative primitivity of Susan's ego, which reacted to these forces with overwhelming anxiety in one instance, and pavor nocturnus and acting out in the other instances. I therefore limited my interpretations of the material to the minimum that her ego could integrate and concentrated on analyzing the nature of her object relationships. These expressed themselves in the various aspects of the transference, particularly in the different forms of many almost silent nonparticipating months. It is difficult to convey adequately the seemingly interminable length of these months, compared to the seeming brevity of the few hours of the patient's active work.

In trying to understand Susan's weeks of silence following the monster anxieties, I became aware of a slightly provocative messing when she sharpened pencils or scribbled on sheets of paper. I wondered whether she was trying to make me angry. She agreed that she wanted to make me angry, for "then there'll be at least two of us." She felt very guilty about her anger because she really knew of no reason for it; on the contrary, "I really like you for what you have done for me." I had stopped her parents from leaving her alone with her fears the night of their telephone call to me, and I had changed one appointment for her to make a special school trip possible. At that time I did not yet know that Susan's unconscious reason for her guilt was that she had pushed me aside in reaching out toward my husband, just as a year before she had felt guilty over playing tic-tac-toe with me and reaching out to me, thereby pushing aside her mother. But Susan relaxed her defenses to some extent after allowing herself to feel some anger. She wanted to learn some of the things I was doing during sessions—knitting, crocheting, sewing. She grasped the rudiments of these skills very quickly, but then lost interest and only virtuously listened to my attempts to teach her. After a while she forgot what she had learned.

In her treatment at that time, Susan learned just enough to make one think she was making a steady effort. She would point out the day she had worked, denying the silent weeks of resistance. I suspected that this righteous "see, I'm doing my best" attitude had been typical of her at school. It also reminded me of the mother's telling me once, "What I remember best about Susan's toilet-training was how virtuous she looked when she sat on the potty." I only learned now, however, that Susan had never really produced anything during those virtuous potty sittings. I showed her that she was hiding a strong defiance under an attitude of superficial compliance, and I suggested that some great anxiety must have made it necessary for her to disguise her opposition so much. Susan became openly sullen and hostile. Around that time, her teachers changed their protective but low opinion of Susan and became increasingly adamant in their belief that she could do a good deal better, that she simply would not make an effort. This attitude also characterized Susan's homework and some of her sessions. At the same time, another change had taken place. Susan's face was no longer a mask. She very obviously had feelings and took in diligently all she could, but kept it a secret, from me especially. I interpreted her anal withholding in the past, linking it to her schoolwork and to her uncooperative attitude and silence in the analysis.

Susan now took up a particular position in her sessions, making a part of the couch into a virtual prison. She would sit crouched, with knees pulled up, and her paper and pencils cluttered closely around her while she drew secretly and silently. She never moved from there from the first to the last minute. This lasted for weeks. I now learned from the mother that Susan had occupied the playpen till two and a half years of age. She would sit in it, taking great pleasure in having Emmy bring things to her. She did not seem to miss muscular activity, but basked in being served. From time to time, though, she would have overwhelming temper outbursts, screaming and shaking the playpen bars. Emmy liked Susan to be in the playpen for, although tolerant in toilet-training, Emmy was obsessively clean in other respects. Susan was her ideal girl, neat, nice and quiet. Susan was already aware that her repetitive behavior on the couch was an attempt to convey particular feelings or thoughts and that these were probably related to our last analytic topic, namely her experiences as a toddler. Utilizing her mother's information, I now reconstructed this behavior for Susan in terms of her preverbal period in the playpen. I stressed that her great wish to control her feelings must have been based in part on her fear of losing Emmy on whom she depended so much at the time, just as she depended on me now. I related the silent nonconformity of her toilet-training to the form of her analytic sessions; her inability to use her mouth, to her fear of her screaming and biting impulses which she had not been able to contain in the past; and her sitting passively and having all the good things brought to her, to her attitude toward the analytic work. Susan responded shortly by showing me her drawings which she had so carefully hidden from me. They were beautiful horses and flowers, the very things she had earlier always insisted I draw for her. We had already had many opportunities to point out Susan's defenses against oral intake in her refusal to look, to learn, and to eat in front of me. (She insisted on gobbling her lunch in the car instead of bringing it to the session to eat.) In addition to the anal meanings, I now told Susan in regard to her art work, "It seems that, to you, learning from me is like stealing something, biting off something and keeping it for yourself. Young children often feel that if they want something another person has, they can get it only by really taking it in, rather than learning it by working for it. That makes them feel guilty and afraid that the other person will be hurt and be angry with them." I linked this to her reluctance to let me know that she profited from interpretations, as though they were forbidden food. She had always ignored interpretations and never informed me of improvements in herself, much less related them to the analysis. I now learned that Susan had recently made great strides in her art work, for the first time showing imagination, skill, and pleasure. Her school suddenly graded her creative art work as well above average. Moreover, there had been a big spurt in her schoolwork, real effort and success in doing her assignments well and on time.

What did not change, however, was Susan's inability to work actively with me. Her attitude changed. She acted like an aloof, self-satisfied adult and treated me in a condescending manner. A point came, however, when Susan showed her conviction that I had master-minded the family's vacation plans. I told her that, in contrast to her recent behavior, she now regarded me as very powerful in an unrealistic way. We understood this better only after the vacation, when I mentioned to Susan that her mother had spoken of Susan's sloppy table manners at home in contrast to her very good manners in retaurants. I pointed out how frequently we could see such marked discrepancies in her behavior, including the analysis, and that her eating was one example of such discrepancies. Since Susan had by now become aware of this tendency, I attempted a reconstruction. I told her that I could not help but feel there must have been a precedent for this in her early life, perhaps the weekly Sunday meals with Maman, when she was expected to behave very differently from the way she did at home. Susan laughed. "Sunday dinners, ha! They were mild. Jeff and I had to have breakfast with her every day for years. Mush! I hated it! It was all right for Jeff. He likes it." —"What did Maman say or do when you told her you didn't like it?"—"You don't tell Maman if you don't like it. She is the sort who then makes you eat it all the more." Susan had complained at home, but neither parent ever crossed Maman. I replied, "Now I know why you thought your parents would go on vacation where I told them to. I am like Maman. You have your daily breakfast with me. There is no appeal and no point in protesting. I just wonder where your anger went." It went in two directions, we learned. On the one hand, each spoonful of mush was devoured with an imagined piece of Maman in it; then Susan would spit back some of it when she returned home. On the other hand, some of the mush and Maman remained inside Susan. In this way she acquired the great power and control which characterized Maman, and solved, in part, the helplessness and out-of-control feelings which characterized herself. If one is Susan, one needs things and gets angry; if one is Maman, one has everything and does not need to get angry. I learned the interesting fact from the mother later that Maman, the unopposed ruler, felt she had met her match in little Susan. By the time Susan was three, Maman was reduced to helplessness when Susan spoke to her in the same authoritative, short manner that was so typical of Maman. Susan's identification thus helped her to achieve a measure of real power.

Susan, we learned, had been very impressed by her parents following my telephone advice on the night of her panic, a year earlier. She felt that I was the only one, except Maman, whose opinion counted with father. The more power I had, the more Susan feared and envied me; the more I came to represent Maman in the transference, the more she identified with the traits with which she had invested me. As we traced Maman's influence in the family, Susan herself pointed out that father was, in essentials, like the grandmother, and that therefore her identification included him. Actually, her rigid attitude of "I have everything, I need nobody, I can control myself and others" was a caricature, consistent with the warped reality picture that a very young child would perceive. The analysis of Susan's penis envy which formed a part of this identification was not undertaken until much later.

But the understanding of Susan's angry eating of mush and of Maman led to a further insight into Susan's lack of cooperation in the analytic work. I had often pointed out her inability to ask me for anything, however innocuous. This seemed an extreme extension of her failure to ask for help with any problem by simply admitting it. We could now see that, in addition to previously analyzed meanings, Susan's cold self-sufficiency was a defense against overwhelming oral-aggressive demands. If she allowed herself to express any demand, she would be in danger of opening the door to an avalanche of greed. I had surmised this when I noticed how greedily Susan "lapped up" everything about me on the few occasions when she saw me briefly outside the analytic setting. At those times it was almost as though she were caught without her defensive armor, and her great wish to take in broke through temporarily. Susan had warded off any discussion of these instances in her hours by her habitual silence and passivity. At this point, however, an opportunity arose. Susan was quite unable to ask me for a change of appointment to attend an optional school function. I refused to handle it through the mother on the basis that only Susan could tell me whether she did or did not want the change. In the nick of time, Susan asked me to accommodate her. When I gladly agreed, she became silently furious for days. I finally made this interpretation: She felt like a person who had wandered through the desert, dying of thirst and hunger, until at last she met someone and asked for help. The person gave her a mere drop of water. What could be more frustrating? What could arouse need and anger more? Susan sadly agreed.

The primitive introjection of Maman and the "mere drop of water" feeling also enabled us to understand one aspect of Susan's inability to give, beyond the previously analyzed anal meaning. She could not give presents, and she could give of herself, e.g., in words, only if the other person gave her something back right away. In her initial psychological test, the examiner had to give her one cookie for each answer. The giving away of words, especially of knowledge and feelings, left Susan empty and aggressively greedy. It represented not only food, but essential parts of herself. She felt she had acquired these by incorporation and would feel overwhelmed with impulses without them, endangering her own and the object's integrity. Similarly, Susan looked upon interpretations as offerings of myself. At times she rejected them; at other times she devoured them, secretly hoping to hide their effect from me, and often enough she "ate" them but spat them out upon leaving me.

Prior to this period, Susan had done very well in horseback riding, thriving under the instruction of a woman to whom she had displaced some of her positive feelings from me. For some years it was the only activity to which she was truly applying herself. Now, Susan had a man teacher whom she found gruff. Once she fell off the horse. She did not want to return to her lessons, complaining of a hurt arm. She told me that the teacher had scolded her when she fell and that she was very angry with him and was not going to see him again. She was going to stop riding. I showed Susan that she was identifying with him in her angry and rejecting attitude and that she felt her deep hurt in her arm instead of in her feelings. Susan admitted she had felt very hurt, could cry, and the arm pain left. She soon brought similar examples of identifying with her father, of humiliating or rejecting him when she felt he had turned her down, e.g., by not playing a game. As Susan began to understand this, and as I helped her to understand father's character and some of his weaknesses, she became much softer and warmer toward him. She could be shown in this context that her inability to give was a defense against incurring a narcissistic injury. She dreaded any situation in which she would offer herself to a beloved person or would demand love and be met with rejection. This, she felt, had happened with her father, and of course in the analysis with me. Now, for the first time, she turned to her father. He was able to respond to her new approach, and both began to enjoy each other in an appropriate way.

It was at this time that Susan's mother became psychotic.

Susan was ten years old and had been in analysis for over two and a half years. Although Susan never learned of some of the mother's symptomatology, certain pathological changes affected her directly: withdrawal of interest from the children, absent-mindedness, excessive sleeping, confused reality-testing, and labile irritability. Both parents initially spoke of the illness in terms of great fatigue, implying that the children had partly contributed to tiring mother with their demands and could help her to recover her strength by being good and quiet. I had to be instrumental in referring the mother for psychiatric care and in helping the father toward a realistic assessment of the situation. Within a few weeks, just prior to the summer vacation, the mother was hospitalized and did not return home until three months later. The children visited her in the latter part of her inpatient care.

Susan's initial reaction to the mother's symptoms consisted of denial, secrecy, and guilt, partly in keeping with her parents' early attitude. She badly missed her older brother, currently away from home, but added flatly that mother did not even think of him, as though this were just as it should be. I pointed out how strange a reaction this was and how scary for Susan because it must make her wonder whether mother would ever miss her. Susan confirmed this by telling me that she still had not received her long-promised ring because mother had to sleep or had forgotten. Both parents greatly helped Susan when they agreed to tell her that mother had a mind sickness for which the children were not responsible, that mother was getting proper help from a doctor, and when they encouraged Susan to talk about it with me. Step by step, as Susan brought the material, I clarified with her her mother's behavior in terms of symptoms and explained her sickness and hospitalization.

In her sessions, Susan had many times of being "little," as

she had been at moments in the early months of her treatment. She resumed writing her name over and over. To Susan, her mother's behavior was not entirely new. It was in some respects a repetition of her first two and a half years. We were able to reconstruct her fear then that mother would never return because she had forgotten her. Susan remembered how scared she was lest she be lost in every sense of the word. That is why she kept writing a "name tag" for herself—to find herself and to be found. I learned that although mother had never been ill to the extent that she was currently, her earlier disturbance had had similar features, particularly in some areas already mentioned which directly affected Susan. In the analysis, we were able to fit together a number of things, e.g., Susan's need to have her mother physically present because she had not been able to count on mother's feelings for her when absent, and Susan's identification with her mother in her earlier attitude to separations by erasing the mental image of the object or by throwing herself away. Susan became overtly sad, allowing herself to experience a wealth of feeling. As the vacation neared, Susan asked me to help her group the colored pencils, saying, "Which family does this one belong to? And this one?" We discussed her deep wish to belong to my family and to have me take her with me. Throughout this time, Susan left little notes of love or gifts for her mother. She continued to write to her during the vacation. A big change took place in Susan. She became competent and independent. She mastered many new tasks by taking care of herself, the household, and her siblings, and she enjoyed her activities. Her relationship with her father improved even more. He was happy with her and found her a reliable helper. On her return to school, Susan made a good start, adjusting well to the many changes of the higher grade. She took conscientious responsibility for her homework and arranged her own school transportation. In her sessions, her attitude reflected the general change. She became a good reporter and talked and worked with more mature ease.

The only area of relative silence was that regarding mother's slow improvement. Susan showed me some of mother's symptoms by identification with her and expressed an impatient wish for her return. She knew that mother only gradually would resume all her responsibilities, even after her return home. Once mother was home, Susan was thoughtful of her but became helpless in tackling her schoolwork, insisting that mother help her. Repeated long homework sessions with mother resulted in mother doing more and more of the work and Susan acting increasingly uncomprehending. She began to fail at school. I interpreted Susan's guilt over her recent competence and independent successes, told her that she apparently felt any achievement to be an aggressive rejection of mother, and that she was now atoning for her "crimes" by making herself stupid and by showing mother that she needed her as much as ever. In the sessions, a similar trend could be seen when we understood Susan's repeated "What time is it? How much longer?" as a fear that I would send her away. This, in turn, represented her wish to get rid of me, not to give me any more time. Susan now also realized that she had felt her turning to her father had made mother sick and had sent her away. Susan's aggression, however, soon turned against her father when he again started to go out alone with mother. He was rejecting her in favor of mother. During several short paternal trips, Susan was very anxious lest a tragedy befall him. This she could analyze. Intermittently, Susan turned to her mother with infantile dependency because, "How could I be angry at her when she is sick or would get sick?" and "If father won't have me, I only have mother left."

Shortly afterward Susan was quite sick for two days, and I did not expect her the third day because a severe snowstorm had paralyzed all traffic. She arrived, nevertheless, quite late. Her transport had got stuck one and a half miles from my house, and Susan had waded through waist-deep snow on her own. When questioned by someone at the door as to what she might want, she replied firmly, "I belong here." It was the only session in which Susan could fully express her love for me in words, her wish to belong to me, how much she had missed me, and her fear lest mother find out she walked. I told Susan how glad I was for her that she could have so much feeling, and that her ability to have such strong feelings of love would help her to cope with what I had to tell her, namely, that the aim of therapy was not to fulfill needs but to learn to understand them, to modify wishes and to accept frustrations. By helping her in this task, I could truly show her my love for her. I would not be a good friend or therapist to her if I acted as her parent; rather, I wanted to help her understand her feelings for her parents so that she could gain happiness with them and with others in her life ahead. After a few days, Susan reacted with the first direct aggression toward me. In the context of a fortune-telling game, she told me her Christmas wish this year—"Drop dead." She had an excellent Christmas vacation and surprising successes at school, while more detailed sadistic wishes came to the fore. In working through this material, some aspects became clearer, apart from the phallic ones:

1. Susan feared that her love for another person or her independent mastery and growth in any area of ego functioning would destroy her relationship with her mother and would

even hurt her mother. This was in part due to the fact that Susan's turning to another love object was motivated by her anger at mother's failure to meet all her needs: "I'll get myself a better mommy." In part, however, Susan's fear was due to a correct understanding of mother's difficulty. A number of instances from the past and present showed that the mother could relate to Susan best on a very early level, even though she could not do so consistently, and a part of her did regard independence in choice of objects and in activities as a serious rejection. With each new step toward bodily independence (bathing herself, caring for her hair and clothes, providing little things for herself from her allowance), we had to analyze Susan's fear of thereby harming her mother, and in each instance Susan had to handle mother's initial angry and hurt reaction. Susan had to learn to understand her mother's problem in this, as in many other areas. In the treatment we could analyze Susan's fear that she would outgrow and lose me if she worked with me toward an improvement.

2. Susan's turning to objects other than her mother was always bound to lead to new disappointments, thus throwing her back to the relative safety of her early relationship with her mother. Again, this was due in part to her reality experiences—her earlier relationship with her father, with people who left, and her encounters with sexual traumata. But in part it was due to the arrest of Susan's personality at an early stage of development. Since she had never coped with the frustrations and ambivalence in her earliest relationship with her mother, she sought new objects as mother substitutes. She transferred to them the bulk of her unmodified greed, impatience, and dependency—her total wish to control and to possess. She expected unconditional fulfillment of needs and wishes on all levels of instinctual development. Her love for

her father contained phallic and oedipal impulses, but her object relationships were fixated on a much more primitive level. Susan showed this very clearly also in her relationship to her pets. At that time she wanted to send away her cat because its squeaky voice was a nuisance. She wanted to get one, preferably from me, that would be just perfect. Susan could see that she was the kitten who had felt discarded and replaced by beloved adults and by her younger siblings because she was not perfect. She applied the same rule to her parents when they did not come up to her expectations. She had no wish to repair, to compromise, to tolerate failings. Also, of course, she expected me to change her into the perfect kitten, not only in the phallic sense, but in order to spare her all pain and frustration. In the analysis at that stage, Susan bounced rapidly between love for and rejection of either parent, with accompanying feelings of guilt and acts of mental self-damage. I had to show her repeatedly how unclear at times was her delineation between self and object representations, how she punished her parents and me—by failing tests, by neglecting herself, by refusing to make progress in the analysis—and how she failed to see the damage in all this to herself.

The most difficult step for Susan was to give up the therapist as the potential ideal, all-satisfying parent. Again she was often silent in her sessions and drew secret pictures. She alternately teased her mother by wishing for a house and life like mine, and then atoned for this by disparaging me in front of her. Susan never asked questions about my life and, indeed, refused information. I interpreted this as a wish to maintain an idealized concept of me, unmarred by reality. As long as she could keep this ideal image, she did not have to give up her unrealistic expectations, such as being magically changed by me instead of working for relatively minor improvements with me.

Susan could integrate this interpretation and achieved a new phase of maturity in her treatment relationship, as well as in her daily life. After more than three and a half years of treatment, Susan was now functioning age-appropriately for a girl of eleven. Her school and camp reports were very good. Her newly discovered sense of humor and tact helped her to get along well with her family. She handled their weaknesses realistically and kindly, but without giving up her rights and feelings.

The Patient's Attitude to the Therapist and the Analytic Work in the Latter Part of the Fourth Year

One area of major difficulty was left, that of Susan's sexual fantasies and activities. I knew from the first year of treatment that Susan sucked on a blanket comforter from babyhood and bit her nails. During the early years of Susan's analysis, her mother still used to alleviate Susan's periodic itching by scratching her feet and rubbing her back. Later, Susan herself had admitted that she used the analysis similarly for protective purposes, but we now saw increasingly that this did not sufficiently tide her over periods of even short separation. Susan was often guilty and anxious by the end of the week, and actively rejecting of me on Mondays. She was, however, unwilling and unable to work on her own sexuality, and could not discuss her thoughts and feelings about my private life. I had often drawn her attention to her defenses in this matter, as well as to the momentary breakthroughs, such as her surreptitious looking, and her phallic wishes for a magical change.

Now, in the latter part of the fourth year of her treatment, Susan spontaneously brought her concerns. "Could you help me with my nail-biting? I guess they'll never grow again."

She felt utterly guilty after separations from me, ready to accept blame for anyone's crime. Most striking, however, was the fact that she continually drew horses, the theme that had been with us from the very start. She could not and would not stop drawing horses. Susan was an excellent horseback rider, but those were not the horses she meant. She told of her first experiences with horseback riding at age six, when this activity represented an enjoyable closeness with mother. Mother and Susan had been surprised then at the masterful ease that Susan brought to movement and control on horseback. This led me to reconstruct Susan's extensive previous joyful experiences in riding horseback on daddy's shoulders. The moment I said this, Susan's whole body involuntarily went into riding motion, her head nodding agreement. She recalled being the only one for years to ride on Daddy during long family walks. She was the smallest and lightest child. She clearly remembered her feeling of power, mastery, and possession as she looked down on the others. She also rode "horsie on daddy's knees" and engaged in a lot of "horseplay" with him. The parents confirmed these memories. Susan came to understand now that her pictured horses represented earlier excited feelings about and with her father.

Several days later, Susan asked me to teach her to crochet again, the first time since the abortive attempt of over two years before. Susan not only learned within minutes, she remembered what she thought she had forgotten. This time she really enjoyed it and crocheted for days. The first thing she made was a blanket for "Thunder." I learned that that was the name of her stuffed horse, which was her sleeping companion. It was a gift from mother two years before, and she had slept with it ever since.

The important material connected with Thunder apparently could not be brought in without its physical presence. The following three sessions show Susan's conflict in this matter and how she dealt with it.

Session 671. In this session, a Monday, Susan withdrew into silent crocheting after an initial welcome smile. She eventually told me that when her parents returned from their short trip, her mother had been occupied in catering to the various needs of her younger siblings. "What did you do?" "First I had to finish my homework, then I watched TV for a while." I told her that she indeed did not need mother any longer in that sense, but she seemed to have needed me and felt rejected over the weekend, as she had shown me by turning away from me at first today. Susan suddenly had several urgent demands for help with her crocheting, but in each instance found she could manage the trouble before I even had a chance to answer her. I suggested, "Maybe you are telling me in this way that you feel you ought to have needed me during the weekend and that you are a bit guilty for having managed without me very nicely." Susan replied, "I don't know if I have enough wool. May I bring Thunder here tomorrow to measure the blanket?"—"Certainly."

Session 672. Susan arrived without the horse, looking thoughtful and puzzled. I: "Thinking of something?" Susan: "Well, I don't know what it is."—"You meant to bring "Thunder."—"Oh, dear, I forgot." Then she discussed her plans for shaping the blanket, and said she had tried a paper on the horse at home and therefore knew how many more rows to crochet. "Did you think you might forget him?"—"I measured it in case I should forget him." After a while she decided, "I can't really do it properly unless I measure it here. Maybe I better stop until I bring him tomorrow." She put away her work and started to draw secretly. I pointed out that she was hiding something from me and feeling bad about it, but could not stop herself. I reminded her how often she acted like a small child who knew grownups got cross at certain things, so the child went right on doing it but hid it. "It's very easy to hide things from me, but you can no longer hide things from yourself. We have often found that I don't judge things nearly as harshly as you do." Susan showed me her drawing—butter-

flies. I did not have to tell her what both of us knew: She wished
that the hidden secret with Thunder were as pleasant and harm-
less as pretty butterflies.

Session 673. The material in this session was almost all new to
me and its tone was like that of a much younger child.[4] Susan
brought Thunder, a stuffed horse about eighteen inches high.
She tenderly tried on the unfinished blanket. "He looks like a
well-loved horse. He really is. I love him very much." She showed
me the bells on his feet. They tended to make a noise, so she had
to be especially careful in playing with him at night lest someone
hear it. Susan: "He is a good horse."—"Always?"—"Yes, he's nice
always except to Linda. He bucks her off. Doesn't like little people. But he never bucks me off. He loves only me." She tells how she
gallops and trots on him on the bed and floor before he goes to
sleep with her. I: "It's certainly nice to be able to control a horse
so well. Does Linda mind?" Linda, Susan had just told me, was a
little doll. Suddenly Susan's voice was hard: "No, she does not
cry, she does not mind, she doesn't feel."—"That's strange. I'd
think she'd care a lot. Does anyone else ride him?"—"No, the others are too big, really." Susan told me of the "others." There is
Purple, a purple puppy; Silver Streak, a cat; and a very big doll,
Lizzie. When she indicated the size of the doll, she was taken aback
by realizing it was only a foot tall. She had had Lizzie since she
was under two, so we established the doll must have looked very
big then. Also, Susan was surprised to find she had only slightly
modified her mother's name in calling the doll Lizzie. Lizzie had
slept with her up to about three and a half years. Then Silver
Streak took over, named for a real cat by the same name, whose
brother had been owned by her father. The real Silver Streak
had never slept with her. He used to come up and then leave.
Eventually, he ran away. Purple replaced Silver Streak as a sleeping companion when Susan was about five and a half years old,
and eventually Thunder took his place. I mentioned how nice
it was that stuffed animals stayed the whole night, whereas real
ones tended to go off when they pleased. "Oh, not Pansy," inter-
jected Susan. She had Pansy when she was six to seven years old.

[4] D. W. Winnicott (1958) described similar experiences with children in analysis.

"Pansy slept with me. Then my parents would insist on taking her out for the night, but in the morning she was on the window in front of my room waiting for me, and I let her in." As she talked of Pansy, the tears welled up in her eyes. I said after a while, "Pansy was a fur person."—"What's that?" "An animal that we feel with, like with a person. When we love an animal and it loves us, we forget that people and animals are different. When we are very little we even don't know they are different. We feel the same way about them." Susan was crying quietly, trying to crochet at the same time. "I goofed on the stitches, making silly mistakes."—"How could one not make a mistake when one can't see for tears? But you did not make a mistake in having so much feeling for your animals and the things they meant to you." Susan did not remember, when I asked her, that the first thing she had ever told me about was the death of the pregnant Pansy when Susan was away from her. Susan could hardly bear to leave. She struggled with the thought of leaving Thunder, but decided it would be too hard to sleep without him. She would bring him again tomorrow, and she did.

The first two of these sessions show that Susan used old defenses against the anxieties springing from her relationship and activities with Thunder, who represented her masturbatory fantasies and acts. In the first session, she returned fleetingly to the "I need you" relationship. In the second session, she externalized her guilt regressively. Both defenses, employed in the face of pressure from id and superego, were pervasively present at the very start of her analysis. At that time, interpretations of these defenses did not help her to master her feelings consciously nor could she bring them into the analysis indirectly. Instead, she used the interpretations as the therapist's supplies or gifts, within the framework of her infantile object relationship, and her ego evoked a strong denial of affect in order to ward off the threatening feelings all the more effectively. Now, however, brief interpretative reminders helped her to manage without these defenses. She could attempt to cope consciously with the underlying feelings. Session 673 shows that she initiated this by bringing her problem actively into the analysis.

Shortly, afterward, Susan brought additional material to show that her activities with her horse were closely linked to her forbidden transference fantasies. In her play with the horse, she acted out, to an extent, what she imagined my husband and I were doing. In this way she warded off thoughts and feelings. Slowly, Susan began to relate her preoedipal sexual fantasies directly and indirectly, and attempted to face her feelings of jealousy and excitement. Much later, she could analyze them in terms of her early experiences, e.g., the primal scene. As the treatment progressed, it was found that Susan's ego could integrate this material sufficiently to maintain relatively normal functioning in her daily life and to continue her active work in her analytic sessions.

Piecemeal work on this material brought us close to Christmas. Susan had been in analysis just over four years. She very happily worked on gifts for all the women and girls in her circle, but could not fathom a gift for her father. Simultaneously she refused to admit any interest in, or enjoyment of her social dancing class. She looked very guilty. Her silences around these topics increased. She was almost as uncommunicative as of old. This time I could interpret her not giving as a defense against a great wish to give all of herself to her father, to give him the best a woman could give, but she dreaded what this would do to her mother. I linked her conflict over giving to her nongiving silence in the analysis. When Susan was once more unable to ask me for a simple favor, I told her, "I think a part of you treats me now as you used to treat your father in the past. The more you want to give and to be given, the more you fear that I shall turn you down. Perhaps some of you even feels you would deserve that because giving to me means taking someone's place." Susan replied by making a baby of wool. She showed it to me and agreed with my interpretation that she must have wished to give father a baby, just as mother did.

Susan's treatment was not concluded at this point. Much work and working through was still to come. Her beginning pubertal conflicts had barely been touched. Yet, at eleven and a half years of age, after just over four years of analysis, she was symptom-free at home and an interested, conscientious student at school, with above-average grades. In her sessions, she had essentially reached the level of development in ego functioning and in the relationship to the therapist at which she could consistently participate in the analytic work and communicate with the therapist.

SUMMARY

An attempt has been made to describe a patient in her latency years whose early fixations, particularly in the area of object relationships, and whose defensively crippled ego made it very difficult for her to participate actively in the analytic process. Some sections of the girl's analysis have been presented to illustrate the technical measures that were taken to help the patient in her task, as well as to point up certain layers of the dynamic, genetic, and structural aspects that were found to underlie her difficulty.

It is by no means an exhaustive presentation; for instance, many facets relating to the topic directly have been left out, and hardly anything has been included of the analytic work in regard to the superego. Further, almost all of the material relating to the patient's phallic and oedipal conflicts has been omitted. The reason for this is as follows. During the first four years of treatment reported here there was ample evidence of Susan's penis envy, homosexuality, oedipal conflicts, and masturbation, as well as signs of her reactions, on all levels, to her traumatic sexual experiences (primal scene, miscarriage, etc.). However, it was not till the end of this period that the analysis of these topics could begin fruitfully. It forms the main content of the fifth and sixth years of treatment. The preceding years described in this paper contain the unusually long analytic "preparation" necessary for that work.

One focus of the analysis was to understand the patient's disturbed attitude toward the treatment and to bring to her consciousness the different transference reactions which precluded her utilizing the therapist as an assistant in the analytic work.

Which level of development had the patient reached when active participation in the analytic work became possible for her? As far as the patient's relationships are concerned, she had reached the developmental level of the object-centered phallic oedipal phase (A. Freud 1962, 1963). She could maintain her love for the object in the face of the absence of the object and of frustration by the object, and despite her own aggressive impulses which had sufficiently abated and become libidinally fused. In line with this, she could begin to form object relationships with people outside the family (teachers, friends, therapist) to whom she did not relate as to early parent substitutes.

In many of her ego functions, considerable changes had occurred. Her inner and outer reality testing were largely age-adequate. Her memory function was at her disposal in her current life. Her speech had become largely neutralized (A. Katan, 1961). Her motility was freed from defensive restrictions. She could better integrate her impulses and experiences. Perhaps most important, she could adequately tolerate pain and frustrations, modify wishes, and delay gratifications. These ego functions and activities had come to be employed more in the service of the reality principle than of the pleasure principle. In line with these changes, she had taken such developmental steps as being able to use toys and play materials for the direct and displaced expression of drives, and being able to gain gratification from work as well as play (A. Freud, 1960, 1963). She had become physically independent of her mother and could provide for her own care and comfort within the home setting, at school, and in other age-appropriate environments.

Libidinally, she had come to experience her phallic and oedipal impulses. These had been present from the start, but had shared their urgency almost equally with other component drives. Shortly after reaching the age of eleven years, the patient began to show some pubertal interests.

Her aggressive impulses had become more adequately attached to the phallic and oedipal stage of development, relinquishing to a considerable extent their earlier oral- and anal-sadistic fixation points. The effect of the newly matured ego functions in modifying the expression of aggressive impulses and in neutralizing aggressive energy was striking. Previously, the patient's aggression had been either tacitly turned against the self or had erupted in outbursts.

Implicit in these developments is also their contribution to the maturation and integration of the superego. It seems to me that the patient needed to attain these particular levels of development before she could age-appropriately master the task of actively participating in the analytic work. Initially, her disturbance had made many functions required for the analytic work unavailable to her during the treatment hours, and had forced the patient into an early type of transference relationship which was of itself unconducive to successful participation.

REFERENCES

Freud, A. (1944), *The Psycho-analytical Treatment of Children.* New York: International Universities Press.
—— (1960), Four Contributions to the Psychoanalytic Study of the Child. New York Lectures, unpublished.
—— (1962), Assessment of Childhood Disturbances. *The Psychoanalytic Study of the Child,* 17:149-158, New York: International Universities Press.
—— (1963), The Concept of Developmental Lines. *The Psychoanalytic Study of the Child,* 18:245-265. New York: International Universities Press.
Katan, A. (1961), Some Thoughts about the Role of Verbalization in Early Childhood. *The Psychoanalytic Study of the Child,* 16:184-188. New York: International Universities Press.
Winnicott, D. W. (1953). Transitional Objects and Transitional Phenomena. *Internat. J. of Psychoanal.,* 34:89-97

Mary Hamm

Some Aspects of a Difficult Therapeutic (Working) Alliance

FIRST AND FOREMOST in the treatment of any child, it is necessary to establish a relationship with that child. In the early days of child analysis it was generally believed that the relationship had to be positive. This is no longer considered to be the crucial factor. Now we think in terms of the necessity to have the cooperation of the child. Briefly, this means the child must be able to, or enabled to, participate in his treatment in an emotionally dynamic way. Frankl and Hellman (1962) refer to this participation as a "therapeutic alliance." They discuss various difficulties which interfere with the establishment of a therapeutic alliance in child analysis and show ways these can be approached and overcome.

The aim of this paper is to illustrate some of the technique used in a particularly difficult and complicated analysis of a child. A selection of material has been made which focuses mainly on the problem of the establishment and maintenance of a therapeutic alliance (or working relationship) with the patient. No effort is made in this restricted and short exposition to discuss fully, either clinically or theoretically, the innumerable aspects of the child's problems and her analysis.

The child to be discussed came from an upper middle-class English family. The parents were most eager for their child to have treatment and made considerable personal sacrifice to carry it through. They both had many deeply rooted problems of their own which, without their awareness, had unwittingly affected the child. The main reasons for referral to treatment were stuttering, underachievement in school, and lack of friends. The analysis began at age nine, in late latency, and continued well into adolescence. It was especially during the first three and a half years of treatment that the difficulties in forming a working relationship were so prominent. Anne could not establish a real contact with her therapist. It soon became clear in the analysis that one of her most painful problems was the inability to be in contact with herself or even to feel that she had a self, that she was a person. Frequent experiences of derealization and depersonalization were two ways in which this was manifested.

Anne was initially very happy about the idea of coming into treatment. Her original enthusiasm, however, quickly turned into ambivalence because she became disappointed in the treatment situation, felt it to be a hardship, and protested vehemently that anything was expected of her, that she herself had to work. The treatment had value for her insofar as it gave her permission to express her anger and to complain about her life. It was difficult to sort out which were realistic difficulties in relation to her environment, particularly her mother, and which were Anne's own inner problems. For instance, Anne hated and despised her flute, an instrument which had been presented to her by the mother in the most glowing terms. The mother's insistence that Anne continue her lessons gave Anne the feeling that her mother put pressure on her.

It was around the flute that the first important contact was made with this child, eight months after treatment began. When, on my suggestion, the mother, to the best of her ability, left it up to Anne to decide for herself whether or not to continue her flute lessons, Anne became quite desperate. "Why did my mother ever start it? How awful to have a chance to give it up and not be able to!" Then she pleaded, "Did my mother tell you anything that could explain why I hate my flute so much?"

It occurred to me that the mother had perhaps revealed some information in her regular sessions with me that might be related to the problem. Anne had been successfully breast-fed for the entire first year of her life. At eight months, when she was already drinking from a cup, she had turned away from the breast. The mother and her pediatrician had not understood that this was a signal from the child indicating a readiness to be weaned. For various reasons, including advice from her pediatrician and the convenience of the mother, the child had been persuaded and coaxed to go back to the breast. A few months later, when the mother became pregnant for the second time, breast-feeding had been discontinued. Bottle-feeding had then been instigated and continued (again partly on medical advice) until at age five and a half, after a tonsillectomy, a doctor ordered its cessation. Until then, through the years, the child had been allowed to have as many bottles as she wanted, whenever she wanted them, day or night—two or three on going to bed, and several during the course of the night.

Because of the quality of the child's words, "Why did my mother ever start it?" and "How awful to have a chance to give it up and not be able to!", it struck me that some of the current feelings about the flute might be connected with feelings the child had had about her bottle. Because of the nature and urgency of her plea for help, I decided to use the information gained from the mother and suggested a possible connection between the two. Anne was strikingly relieved. "Yes," she said, "I always felt I was just an experiment, that

Mother learned on me, then *took what should have been mine and gave it to Susie."* (A younger sister was born when Anne was 19 months old. At that time the mother's feelings toward Anne had changed very dramatically from adoration to annoyance. The reason for this was that the older child came to represent to the mother one of the mother's older sisters.)

It had occurred to me that it must be most humiliating for a child at the height of the oedipus complex still to indulge in such a totally infantile activity as having a bottle. Anne's response, however, also indicated another aspect, namely, the feelings of rivalry and of being deprived by mother.

Though Anne had left the above session claiming to feel much better and not to be so mixed up any more, it took several more months of analysis before I achieved a better working relationship with her, gained her cooperation, and enabled her to participate actively in her treatment. It was an interpretation of the transference and her defense against it that turned the tide. There had been three breaks in treatment during the year. Any feelings about these breaks had been completely warded off, and Anne's defense against them had not yielded to any of my efforts to uncover them. However, one day after the third break, I interpreted to her that behind her specific and persistent complaint that mother loved her younger sister more and gave more to her, Anne must be hiding her fear of being deserted and deprived by me. Startled and looking frightened, Anne very unconvincingly tried to deny that my interpretation was valid. However, the following sessions showed the effect of my interpretation. She was now more ready to enter into a therapeutic alliance with me. Thus she was able to begin a most painful and tedious process of revealing herself to herself and to me.

This readiness to reveal herself increased when I could

make the next interpretation. This was when Anne reported that she was angry because her mother had to care for her younger brother and sister, who were ill. I commented, "These feelings originated in your childhood. It must have been very hard for you to share your mother when you were little." Anne's response was again of the greatest importance and opened up the analytic work on her central problem.

Standing before me, slightly swaying and with great affect, which showed the devastating nature of the episode, Anne recalled that at age three she was allowed to suck at the mother's breast after the newborn baby brother had nursed. "When there was no milk," said Anne in agony, "it felt just as if Bobby had taken all Mother's love." From now on the analysis proceeded more easily and there was a flow of material.

Tediously and painfully, the depth and degree of this child's neurosis became clear to us. There was a serious disturbance in the ability to relate with the parents and siblings, partly because of the interaction with their individual difficulties, with peers and outsiders, because of the child's own problems. There also were severe and pathological structural conflicts within the child. There was an imbalance because the superego was relatively too strong, and the ego too weak and immature. In particular, the impaired ego of this child constituted a great handicap that could not be dealt with or overcome by analytic interpretation alone. For the next two and a half years, a special effort on the part of the therapist was required to maintain the therapeutic alliance. Each day the relationship had to be re-established. If there had been a weekend or holiday interruption, correspondingly more time and effort were needed to get the relationship back on a working basis.

One aspect of this seemingly endless problem arose from the tenacious oral fixation to her mother. This showed up

clearly when it became necessary to make other travel arrangements to her sessions. Up to that time, Anne had been driven
each day by one of her parents. When an effort was made to
begin to prepare her for a change in this setup, Anne became
livid with rage and, in an outburst full of indignation, said,
"I don't want to be bothered by all that. I want to be held by
the hand and led." For a short time transportation arrangements were variable and afforded meaningful material for
the analysis.

When mother had trouble finding people to drive Anne to
her sessions, Anne reacted with shocked surprise and intense
disappointment. This was understood as a repetition of an
earlier experience when Anne must have felt suddenly deprived of mother's care. When a lady driver had to quit this
job after a short period, Anne felt utterly deserted. When she
finally took a taxi for the first time by herself, she cried like a
toddler, "I want my mommy."

To show some of the complicated interactions of this analysis, material will be given in detailed sequence.

One day, before Anne started to take taxis, mother again
had to bring her and they arrived early. Anne complained,
"While we were waiting Mommy scolded me for not washing
my hair on Sunday." Evidently the mother's annoyance had
taken Anne aback, for she said, as if shocked, "Mommy never
spoke to me like that before. Why should she be cross? I didn't
have time to wash my hair." I asked her, "Why does that
bother you so much?" and went on to comment, "Not having
enough time doesn't seem a very good reason to me, and it
certainly isn't too much for a mother to expect an eleven-year-
old girl to take the responsibility for keeping her hair clean."
Then Anne told me the really important problem of the moment, "Mother's thinking of having me take a taxi alone, and

I don't like that idea." She continued in a whiny manner, "I want a lady to bring me." I reminded Anne, "Not so long ago you told me that you wanted to be held by the hand and led. Wanting a lady driver is part of that same problem." Then I explained the current reality. "It isn't possible for either your mother to drive you or to get some other person to be your regular driver. Besides it wouldn't help you to find someone who would just lead you around. What is very important is that we tackle this problem so that your treatment can proceed. Our aim here is to help you grow up, not to let you escape every time you meet a difficulty, as you did by sucking your bottle when little." Anne explained, "But I'm afraid I might not be able to talk to the taxi driver. I might stutter." I reminded Anne, "Your stuttering isn't really all that bad. You're quite capable of giving a simple direction. It seems to me that you're telling me again about the feeling that your body can't function properly. We have already found out that this feeling is connected with a very strong conviction that your body is damaged." Anne's penis envy had been a very prominent theme in the analysis for some time. At this time I connected her stuttering to it in the following way. "Your stuttering isn't, in reality, a result of a damaged body. Rather the feeling that you're damaged must be one of the reasons for your stuttering."

After a quiet spell, Anne wanted to talk about a bracelet that she had lost about two years previously while square-dancing in a church. We had previously discussed this bracelet as symbolic of a firmly entrenched mother-breast-penis equation. But, as on previous occasions, Anne had the greatest difficulty discussing this topic and she could not say the word bracelet. In like manner, she was adamant in believing that the bracelet could be found. The reality that it either had

been thrown out in the trash or was in someone else's possession was intolerable. As on previous occasions in connection
with this topic, Anne dissolved into tears.

When her tears ceased, Anne's thoughts turned to the topic
of another loss, the emotional significance of which was apparent because of the presence of a typical defense, repression
of affect. "My last health class is tomorrow. But I can't *feel*,"
she said, "that I won't be seeing Miss Lowe any more."
I explained, "Its the pain of the feeling of desertion which
makes you unable to be in touch with your feelings. As we
have said before, these feelings of loss belong to your babyhood. It is very important for you to understand them so that
you won't constantly continue to get them mixed up with
your present-day life. After all, why should it be so hard to
lose a lady driver you hardly know or a teacher whom you
have had relatively little contact with?" Her response was to
say, with obvious pleasure, "Yesterday when I got home
Daddy gave me a sandwich which he had just made for himself." I sympathized, "It must have been especially nice after
being so upset yesterday about losing things to arrive home
and get something nice from your father." Anne suddenly
leaped into the air. We had already reconstructed that Anne's
sudden leaps were a way to repeat a childhood experience of
being thrown into the air by father. I reminded her of this
and added, "It seems clear that when you were little and felt
you had lost your mommy, you must have for a time gotten
some nice pleasurable things from Daddy."

Anne then called attention to a tie she had on and related,
"I wanted to wear it one day last week, but both Mommy
and Susie said it didn't match the skirt I was wearing. I was
cross and wanted to wear it anyway." I could then take the
step to interpret to her, "The tie must stand for boy things,
for the penis you so much want." Anne readily admitted this.

But then came an often-repeated question which always had had an urgency about it and the meaning of which I had never been able to understand. "Are you a Catholic?" After some puzzling and exploratory questioning as to why this was so important to her, I reminded Anne, "Once you told me that, though you know from your parents that there is no God, you sometimes prefer to think there really might be one." I then suggested, "Perhaps you are wondering if it is all right for you to have a religion." Anne replied, "Well, recently I have been thinking that I would like to go to Heaven, then return to earth and have another life." Her reason, expressed very sincerely, was, "I can't bear to think that what I have in this life is all I'll ever get." In this complaint, besides her dissatisfaction with her body because she was a girl and had no penis, lay Anne's extreme unhappiness that she had not received an adequate supply of love, devotion, and understanding from either parent.

Anne's fixation to the oral phase expressed itself in many ways in the transference and involved her use of the whole treatment situation. It was impossible for a long time for her to express transference feelings. All attempts to discover directly what they were had met with a blank. Anne claimed that she never thought about me and had no feelings toward me. There came a day when, while waiting for a late taxi, Anne overheard various of my household activities. Later, I learned that this had given her quite a shock. She explained, "I never thought of you as existing outside this room, here, with me." I could then understand and explain to Anne that the treatment was used as an expression of her wish to repeat the early unconflicted relationship with mother, when she had felt alone with her. This strong wish could serve as a most powerful defense, for it protected her from experiencing conflict, frustration, and anxiety in the transference. It

took another whole year of analytic work before she could let
the transference develop, reveal its daily manifestations, and
tolerate a discussion of it.

Another consistent device of Anne's was to use the treatment situation as if it were her baby bottle whenever she
needed comfort. If things got difficult at home, she would
tell herself that all she had to do was come to me, then everything would be just fine. Just as the baby bottle stood for the
magical fulfillment of all wishes, so did treatment, and just
as the baby bottle had been one of her ways to enslave the
mother, so Anne wished to use me. She revealed this by representing me in a drawing as a naked little brown slave kneel-
ing at her feet. (During the first five years of Anne's life,
mother had taken for granted that it was her duty to run to
Anne in the night at the slightest whimper from her.) Just
as Anne tried to blame her mother for her baby bottle and
take no responsibility for her own role in regard to it, so she
tried to make me responsible for her inner life. "I wouldn't
even know what my thoughts and feelings are," she snapped
one day, "If you didn't tell me about them. I shouldn't have
to work so hard to try to tell them to you. You should tell me
what they are, then I would know just what to tell you." She
constantly, in ever more subtle ways, tried to make me do her
thinking and her verbalizing so that she could avoid responsibility, frustration, and anxiety.

The first interpretation which contributed to the precipita-
tion of severe anxiety dealt with a subtle but powerful defense used to ward off the transference. The problem of analyzing her relationship to me was a seemingly insurmountable obstacle. At times, when some incident, such as seeing
me come in the driveway, had reminded her that I had an
existence other than in relation to her, she had been able to
bring some transference material, such as the wish to live

with me and the accompanying fantasy that I would give her everything. However, it became apparent from some aspects of the way Anne brought material that she managed to ward off awareness of her transference feelings by identifying with me.

Some of the factors which had become increasingly frequent in the over-all style of Anne's presentation of material and indicated an identification with me were the following: More and more, Anne adopted my role of interpreter, explainer, the one who understood and made sense out of things. She now supplied her own explanations for her behavior and moods. Previously current material had often been explained in its relation to the past, and this became the repetitive pattern of Anne's own understanding. But she sounded like a student who had learned one pattern of dynamics, i.e., repetition of the past, rather than a patient involved in an emotional relationship with her therapist. Further, Anne's explanations and verbal material ignored me. My presence in Anne's emotional life was apparent only in the subtle form of taking over my role and my way of thinking. She voiced, as her own, attitudes and ideas learned from me and echoed interpretations which had been given previously, sometimes seemingly appropriately, but more often the explanations served only to show superficial layers or sounded as if they were what she imagined might result from my way of thinking.

Though Anne's treatment was a constant struggle to deal with increasingly more complicated defenses and resistances, all reports from home and from school had been of a steady though mild improvement. Shortly after the end of the second year, there was a father-daughter dance sponsored by Anne's Scout troop. This incident caused a setback of no small magnitude.

Always the most serious stumbling block in the analysis remained my contact with this child. Now again it was gone. The hard-earned and forever tenuous working relationship had to be refound. The timing, wording, and tone of interpretations, even comments, had to be more than ever scrutinized, otherwise Anne would withdraw into her own world and shut off any contact with me.

Although withdrawal had been a constant problem throughout, heretofore it had always been possible to deal with it more or less immediately in the session. Sometimes she would turn back to me if I could verbalize for her the painful feelings she could not tolerate. Other times she could be reached by my showing her firmly and emphatically that to withdraw, to turn her back on the world, to turn away from people who could help her, to close her mind to her difficulties, really only made things harder. Instead of opening up avenues to gain strength and some mastery over her feelings, by withdrawing she prevented any further understanding, any participation, any sharing, any relationship, i.e., any therapeutic gain.

On this particular occasion the withdrawal from contact with me and her environment was more difficult to overcome. Eventually one could understand this particular regression as a defense against the wish to castrate father which had been aroused by the close contact while dancing with him. This child's fixation to the earliest phase of development and the easy regressions to this phase presented a constant challenge. Her orality, the wish for narcissistic gratification, her primitive mode of relating to a love object, and the complete rejection due to the intense aggression were most powerful resistances in the analysis. She found such comfort in being alone, physically and psychologically. Only after four years of treatment did she become aware of not wanting to be alone and realized, for the first time, that this was the way most people felt.

As mentioned before, Anne made extensive use of the mechanisms of derealization and depersonalization. At the time of the father-daughter dance these became more prominent than ever before and occurred also in the sessions. Later, when I understood more about her and could give effective interpretations of other defenses, she had a few weeks of constant experiences of derealization and depersonalization, which were usually preceded by withdrawal. The psychological withdrawal was accompanied by physical retreat to the furthermost corner of the room.

As mentioned earlier, the interpretation of Anne's defensive identification with me illicited severe anxiety. However, it also had enabled her to acknowledge her feelings of needing me. This made the treatment more meaningful therapeutically. When she was shown that, instead of working with me, she had become like me for the purpose of warding off strong feelings about me, her immediate reaction had been one of anger. In one of her rare outbursts, but with true feeling, she complained that our relationship was unfair. "I have to rush to get here," she protested, "but you can take your time about starting our sessions. You just sit there and don't do anything while I have to tell you more and more and more." In the following sessions, however, Anne experienced intense anxiety and frequently became depersonalized. She wondered whether I said prayers at night, which led to thoughts about God, whereupon she became depersonalized. This happened three times in consecutive sessions. In discussing this, I explained, "For you, thoughts about God seem to be forbidden. But I don't think the real problem is because your parents don't believe in God. All kids your age think and talk a lot about God without getting frightened like you do. You must have connected some other kind of thoughts with God, some kind of thoughts you yourself feel you shouldn't have." At the very end of the session, when she could escape further discussion, with great difficulty and in a most faltering voice, Anne whispered, "Thoughts about God have to do with sexual intercourse."

But one of the most severe attacks of depersonalization came as a result of interpreting the defensive use of identification in relation to her father. Again my clue came partly in the form of the material rather than in its content. There had been a mixup in which a young man who was supposed to drive Anne to her sessions had not shown up. When he telephoned the parents to explain, he had reversed the charges. Anne dissolved into tears trying to tell of this. But her manner of relating the above account was a typical and striking characteristic of her sessions. Everything came in little fragments, and I had to question and encourage her in some way for every detail. This was typical of the way her father, who was a withdrawn person, communicated with the children. When I showed Anne that, as with me, she became like her father in order not to have feelings about him, and that the strong emotional reaction had to do with her feelings for father, she was very quiet. She then remarked, "You don't seem real to me. I feel as if I am a stranger to myself, as if I were two people, as if I were outside myself watching myself."

Anne suffered one of her most intense rage reactions a few days after I had shown her the defensive use of identification in relation to father. Anne was not able to return the friendship of the boys in school and ignored them in the same way her father ignored her. When I explained this to her, the aggression bound in the identification was freed. Anne became enraged. This was almost intolerable for her. For two days she dashed and darted about the room, fearing she might explode and dreading to leave lest she couldn't get herself back together.

(Anne's experiences of depersonalization lessened considerably nine months later as a result of an interpretation of her death wishes. Anne described an incident when, in the middle of an altercation with her mother, with whom she was furious, she had suddenly felt estranged from her mother. "It felt as if Mommy just wasn't there," she explained. I showed her that the feeling her mother wasn't there was Anne's way of doing away with her mother. Usually, however, what she felt was a loss of herself [depersonalization]. It must have been that when this happened [when she became depersonalized] she was really doing to herself what she would have liked to do to somebody else–to get rid of them, demolish them, kill them. Following this interpretation, although there were occasional temporary returns of the symptom at moments of acute anxiety, depersonalization played a minor role in the analysis.)

After repeated reassurance in many sessions that she would be better able to tolerate such strong feelings if she could become aware of the thoughts that accompanied them, Anne managed to give another clue about the content of her rage. "I think the reason why Daddy is always tired and ignores me," she explained, "is because Mommy uses him all up at night when they have intercourse. There's just nothing of him left for me." She added in a sad and woebegone voice, "I don't even have a chance with Daddy." To my query, "Just what do you mean when you say 'using up'?" Anne brought a memory about her baby bottle. "I remember once when I was about three years old I woke up one morning and couldn't find my bottle. Then I found it on the floor, broken." She had told me this memory several times previously, and its significance became clear only now when she finished the

above thought with the words, "That is what Mommy does to
Daddy at night, break him." Thus Anne revealed that the
thoughts about the baby bottle were mixed with sexual fantasies. Also, one could now understand that Anne's fantasies
of castrating her father, which were so frightening to her,
were reinforced and complicated by the fantasy that this was
the way her mother treated the father. (Some of Anne's reactions to the primal scene had been discussed earlier in the
analysis.)

Before and simultaneously with the bursting forth of anger
toward the father, which included almost overt death wishes
toward him, Anne brought many anxieties centered around
the idea of being too late, and much resentment toward those
who came ahead of her. Many times she had proclaimed that
her lot in life was expecially difficult due to the fact that she
was the first child. In the session following the sequence described in the preceding paragraph, she brought a dream
about two dried-up lakes in a mountain, below which was a
home for deprived children. Associations clearly indicated
that the two dried-up lakes stood for her mother's empty
breasts. This, together with the above material revolving
around the feeling that her turn came too late, was understood
to mean that Anne imagined it was father who had got the
mother's breasts first. This fantasy was connected with some
material Anne had brought a year previously. She had been
furious when father had eaten a biscuit which mother had especially saved for Anne, and she had become very anxious at
that time when I had suggested it had made her feel that her
father could do forbidden oral things not permitted to her.
It was now clear that one aspect of Anne's rage toward her
father resulted from the fantasy that he was allowed to suck
the mother's breasts and that he had gotten them first, before
she arrived.

However, though Anne agreed with the above, this insight again drove her away. In the following sessions the contact with me was lost, the contact with reality was lost, and the contact with herself was lost—nothing felt real to her. She commented, "I know where I was born, but that doesn't seem real to me either." I replied, "It seems you feel as if you have lost your past. What do you think the past stands for? Don't you think that is just another way to say your mother's breasts? After all, we know so well that that is the part of your past that you have the strongest feelings about." Anne complained, as she had done previously, "I don't like to see your other patients. It bothers me, especially when I see the ones who come before me or when I imagine they have been coming to see you longer than I have. Why don't you get rid of them? I still hate to have to leave every day. It all just makes me feel hopeless." I translated this transference material into the language of the above fantasy. "It seems that you are now telling me that the same feelings and fantasies that belong to your parents and originated in your past have become connected with me. Now I have become the depriving mother who prefers and gives more to the one who got there before you. It is as if you feel I am the mother who lets the father suck my breasts." This caused Anne to go blank. Previously such moments had seemed to be related to Anne's feelings of phallic castration. In the present context, however, I interpreted to her, "You have become like the dried-up, empty breasts you dreamed about recently and actually experienced when you were little." Anne's thoughts immediately began to flow, and my contact with her was better than ever before and became increasingly more so from then on.

Some material in sequence will show that one reason Anne needed to cling so strongly to her early mother fixation was to ward off anxiety connected with more current and more

grown-up but forbidden feelings revolving around her oedi·
pal complex. After this interpretation, she brought many
thoughts and feelings about her father. "Yesterday I was so
disappointed. All the way home I was thinking about Daddy
and looking forward to talking to him. But just as I came in
sight of the house, I saw him pulling out of the driveway. I
don't know what made me do it, but I cried. Last Sunday we
went on an outing. We all went except Mommy. She hates
outings. She always sits up front next to Daddy, but I sat
there this time." Suddenly, in the session, Anne didn't feel
well. She had a tummy ache. I commented, "That's a funny
thing. Why should you suddenly get a tummy ache at just the
very moment you tell me about sitting in your mommy's place?
It must be that you were reminded of some other thought
about Daddy, some thought you feel is forbidden. We know
that every once in a while you get an ache or a pain when you
are frightened of something that is going on in your mind."
Anne then began to complain about her treatment. "I wish I
could leave. I have a dancing class when I get home. I'm worried I might be late. I might miss my bus and it would all be
your fault." "Once again," I told her, "I have become a person
who deprives you, just as you feel your mother does." Anne
then revealed that a typical conflict with her mother had
flared up again. "I've been fighting with Mommy over clothes.
She won't buy me the new dress I want." I reminded Anne,
"In the past we have understood your troubles over clothes
in terms of your feelings about your sister." (Anne's sadness
and crying attacks when her old clothes were handed down
had seemed to reflect the feelings she had had when her sister
had been nursed by the mother.) "Perhaps, now, other problems are mixed up with your feelings about clothes." Anne
recalled, "When I was little, Mommy told me to draw a picture to express my angry feelings. Once I drew a picture of

Susie in a dress full of holes. I got worried that Mommy would be angry and punish me." I said, "I wonder if perhaps you aren't still worried that mother will be angry and punish you. But I think the reason for this worry is different at the moment. It must be you feel guilty for the thoughts you had while sitting next to your daddy on the front seat of the car in your mother's place. But you also seem to be frightened in yourself to know what those thoughts are, and so you got a sick feeling in your tummy instead."

As Anne became emotionally stronger, the wish to be free from her too-close bond with her mother emerged. Several months later, for the first time, the direct wish to rid herself of her fixation to her mother's breasts came to the fore. One day Anne's parents brought her to her session, then went on to a French restaurant for lunch. Anne was again in a depersonalized state and explained, "I feel pointless, as if I have no self, no personality. I only smile when others do, laugh when they laugh, stop when they stop. I agree with whatever anybody else says." I pointed out, "It seems you feel this way in order not to let yourself know how angry you are that you have been left out of your parents' life and pleasure.[1]" Anne started talking about a problem of which she had complained many times, namely, her inability to hit a volleyball. But this time she clarified the problem. "I never have any trouble coping with a football. It is only round balls I can't hit away from me." Therefore, I replied, "Well, what do you think those round balls that come flying in your face and make you feel helpless stand for?" "Of course," said Anne, "my mother's breasts." This helplessness must have originated with the in-

[1] In the analysis, much work had been done on Anne's resentment about being left out of the excitement of the primal scene. The mother would have been very exhilarated by the treat of going to a French restaurant. Not being able to go to the restaurant with the parents meant to Anne to be left out of the excitement of the primal scene in terms of the oral concept of intercourse.

terfering influence of the mother at eight months when Anne's readiness to take her first step away from the mother was thwarted. The complicated interplay of forces following that episode seemed to have entangled Anne more than ever in her feeling that she was in the power of her mother.

A connection between the oral and phallic deprivation and Anne's inability to feel herself a person came together as follows. Anne's efforts to use my, rather than her own, mind were understood and dealt with in various ways. (One of the meanings ascribed to my words was that they stood for the flow of milk from the mother.) Analyzing this problem, instead of gratifying Anne, made her become extremely frustrated. She explained her inability to express the resulting anger by claiming, "Of course, it's because of your magic. You can punish me or hurt me in any way your choose." I answered, "Why, after all this time and work, do you still insist that I have magic powers? It seems that you have a *need* to make me omnipotent. But it doesn't make sense that you want me to be omnipotent in order to harm you. I don't believe that is the real reason." Anne replied, "You're right. It's because I don't want to lose my chance to get a penis from you." The oral and phallic fantasies could then be linked to the trauma Anne had suffered at the age of three. "You must have imagined, when you were only three years old and your mother let you suck on her breasts, that the reason there was no milk for you was because you were a girl and had no penis. It certainly seems that you must have thought you could get a penis if you could go on sucking milk from your mother. Now we can understand why you clung to your bottle for so long. The bottle stood for the two things you wanted most, mother's full breasts and a penis. But you still cling to the idea of getting both, and it seems as if you feel that if you can get one, you will automatically have the other." Anne then could connect the meaning of this fantasy to her sense of self by replying to my explanation with the words, "Now I feel like a person."

The analysis of these sessions highlighted the impact on Anne's neurosis of the prolonged bottle-feeding which increased the oral fixation and thus the early infantile, dependent relationship to the mother. The rage against the mother as the oral castrator, as well as the rage toward the father as a competitor for the mother, was relived in the transference. Strongly interwoven and practically inseparable from these feelings was the longing for the father as a substitute for the mother of the oral phase, in the hope of receiving a penis from him. The feelings for both parents then became even more contradictory, as well as intense, when the sexual love for father developed in the oedipal phase, and her mother was experienced as a competitor for father's love. All these feelings were expressed in the dream of the dried-up lakes, as well as in the transference reactions of rage at the analyst, the feelings of emptiness in the analysis, and the "tummy ache."

The feeling that she was a person, of course, did not last. This problem, as well as all others she had, only a few of which have been touched on, had to be worked on over and over, making Anne's treatment very long. She developed considerably with the help of treatment, which proceeded much more easily after the initial work of the first three and a half years had established a real therapeutic alliance due to the insight gained through the interpretations.

REFERENCES

Frankl, L. & Hellman, I. (1962), The Ego's Participation in the Therapeutic Alliance. *Internat. J. Psychoanal.*, 43:333-337.

Elizabeth Daunton

Some Aspects of Ego and Superego Resistance in the Case of an Asthmatic Child

IN HIS DISCUSSION of resistance, Freud (1926) first equated what is experienced in analytic treatment as resistance with the defensive action of the ego, undertaken to protect repression, an action "which is made secure by a permanent expenditure of energy." He further identified three of the varieties of resistance met in analysis, namely the resistance due to repression, the transference resistance, and the resistance proceeding from the epinosic gain, as having their source in the ego. The two remaining varieties of resistance Freud traced to their sources in the id and the superego, respectively.

In presenting material from the treatment of an asthmatic child, I shall first consider the ego resistances, with illustrations chiefly of the transference resistance and the resistance due to repression. Second, I shall give detailed material from

From the Department of Psychiatry, University Hospitals, Western Reserve University, Cleveland, Ohio.

A shorter version of this paper was presented in a Panel on Resistances in Child Analysis at a meeting of the American Psychoanalytic Association in New York, 1960.

My thanks are due to Dr. Anny Katan, Professor of Child Analysis, Western Reserve University, for her many valuable suggestions concerning the treatment of this patient.

one phase of the treatment to show how the analysis of certain ego resistances led to a clarification of the superego resistance and to some further understanding of the interaction between ego and superego.

PERSONAL HISTORY AND FAMILY BACKGROUND

Tom, who suffered from severe asthma, had entered the Nursery School of University Hospitals, Cleveland, when he was three and a half years old. A colleague[1] had worked with Tom's mother during his first year in the school, helping her to handle with Tom certain problems related to his asthma and to the stillbirth of a sibling, born when Tom was two and a half years old. Another important aspect of this work was the help given to the mother in explaining his need for treatment to Tom.

Tom already had a long history of asthmatic illness, having developed his first asthmatic symptoms at six months, following a bronchial infection for which he was hospitalized for five days. Tom showed persistent wheezing during the rest of his first year. In his second year he had severe recurrent laryngitis, accompanied by wheezing and nocturnal coughing, which led to hospitalization six times between the ages of twelve and eighteen months.

By twenty-one months, Tom had a constant cough, continuous breathing difficulties, marked emphysema, and weight loss. At this time he was again admitted to the hospital for evaluation and the working out of a treatment program which included antiallergic injections, cold humidity, and various bronchodilators for the more severe episodes. Subsequently, Tom had few severe infections, but his breathing difficulties continued until his mother's confinement, during his third

---

[1] Dr. Robert Furman, Assistant Professor of Child Psychiatry, Western Reserve University.

year. Tom woke in the morning to find that his mother had left for the hospital in the night. His wheezing stopped abruptly and he remained symptom-free for the next two months.

After that the wheezing gradually returned, but for the remaining year was mild and intermittent. During his fourth year, Tom's condition again deteriorated. He had severe coughing episodes as well as constant difficulty in exhaling, and was only briefly relieved by medication. At this point it was noticeable that Tom's asthma became worse in certain situations. His father's work required him to spend one or two nights a week away from home. Tom would protest about his leaving, ask anxious questions about his father, while his coughing became more pronounced during his father's absences. Tom was also more troubled by his symptom following visits with his maternal grandparents, who lived in another state. During Tom's infancy, his grandfather had become asthmatic as the result of a heart condition. Tom noticed his grandfather's labored breathing and asked about it anxiously. On these trips away from home, Tom, who was accustomed to sleeping alone, shared a motel bedroom with his parents and had disturbed nights at these times. It was thought that unconscious conflicts relating to these experiences, as well as the repeated illnesses and separations of his first two years, were contributing to the establishment of Tom's asthma as a chronic symptom. Analysis was therefore recommended.

Tom's mother lost her second child at birth when Tom was two and a half years old. She became pregnant again shortly before Tom began his analysis at the age of four and a half. His brother, Danny, was born when Tom was five. His mother later had a miscarriage when Tom was seven years and nine months old. The father has always been an active and responsible provider for his family and a support to his wife in her care of their children. During Tom's first two years, when he took over some of his nighttime care, he experienced some attacks of anxiety. At this time he was inclined to respond to Tom's requests for bodily contact and stimulation by lying down with him, playing a bedtime chasing game, and, at a time when Tom had a pronounced fear of water, getting into the tub with him. The father was later able to refuse Tom's requests for these forms of bodily contact while continuing to spend time with him and share his interests.

Tom's mother is an intelligent, capable woman, who has been exposed during her marriage to many distressing situations, as well as having to cope with the anxiety of having a recurrently ill child. This mother's characteristic way of dealing with such situations is to ward off feelings of anxiety and sadness by active control. This defense is not always effective, and at such times she is liable to an outbreak of anger.

This mother's defense of active control has had many repercussions in her relationship with Tom. It has had far-reaching effects in her management of his illness, in her handling of him during certain phases of his development, particularly the anal phase, and in her response to the child's own defensive pattern. When the medical program was established for Tom at 21 months, it was a relief to his mother to play an active role in his treatment, particularly at times when his asthmatic attacks were extremely severe. She assumed responsibility for giving him the prescribed allergy injections. These were discontinued when Tom entered the Nursery School and guidance work was begun with the mother. At this point, she could recognize her own ambivalent feelings about giving the injections as well as the fear and anxiety which they aroused in the child. There had been times when Tom's paroxysms of coughing had led his mother to impulsive action. She had tried to get him to cough up the irritating mucous by putting her finger in his mouth and making him gag. There were several occasions during Tom's first years when the mother's attempts to master anxiety through activity caused her to lose contact with the child. When Tom was eight months old, his father was admitted to the hospital for a week for investigation of a back injury. His mother spent much time at the hospital, leaving Tom in the care of sitters, some of whom were strangers. She had felt fortunate that he had appeared unperturbed and had seemed not to miss her. By contrast, when Tom was himself in the hospital, the mother focused all of her attention on him, and she was well aware of his fear and separation anxiety at these times. She also prepared Tom well for the birth of his first sibling, although she did not say good-bye to him as she left for the hospital in the night. Following the baby's death, she maintained rigid control over her own feelings and could not discuss what had happened with Tom. He responded by ignoring his mother and crying continuously for his father. Within a few days of her return from the hospital the mother had news that her father was ill, and she left at once to visit him in another city, leaving Tom at home with her husband.

Tom's mother had a genuine wish for help. During her previous guidance interviews and work with the present therapist she was able to verbalize some previously defended feelings and, consequently, to recognize some of the same feelings in her son. As she became able to express her anxiety about Tom's illness and her paramount fear that he would die, she could help with his own fears about his asthma, his medical treatment, and hospitalizations. Similarly, when she could voice her own feelings of sadness about the death of her baby, she could discuss this difficult time with Tom and sympathize with his feelings about it.

Tom's toilet training was not completed until after his third birthday. Bladder control was achieved first. His mother had tried to adopt a patient attitude during training, recognizing that slow progress and setbacks were connected with the separations Tom had had from her. Nonetheless, the mother had, in part, seen the training as a contest of wills, in which she was afraid she would be the loser. She often recalled that the last time Tom had wet himself he had done so in a provocative way, and she had responded by slapping him hard. She felt satisfied that, in this way, she had prevented further difficulties with Tom in this area. However, it became apparent from the work with the mother and child that, while Tom had submitted to his mother's wishes over toilet-training, the contest between them had been displaced, leading to arguments about other daily routines, such as dressing. In his analysis, Tom staged many wars between nations and showed much interest at one point in the "cold war." When asked what kind of a war this might be, he replied, "It's when people fight with their mouths, of course."

As previously stated, his mother was able, with help, to recognize some of Tom's defenses and find ways to express his underlying feeling. She acquired understanding of his use of bravado or extreme stoicism in certain frightening situations connected with school or visits to the doctor's office. She could not help in this way where she and Tom had defenses in common. It was hardly possible, for example, for her to understand that Tom sometimes became angry about some trivial happening when he had reason to be extremely anxious about some other situation or feeling. Similarly, she could not recognize that the managing attitude characteristic of Tom during a prolonged phase of his analysis was based on an identification. One of the major tasks of the analysis was to help Tom to understand the use made of these defenses including their role in his relationship with his mother.

TREATMENT[2]

Tom is a small, dark-haired boy with big brown eyes and an alert expression. When he is having breathing difficulties, his face has a puffed appearance; he is pale and watery-eyed, and walks slowly with hunched shoulders. At other times he is energetic and has a certain robustness of manner. He is observant and has a good sense of humor. Tom brought much of his material in the form of fantasy games which, in the beginning, had a family background and later bacame baseball epics. Through his early games, it was possible to approach the affects of sadness, fear, and guilt aroused by early separations, by the death of his baby brother, and by his mother's present pregnancy. In his later play, Tom, who always had the role of the father or hero who could cope matter-of-factly and successfully with any odds, defended himself by denial in fantasy. Actually, he often felt weak and easily overwhelmed both by his asthma and by instinctual pressures.

After a few weeks in treatment, the transference resistance became noticeable in Tom's reactions both to everyday conversation and to any comment I would make about feelings. At the beginning of the sessions, Tom would often refer to some happening at home or at school and, when I would express interest, he would quickly change the subject, usually with the refrain, "I want to play our game." When I would pursue the topic, Tom would cover his ears and be hurt and resentful. Other material helped to reveal the transference

[2] The material described is drawn from the first three and a half years of Tom's analysis.

meaning of talk for Tom. Comparisons of my room with the doctor's office, and a game in which a boy gets into a fight with his mother and is about to lose when his father comes to the rescue, indicated that Tom was terrified of me, in the same way as he had been of the doctor and his mother, for what I might put into him, words here having the unconscious meaning of shots. Subsequently, Tom showed that my talking had other frightening and unpleasant connotations. At a time when he particularly disliked my talking and his mother was commenting on how uncommunicative Tom was, he began to have spells of coughing at home in which he threw up. One day Tom volunteered that, while coughing, he had tried to throw up. I expressed curiosity. Later, since his mother was in the first stage of her pregnancy, I wondered whether Tom's throwing up could have anything to do with her. Tom gave an unexpected reply, "Do you mean because of her hurt finger?" I recalled then that, shortly before, his mother had cut her finger in opening a parcel which Tom had thought would contain gifts for the new baby. In linking injury to his mother's finger with throwing up, Tom was recalling his mother's earlier frantic attempts to relieve his coughing by putting her finger in his mouth. By throwing up, Tom was attempting to forestall his mother's action and to protect her from his impulse to bite her finger. It could now be seen that Tom feared any inquiries and comments as an attempt to get something out of him, just as his mother had done.

As might be anticipated in a child with such a history, the mouth and throat were highly cathected areas and allowed for the displacement of anal and phallic conflicts and their expression in respiratory and oral terms. Thus the taking in and throwing up of food, listening to speech and producing it, holding breath and expelling it, had many unconscious meanings for Tom.

The anal content of the transference resistance could be understood at a time when Tom's brother was being toilet-trained. Tom, who was now seven, was particularly uncommunicative at this time. He would usually throw out a few words and then retreat into a book. When we finally reached the topic of his brother's training, Tom volunteered that sometimes he, too, put off going to the toilet. He found that the need to go often came just when he was in the middle of a baseball game. He enjoyed baseball so much he did not want to interrupt it. Tom's resistance could now be approached by telling him first that he must have felt his training interfered seriously with his pleasures; in the same way, he did not want the pleasure of his games in the office to be interrupted by troublesome talk; later withholding aspects of his silence were interpreted to him as a wish to hold on to his worries in the way that, when he was little, he wanted to hold on to his feces.

Interpretation of these aspects of the transference resistance led to an improvement in Tom's relationship with his parents. He had been both obstinate and provocative for a long time. However, Tom continued to have frequent coughing spells which sometimes culminated in vomiting, and he also developed an eating disturbance, refusing foods that he had previously enjoyed. Tom's knowledge that his mother was pregnant again (when he was seven and a half), led to an exacerbation of these symptoms and to the appearance of a new one. During his sessions, Tom would periodically touch his throat with a quick, upward, stroking movement. The material showed that the central conflict expressed in these symptoms was between Tom's passive wishes toward the father, strengthened by envy of his mother's pregnancy, and the forces of repression, activated by fear of the mother's reprisals and by his own guilt feelings. The function of the resistance here was to maintain repression and safeguard anti-cathexis. The negative oedipal conflict was approached by helping Tom to recognize the affects aroused by the mother's pregnancy and miscarriage, by interpreting his conflict over masturbation, and by showing him he warded off castration anxiety by displacement from the genitals to his mouth and throat. Some material from this phase of Tom's analysis will be presented in detail.

Tom gave the first hint of his masturbation problem when he explained one day that when Danny is quiet, he goes with his parents to find Danny and see what mischief he is getting into. Just before his mother told Tom of her pregnancy, Tom showed his preconscious knowledge of it in a session which also brought his anxiety about masturbation into the open. He asked me whether I thought a person could run all day and all night without food. When I replied, doubtfully, that I thought it would be difffficult, Tom said that he had been reading a story about Tom Savage and Pocahontas, and that Tom Savage was the runner who had done this. His mother had told him that it was not possible. Tom then questioned me about another aspect of the Pocahontas story. Did I think that she had married Captain Smith? She really had not; it was just a legend because Captain Smith had died when Pocahontas was only six or seven. I remarked that today Tom seemed to be thinking mostly about what to believe and about what was really true and what wasn't. After I made this comment, Tom sat on the floor with his back to me and began masturbating, which he had not done previously in his sessions. After a while, I said that a boy may touch his penis when he is having certain worrisome thoughts, and that today he might be worried about whether something was true or not. Tom showed acute anxiety at my comment on his masturbation. He shouted angrily, "I didn't. I didn't. I didn't." I replied that I was sorry that I had scared him by noticing that he was touching his penis; I thought that he said, "I didn't" in such a scared way because it felt to him that I was saying he was doing something bad. Tom remained very unhappy and hurt. He could not respond when I asked if someone else had made him feel bad before when he touched his penis.

Before his next session, Tom had been told by his mother of her pregnancy. He came to his session with a box of baseball cards. Half opening the lid, he said he hoped I did not know already what was inside. He then revealed that these were treasured new baseball cards for the following year. After much news about the local baseball team, I wondered if there might be other important new happenings in the following year. Tom replied smilingly that there was going to be a new baby in their family. He had wanted to be the first to tell me and did not like it that his mother had told me first. I sympathized that it happened so often that grownups knew and told important news first. Tom then wondered how his mother knew she was having a baby and how long she had known. I replied that these were both good questions and suggested we might be able to find the answers. Tom, however, had quickly changed his mind and told me now that he *did not* want to know the answer and he "wasn't supposed to know." When I asked if he meant that his mother would not want him to know, Tom muttered, half under his breath, and with great intensity: "I can't know, because I'm never going to be a mother myself." I answered that I knew boys sometimes wished very much that they could be mothers themselves and sometimes, too, felt bad about this wish. Perhaps if they did not think it bad to want to be a mother, they would think it was all right, as I did, to know the answers to their questions. Tom made no reply to this but, as he left, he remarked that his box of baseball cards might get a lot fuller during the next year.

In the following session, Tom threw more light on his masturbation conflict. It became possible to show him some reasons why he was so afraid to know and to talk about it. Tom began by complaining about his teacher at school who, he thought, gave far too many orders, telling the class just when to stop writing and to put down their pencils. He added, "Sometimes I don't, I write two or three words more." He told, further, how sometimes the teacher cuts short recess, telling the children that if they take too long sharpening their pencils they will have less playtime. Tom's tone of great indignation reminded me of his explosive reaction when I had commented on his masturbation. I therefore linked the material in the following way. I said I thought Tom had been so unhappy the other day when I mentioned his touching his penis because it felt as though I were ordering him to stop doing that, just like his teacher ordered the children to stop writing and put down their pencils. The "Stop that" feeling must come from a long time ago when his mother, I knew, had told him that he shouldn't touch his penis in front of people, only when he was by himself. This must have seemed to him like an angry "Stop that." I thought a lot had happened since then and it was now Tom himself who seemed to have opposite feelings about touching his penis. One feeling was, "I want to do it," and the other seemed to order "Stop that." When he had told me not long ago about Danny, who was always in mischief when he was quiet, Tom had also been telling me something about himself. I thought he was saying that when he was quiet, especially in bed at night, he would feel like touching himself, which seemed like getting into mischief. Perhaps it was just when he was feeling bad about it, and worried that his parents would think he was getting into mischief, that he began to have a loud coughing spell to show his parents and himself that he was not. Tom listened attentively but made no comment until I said that I thought all children had a hard time with their opposite feelings about touching themselves. He looked startled and replied, "Not all boys do it." I answered that I thought all boys did at times, and that he must have felt lonely and scared in thinking that other kids didn't have this worry. Tom showed then that his masturbation had also to be denied so vehemently because of its unconscious connection with a fantasy of oral intercourse. He made a truck crash into some dolls; some of them, he said, were alive a hundred years ago. He then spoke of Hitler who, he thought, had been alive in World War II. His friend, John, told him that Hitler had killed himself with a bullet down his throat. "Some people," Tom continued, "say Hitler is still alive." He then related a joke about Hitler, who said, when his wife was going to have a baby, "Hotsi, Totsi, another little Nazi." I remarked that Tom was telling me now, in a joke, about something he had puzzled me before by saying he oughtn't to think or know about, the beginning of babies.

In the sessions preceding his mother's miscarriage, Tom began to reveal his fear that the expected baby might not live. One day he brought a bird book and examined the pictures carefully. He made a horrified face as he looked at a drawing of an extinct bird, explaining that it was a dinosaur that had died out one hundred and fifty million years ago.

Tom's feelings of sadness following his mother's miscarriage were approached by interpretation of his reversal of affect, his magical thinking, and by talking with him about his mother's way of dealing with her own great sadness at this time. In a telephone call following the miscarriage, Tom told me sadly that this was the second time a baby had died in their family. In the next session, Tom's "cheerful" defense was in evidence. He showed me all his most valued possessions, base-ball cards and candy, and appeared quite contented. After I commented that I could understand it was much easier for Tom to show me he was pleased with what he had, rather than how sad he was about missing his mother and about the baby which had come out of her too soon, Tom recalled an earlier discussion between us. He said that sometimes clowns act like that; they "act happy to cover up their sad feelings." I agreed that they did and Tom was quite right that the sad feelings were there underneath. While his mother was in the hospital, a close friend of the family had taken Tom and his brother Danny to meet his own son after Sunday school. Tom's father had told me that the Sunday-school children had made a big fuss over Danny. Tom used his "cheerful" defense again when he claimed to have liked this Sunday-school visit very much. I wondered about the children making such a fuss over Danny. Tom replied vehemently, "I could have killed him." I said that perhaps this angry feeling was made stronger by all the fuss that had been made over the baby inside his moth-er. This fuss must have made him feel angry with the baby sometimes, and we knew that he had thought before that you could kill someone just with being angry. Tom reminded me then that he used to think that when a baby dies he just swims away, he had thought this about the other baby who died. I agreed and recalled with Tom how he had thought he had made the baby swim away through wishing and how, because he felt so bad about it, he was afraid of the water himself and found it hard to learn to swim.

Tom then gave another explanation for the miscarriage, saying that Nature had "goofed" with the baby and that it was better for an unhealthy baby not to be born. (Tom was quoting his mother's words here.) Later he told me that a neighbor had taken him and his own son to the movies. They did not see the movie "because the house was full and who wants to wait around 'til four o'clock?" Tom could agree that he would really have liked to see the movie and it was his friend's father who thought the wait would be too long. I said I thought that Tom might not have quite agreed either with what his mother had told him about the baby. It might seem that his mother did not want the baby because it was not healthy. Tom answered with conviction, "You can say that again." I told Tom that I thought his mother had really wanted this baby very much and that she talked most about why the baby could not live because her sad feelings were so hard for her right now, just as they had been with the other baby who died.

In the weeks following his mother's miscarriage, Tom's loss of appetite, throwing up, and throat-touching symptom were still much in evidence. It now became possible to analyze Tom's conflict about his passive wishes which found expression in these symptoms. After I had commented that he was showing in sign language that he had a lot of feelings about his throat and mouth and that his loss of appetite was a part of the same language, Tom introduced some thoughts about being poisoned. This happened, he thought, when people ate something especially good. When Captain Hook had wanted to poison Peter Pan he had made a cake with tempting green frosting. Tom then recalled that for his birthday his mother had provided a cake, shaped like a baseball field, with plenty of green frosting to look like grass. By his friendly manner at this time, Tom caused a receptionist at the Clinic to make him presents of candy. He would eat it with guilty enjoyment in the session and indicate his wish that I would make him similar gifts. When Tom expressed the fear that his mother would kill him if she found out about his secret candy eating, I could agree that he was afraid of his mother and what she might do to him, but I could not believe that such a big fear was caused just by candy eating, but must be due to something which he felt much worse about.

The real wish for which Tom feared punishment from his mother became apparent in the following sessions and was introduced first in a displaced form. When Tom was eagerly anticipating a visit from his widowed grandmother, he came early for his appointment and saw another boy leave my office. He complained that he was very tired because his brother woke him at nine, otherwise he would have slept until at least nine-thirty. I remarked that he was angry, too, about my other patient, feeling that if this boy had not been with me in the office he could have been with me sooner.

Tom then spoke of his grandmother's visit, commenting that he would be going to play-school at that time. I said that this might be hard, especially as Danny would be at home and I thought it must be difficult at times to share grandmother with Danny. Tom, who was crouching behind my desk, volunteered that it was hard to share grandmother with his cousin Billy. It was unfair that she lived near Billy and far away from him, and it was unfair also that his friend, John, was able to see his grandparents every week. I agreed that Billy and John do have more chance to be with their grandparents and therefore don't miss them so much as Tom does.

Tom then lay on the couch saying that he was so tired he felt like going to sleep. I replied that I knew he did not like sleeping alone and that he wished he could sleep here with me just as he had told me once he had liked to sleep with his grandmother. Tom corrected me, saying that he had not slept with his grandmother but had taken a nap in her room; she was not there but had come to wake him up. Tom had a blissful expression on his face as he recalled this experience. He next expressed the wish that he could sleep with his grandmother during her visit. He added that his mother had said that he could not and that grandmother would sleep in the guestroom. I replied that Tom must sometimes have lonely feelings, too, when grandmother was in her own home and wish that he could have someone to sleep with at night. Perhaps it was just easier to let himself know about these feelings when grandmother was coming to visit.

Tom's longing for his father was now more openly expressed. Some months previously, he had been very distressed in hearing of a family where the husband, following disagreements with his wife, left home without warning and without leaving an address. Tom now recalled this episode, sympathizing greatly with the son of the family, commenting that if his father planned to go away like that he would be right upstairs packing his suitcase to go with him. In a following session, Tom showed me a number of trophies which he had won at a carnival. He got some free rides at the carnival, he said, because his father was helping by blowing up balloons. He then told with great satisfaction that he had had a ride in a stagecoach and "I was the last to get in, so I had the place of honor next to the driver." This provided the opportunity to show Tom the wish which led both to his fear of his mother and to his eating difficulties. I said that he really wished to be much closer to his father and to sleep in the place of honor beside him. Tom readily agreed to this, saying, "I wish I could sleep with him every night!" I also told him that I could understand better now why he had such a longing for candy gifts and was afraid that his mother would be angry about it. Most children thought that the most valuable gift was a baby, and that their mother was the luckiest because she got this gift from their father. Usually their first idea about how a father gave this gift was by putting something in the mouth. I thought that Tom was afraid of being given some bad and poisonous thing to eat because of his wish to be given a baby in this way; when he stopped eating or threw up, it was his way of trying to get rid of the "baby wish" so that he need not be punished for it.

In further material, Tom confirmed that a baby was the longed-for gift that he was afraid that his mother would take out of him. He recalled with anxiety a television program about disappearing people and the awful warning received by one of the characters that he would be the next to disappear. Tom was also afraid of ghosts at this time, and of being upstairs without his mother. When I wondered what this concern could really be about, Tom referred to his baseball list, pointing out that tomorrow was Ladies' Day at the Stadium. It was now possible to interpret that Tom's worry was caused by his feeling that he could only attain the longed-for position with his father by having his mother disappear, and it was for this reason that he was afraid she would do angry things to him. Now, for the first time, Tom expressed the thought that when his mother had given him shots she had been trying to "disappear him." I recalled for Tom that, earlier in his treatment, when we had spoken of the death of his baby brother and of the baby "which came out too soon," we had seen that he believed he could make his mother's babies disappear by his magic thoughts. Now we could better understand his idea that his mother would want to get rid of his baby wishes and "disappear him."

In a session before his birthday, Tom was discussing the gifts he would like. Meanwhile, he was writing words on scraps of paper, asking me to guess what he had written. Suddenly Tom became quite panicky that I would guess what he had written, and cried out, "Help! help!" I remarked that boys were often disappointed with their birthday gifts; this was sometimes so because they so much wanted what their

Daddy could give as a gift to Mommy. I thought he had yelled "help! help!" because he became so frightened that I would be angry if I guessed his wish, and would try to get his "baby wishes" out of him just as he had thought Mommy would want to do.

Tom now began to relate a number of sadomasochistic fantasies. On a day when his mother had a doctor's appointment and Tom feared she would be found pregnant, he described, with a wealth of detail and a kind of thrilled horror, a series of tortures which he thought Marshall Foch had experienced at the hands of the Germans. These included being strapped down in a small room with walls which could close in on him and then expand again; a knife was suspended over him and, little by little, came closer. Afterward, Tom recounted, in the same mood, a story of a boy who was eaten by red ants. By his own comments on the stories, Tom made it clear that he was identifying with his mother in intercourse as well as in her experiences of miscarriage and childbirth. In telling the red ant story, Tom, who had witnessed his mother hemorrhage during pregnancy on at least one occasion, coughed up a spot of blood. He was also sadistically punishing himself for his wishes. In reply to my query as to what the torture stories might mean, Tom said he knew for sure what I would think of them. I would say that the boy wanted his father to give him a baby through his mouth, that he was afraid that his mother would be angry, want to take the baby away and send the boy to the hospital. I had not, in fact, made a link between these current conflicts and Tom's hospital experiences. In doing so himself, Tom showed that they had been understood as a punishment and that they supplied a model for his later self-punishing fantasies.

While mainly concerned in this paper with ego resistances belonging to the transference or based on repression, I would like to give one example of resistance stemming from the epinosic gain, which illustrates Tom's investment in his asthmatic symptom. Shortly before a vacation, when I was going to England, Tom was reading to me selected passages from a biography of Benjamin Franklin. He was chiefly concerned with Franklin's long absences in England on state business and the effect these had on his wife. Tom explained that Franklin only decided to return after a ten-year absence when he received the news that his wife was dying. There had been times when Tom's father had been recalled from business trips by his wife when she had been sick. I linked his comments about Franklin and his wife both with my vacation and with his father's frequent trips, telling Tom that I thought he believed the only way to make sure of our return and to keep our love was to be like a sick wife. Tom recalled how his father had once returned home because he, Tom, had been sick, adding thoughtfully, "But if he goes away every two weeks, how can I get sick so often?" I reminded him that when he was little he had many illnesses as well as asthma and, while he was healthier now, his asthma was still a way of saying, "If I am sick, you will come back to me."

Analysis of the material relating to Tom's passive wishes and his identification with his mother made possible certain steps in ego and superego development.[3] Tom became more independent, overcame a long-standing difficulty in learning to ride his bicycle, acquired greater status with his friends, and was elected Class President. At the same time, he became preoccupied with certain moral problems, was concerned with correct behavior at school, and wanted to establish the difference between fantasy and untruth. However, material in the

[3] The displacement from the genitals to the mouth, in his fantasies of intercourse, was interpreted to Tom as a way of protecting himself from castration anxiety, at a later date.

sessions showed that his need for punishment had become internalized. For example, Tom related with satisfaction selections from a favorite story-book. The hero had been punished by his mother for coming home late from school and, in his anger at being forbidden to play with his beloved railway, provoked still more punishment from his mother and teachers. Tom was of the opinion that the mother was too soft with her son and that she should have been more severe with him on account of his naughty behavior. In further discussion, he described how he and his friend enjoyed playing school with the friend's older sister as teacher, the fun of the game being to provoke the teacher to still greater severity. Tom was having difficulty in exhaling in this session, and when he began to act out his favorite baseball fantasy, he began to wheeze heavily. This time, instead of his usual outstanding performance, his hero only just made the team and then received leg and elbow injuries. By now Tom was wheezing so much that he had to abandon the game. His comments on the story and the developments in the game provided the key to the intensification of his symptom, indicating that in his asthma the superego was directed sadistically toward the ego, gratifying its masochistic need for punishment.

A further brief example illustrates this same relationship between ego and superego. Tom's mother reported that he had complained bitterly and sometimes refused to comply when she had wanted him to wear warmer clothes during an unseasonably cold spell. Tom surprised me in the session by remarking, "Was I glad when my mother made me wear warm clothes to school!" He added that it was harder for him to breathe in cold weather and he therefore felt much better when he was warm. Tom showed here a preconscious recognition of his need to punish himself destructively by exacerbating his symptom, a need which interfered with the reality-testing function of the ego.

Discussion

In following the sequence of material with this patient and in trying to understand the relationship between ego and superego resistances, I have been most helped by Freud's (1924) elucidation of the problem of moral masochism. In "The Economic Problem of Masochism," he first traced moral masochism to its origins in the oedipus complex. He showed that the wish for punishment, originally at the hands of the father, was only a regressive distortion of the wish for passive sexual relations with him: "Conscience and morality have arisen through the overcoming, the desexualization, of the Oedipus complex; but through moral masochism morality becomes sexualized once more, the Oedipus complex is revived . . ." (p. 169). Freud further postulated that a part of the sadism which is turned back against the self finds expression in the ego as an intensified masochism while "the destructiveness which returns from the external world is also taken up by the superego, without any such transformation, and increases its sadism against the ego. The sadism of the superego and the masochism of the ego supplement each other and unite to produce the same effects" (p. 170).

My patient showed how the uncovering of some of the passive oedipal conflicts contributed to the development of an independent conscience. Concurrently, his identification with the tortured Foch, representing his mother, indicated the distortion of his wish for a passive sexual relationship with his father, while he also obtained masochistic gratification from the destructive turning of the superego against the ego. An increase in the severity of his symptom at this time could be understood in terms of the complementary relationship of the superego and ego, observable in the treatment as a superego resistance.

REFERENCES

Freud, S. (1924), *The Economic Problem of Masochism. Standard Edition,* 19:159-179. London: Hogarth Press, 1961.
—— (1926), Inhibitions, Symptoms and Anxiety. *Standard Edition,* 20:87-172. London: Hogarth Press, 1959.

SELMA FRAIBERG

The Analysis of an Eight-Year-Old Girl
with Epilepsy

NANCY WAS EIGHT when she began her analysis. Four months earlier her parents had observed characteristic petit mal seizures. An EEG was confirmatory. A report indicated "spike and wave discharges in long episodes and from many areas," and concluded with the examiner's statement, "This record is diagnostically abnormal and is indicative of a convulsive disorder of the petit mal type with grand mal components." (Later evidence from the clinical picture pointed to the existence of temporal lobe seizures, as well. This was confirmed in a later EEG.) Nancy was placed on dilantin infatabs, 50 mg. each, but during a trial period this medication was found ineffective in controlling the seizures. After further experimentation with drugs and discouraging results, Nancy was placed on 3/4 of a grain of phenobarbital per day, with doubtful effects in controlling the seizures.

With the onset of seizures, the parents observed grave personality changes in Nancy. She had always been a vivacious and active youngster, an excellent student in school, well liked by other children. Now she was withdrawn, moody, and irritable. She no longer played with other children; she was

Mrs. Fraiberg is Associate Professor of Child Psychoanalysis in the Department of Psychiatry, University of Michigan Medical School.

reluctant to go to school. She had become increasingly de-
fiant toward her mother and exhausted the mother with repetitious complaints and accusations in which the theme
"You are to blame . . ." was elaborated in various forms.

The progressive deterioration in ego functioning alarmed
the parents. After a period of diagnostic study, analysis was
recommended. At the beginning we had no expectations that
analysis could bring about a significant change in the convulsive disorder. But we had good reason to believe that we
could restore ego functioning and strengthen an ego that revealed, on close study, a high degree of vulnerability in its
structure. When, in fact, analysis was able to achieve therapeutic success in controlling the seizures, we began to extend
our goals in treatment. When analysis was terminated at the
end of four years, Nancy was symptom-free and there were
significant characterological changes.

HISTORY

Nancy was the youngest of three children. A sister, Barbara, 15, was in boarding school; a brother, Fenton, 11, plays
a significant role in Nancy's analysis.

The parents, in trying to reconstruct the period that preceded the onset of seizures, recalled an event that puzzled
them, one that appeared to have extraordinary significance
for Nancy although it seemed trivial to the parents themselves. In the Spring, roughly coinciding with the onset of
seizures, Nancy had had a fight with her friend Arthur, also
eight years old. Nancy's nose began to bleed. She ran home
in panic, pounded on the door of her house, and screamed
for her mother. Her mother was slightly delayed in getting
to the door. Nancy was hysterical when mother brought her

in. Since then, she had accused her mother irrationally of being to blame for her bloody nose. It was an insistent, repetitious complaint, part of a litany of grievances against mother that poured forth on the slightest provocation.

The parents also described Nancy's preoccupation with sexual matters. Among other accusations against her mother, she complained repetitiously that mother had told her a lie about the male role in procreation. Mother, who felt she had been entirely candid with Nancy, could not follow this obscure argument. As far as we could reconstruct from Nancy's complaints, she accused her mother of denying the role of the male in procreation.

There had been a number of episodes of sex play between Nancy and Fenton, which had come to the mother's attention. (Details emerge in Nancy's analysis.) Mother thought sex play between the children had ceased during the past year.

One detail from the history invites special attention: Nancy was unable to fall asleep unless she took a ball to bed with her. Mother, in checking Nancy at night, would find her with the ball between her thighs, in the genital region.

During a significant portion of Nancy's first 18 months, mother was ill and unable to care for her. When Nancy was one month old, mother developed a hystoplasmosis that was mistakenly diagnosed as tuberculosis. She was actually treated as a tuberculosis patient in the home, and no contact between mother and infant was permitted. For the first five months of her life, Nancy was cared for by maids, with some assistance from the maternal grandparents. When Nancy was approximately six months old, mother resumed care of her. Seven months later, when Nancy was 13 months old, the mother became ill again and once more the question of

tuberculosis entered the picture, and mother was permitted
no contact with Nancy until the child was 18 months old. The
child was permitted to come to the door of mother's room
to see her and talk with her. Mother said she could never forget the picture of this child with her yearning eyes, standing
in the doorway of the mother's bedroom.

There was still another recurrence of illness when Nancy
was two years old, but by this time the diagnosis of hystoplasmosis was made and the mother, while confined to bed, was
no longer excluded from contact with the children. The children were in the care of grandparents at the time. During
the first eighteen months of Nancy's life the father, with
grave concern for the baby who was deprived of her mother,
took over, as far as possible, the care of Nancy in evening
hours. When Nancy was 19 months old, the mother had recovered from illness. The father's work then took him to another city for approximately a year and, except for occasional
visits, Nancy had almost no contact with her father. The family was reunited when Nancy was nearly three years old.

Under these circumstances, we have no history of Nancy's
early development. Feeding was largely in the hands of ser-
vants, and mother only recalls that there were no special feeding difficulties. Motor development and speech appeared to
be normal. Mother had no memory of Nancy's toilet training
and recalls only that this took place during the period that
the maternal grandmother had assumed some responsibility
in the home. There were no unusual illnesses in Nancy's early childhood and no earlier history of a convulsive disorder.

SUMMARY OF THE FIRST TWO YEARS OF ANALYSIS

Nancy, when I first knew her, was a grave, reserved child
with a gentle, strained face and a thin little body which gave

an over-all impression of forlornness and hunger. There was a stillness in her personality that at first gave me the impression of "no contact." However, even at the beginning of analysis, there were rare moments in which the face and voice became animated and I could catch glimpses of what the parents had described as her "old personality." I could see that she must have been a delightful child. The seizures were very frequent and took the form of absences with staring. She spoke of them candidly as "my spells" and "my forgetting spells."

In the early sessions, she described her problems to me. She felt that other children disliked her, she no longer wanted to go to school, and her biggest problem was that she always felt mad at her mother and she didn't know why. I addressed myself to these problems at the beginning and told her that I thought these problems were caused by worries and fears inside of her, and as we talked together and understood the worries she would find the outside problems getting much better.

"Casting a Spell"

The earliest games, stories, and puppet dramas which Nancy produced in analysis furnished important insights into the child's own fantasies regarding the origin of her seizures. One of the repetitive themes in her puppet dramas had to do with "a witch who cast spells" and could make a child, an animal, or a fairy creature do wicked things or change into something else. In one such drama the witch cast the children into a dungeon and changed their good personalities into bad ones. The children went out robbing and killing without knowing what they were doing. There were other dramas in which spells were cast and boys were changed into girls and girls were changed into boys. In a series of cowboy dramas, the theme of killing and coming alive again was endlessly repeated.

Still another recurrent theme in play had to do with "hypmatists." "A hypmatist," Nancy explained, "can make you do anything he wants you to do." As this theme expanded in the early months of analysis, Nancy confided that she sometimes had the feeling that she was "hypmatized," that this was her feeling when she had her seizures, but at other times, too. Later she told me of a daydream that she brought forth at bedtime. In the daydream Flash Gordon comes out of the television screen, picks her up in his arms, and carries her right through the television screen with him. Then, in her daydream, she is his girl friend, and accompanies him on adventures in space. At the beginning of the daydream, she explained, when she goes through the screen with Flash Gordon "it's like I'm hypmatized."

Defenses Against Affects

The major work during the first year of analysis had to do with the defenses against affect. In the area of aggressive thoughts and feelings, the defenses were nearly impenetrable at first. At home, the anger toward mother was expressed in the form of nagging accusations and tears. As I made careful inquiry of both Nancy and her parents, I saw that at such times the anger had no affective quality. When Nancy described quarrels with her mother, her voice was flat, or at the most querulous. It was this, I learned, that had been described as "anger" at home. Similarly, sadness and grief were expressed in a tiny, still voice, as if she still owned the vocabulary of grief but had lost the tune. When, in analysis, I began to see slight stirrings of anger, discomfort, or sadness and encouraged their expression, she would deny flatly that she had any feelings. More than once, she said defensively, "You're trying to put ideas in my head!" Many months passed before she was even able to admit that there were times when she did not feel like coming to see me.

I was impressed at the extent to which Nancy had removed herself from close human ties. For a long time in analysis it seemed to me that her affectional ties to parents and to her brother had a formal quality, as if she were expressing obligatory family feelings. Yet I was certain that this was not an incapacity for relationship. Rather, I had the impression from my own observations, as well as from the reports of her parents, that she had once had qualitatively good relationships, and that a withdrawal of cathexis had emptied these relationships of emotional quality and had left them with only their formal characteristics.

Nancy's relationship to animals provided some important clues here. Her love for animals and the range of her feeling for them was extraordinary. When I observed her with my own dog or neighborhood dogs and cats, she was entirely spontaneous and joyful. She had such gentleness and tact in her handling of animals that the most savage dog of my neighborhood greeted her as a friend and walked her to my door. The illness or death of an animal in real life or in a story brought forth genuine grief. She loved all animals, birds, lizards, turtles—worms! Why worms? She brought one in to see me one day, carefully cradled in her hand. "Wouldn't it be sad to be a worm?" she said. "It's so helpless; it can't protect itself at all. And then one day a foot comes down on it and squashes it and that's the end." She was, we saw, identified with the small and helpless animals. In her love and solicitude for them, she was also identified with the protectors of helpless things. As Nancy's analysis progressed, one had the impression that, in the crucial period that preceded the onset of seizures and the personality changes in Nancy, the original love objects had lost their vital roles as "protectors," and that a grave disturbance in these love relations had caused her to withdraw from human objects.

The Balls

The rubber balls that Nancy took into her bed each night first came into analysis on the side of "protection." She needed her balls, she explained, so that she would not be afraid at night. She was unable to fall asleep unless she had one or another of these balls in her bed. Nor could she tell me what she was afraid of, of course, since the balls always served to guard against the unknown danger.

She was candid with me in describing how the ball must always be between her legs, and there was an innocence in her manner of describing this that made me attentive. When I felt that our relationship was such that I could begin making inquiries, I began to ask Nancy about the feelings that accompanied this bedtime ritual. There was no feeling, she said, and I felt she was being truthful. On the chance that her child's vocabulary might be inadequate to describe feelings if she had them, I went a little further and asked if sometimes there were good feelings or tickly feelings when she put the ball between her legs. "No feelings," she said. "Not good feelings and not bad feelings. Just no feelings." It was in this way that I began to understand that she was truly anesthetic in the genital region, and I had the suspicion, later confirmed in all details, that masturbation and its attendant feelings had been lost, and that the ball was a souvenir from the old days—properly speaking, a fetish.

Along with the first exploration of the bedtime ritual with the ball, there came an exacerbation of the persecutory feelings in relation to mother. Again there were the insistent, nagging reproaches to mother that she was to blame for something—for the bloody nose, but also for dozens of seemingly trivial occurrences in the course of a day. When we examined these complaints in analysis, Nancy herself felt the complaints were absurd, but she could not get rid of the feeling that her mother was to blame for something. She even had the feeling, she confided, that her mother was somehow to blame for her "spells," but she knew that was silly too.

Always, it seemed, the feeling that mother was to blame for something led back to the balls. Here, I learned, there was actual conflict with mother. Mother did not like Nancy to take the balls to bed with her. She told her that this was silly and babyish. She was afraid that mother would take the balls away. During the same period, there were repetitious themes in Nancy's play of a witch casting spells, in a variation on the theme of Sleeping Beauty, and I began to understand (without telling Nancy, of course) that the reproach against mother was that mother had taken away her "good feelings."

Gradually, Nancy began to recover genital sensation and reported to me that "sometimes" she could get feelings when her rubber ball was between her legs. I could not explain this partial recovery to myself because very little of the masturbatory conflicts had entered analysis at this point. I can only guess that "permission to talk" and the neutrality of the analyst on the subject of having sexual feelings may have been taken by the child as permission to have the feelings once again. But almost as soon as Nancy reported that she had genital feelings "sometimes," a new anxiety emerged in relation to her mother. She was afraid of mother's anger and, when she tried to tell me what it was that she was afraid of, she could only think of the balls. She was afraid that mother would be angry about the balls, that mother would take away the balls. At this time she actually became provocative with her mother at bedtime, making a conspicuous ceremony of taking the balls to bed in order to test mother's reaction. Mother, who somehow had not understood that the balls were connected with masturbation (she would not, she told me privately, have prohibited masturbation per se) unwittingly played into the conflict provoked by Nancy at this point. In attempting to handle the issue tactfully, mother told Nancy not to worry so much about the balls, that analysis would help her so that she wouldn't need the balls anymore. This was reported to me by Nancy. At an appropriate time during this period, I was able to talk with mother about handling the balls and any other masturbatory incidents in a way that would support the treatment. Mother then withdrew from conflict over the balls, told Nancy that she (mother) had undoubtedly not understood that the balls were important to Nancy in some way and that, if Nancy felt she needed the balls, mother did not object.

We now had a more favorable situation to begin the analysis of masturbatory material. Nancy, for the first time, began to see the connections between the "goings" and "comings" of sexual feelings and her fear of mother's anger. The loss of "good feelings" which she had interpreted magically (witch casting a spell, hypnotist) she now understood was connected with her anxiety. When mother withdrew from the conflict over the balls and thereby gave tacit permission to have "good feelings," Nancy recovered the good feelings and with this came significant personality changes.

With the recovery of genital sensation, the persecutory feelings in relation to mother disappeared from the picture and there was a marked diminution of seizures. At the same time, spontaneity returned to her personality and, in all areas, affect became freer. I now understood that the stillness in her personality, which had so troubled me when I first knew her, was the counterpart in the ego of the genital that was silent. From time to time during Nancy's analysis the anesthesia returned on a hysterical basis. With each recurrence, the same syndrome was reactivated: repression of all affects with the consequent stillness of personality, increases in seizures, and a return of the persecutory feelings in relation to mother. After a time, I found that any increase in frequency or duration of seizures became a reliable index to the total affective picture. In this way I could employ the seizures in analysis in the same way that I could use any symptoms or defense. Nancy, herself, learned to view the seizures as symptoms and to work with me analytically when they appeared in hours. In January of the first year of treatment (after approximately 90 hours of analysis), there was general improvement in the seizure aspect and a marked improvement in her relationship with mother. These gains were also reflected in a substantial improvement in her school performance.

The "Looking Games"

Now I began to hear of conflict with her brother Fenton and veiled allusions to "trouble" whenever the parents went out in the evening. She complained that Fenton "pestered" her and wouldn't let her get to sleep, that he would come into her room and tease her or clown. Her complaints were vague, and I felt that she was concealing something. During the same period, the content of play and fantasies in analysis was heavily loaded with spy stories and criminals who performed daring crimes and escaped the law. She even attempted to bring me into the games, assigning me the role of "a good guy" and taking the role of "a bad guy" herself, who tries to get the good guy to steal.

In March, a crisis occurred. Nancy's mother called in great
distress to tell me that she had come home that afternoon
from a meeting, heard a commotion in Fenton's room, and
found that Fenton and a group of boys had taken Nancy into
a room and were attempting to get her to take down her pants.
Mother said that she lost her temper, "I guess I was really
furious!" and wanted me to know because Nancy seemed
quite terrified. Mother said her anger was really directed toward Fenton, but Nancy behaved as if it were all intended for
her.

When Nancy came in for her next hour, I saw immediately
that the old stillness had returned to her personality. She told
me what had happened the day before in a toneless little
voice. She thought the boys were bad for doing this. She
thought her mother was right in being so angry. And she
closed off the episode from analysis. In subsequent hours, she
told me that "the good feelings" were gone again. I saw a
number of seizures during analytic sessions and several times
I observed that the seizures were accompanied by a mumbling
that I could not distinguish. Once I thought I heard her
counting.

If I asked Nancy about her mumbling when she came out
of her seizures, she was always surprised. She assured me that
when she had the seizures her mind "went blank." There
were no pictures, no words. Then, on one occasion, when I
was certain I heard counting again in a seizure, I drew her
attention to this when she came out of it. Since she already
knew how to give associations to dreams, I asked her if she
would tell me what popped into her mind in connection with
counting. She said, immediately, "Fenton!" In this way, slowly and reluctantly, she told me about the "looking games"
with Fenton. Fenton and she used to play a game when mother and father were out at night. They would close their eyes

and take down their clothes while counting to ten and, at the count of ten, they would open their eyes and look at each others' genitals. She assured me they no longer played these games, not since those boys tried to get her to take down her pants and mother was so angry.

Over a period of many sessions, details of these games emerged. The erotic high point of these games was "looking." The children did not touch each other. From small clues during these sessions, I gathered that Nancy had observed erections in Fenton. When I asked her about this, she firmly denied it. (In fact, it was not until the third year of analysis that she was able to acknowledge that she knew what an erection was.) She assured me that she was not interested in looking at the penis at all. It wasn't the penis that was interesting to her, she said flatly, "It's the balls." She must have been struck by the same thought that occurred to me, because she smiled a bit in embarrassment and added, "Maybe that's why I like my balls at night!"

There were no further episodes of counting in seizures. (I will only mention, in passing, that counting as part of an obsessional ritual appeared later in the analysis, where it had the significance of warding off the death of a loved person.)

Much of this period of analysis dealt with Nancy's guilt about the games with Fenton and her fear of mother's anger. Once again we had to establish the connection between loss of genital sensation and fear of mother's anger and, as before, Nancy recovered sensation and the seizures diminished once again.

During this period, the ball ritual at bedtime re-entered the analysis. This time the connections with masturbation became available to us. The balls were used for masturbation. She never used her hand or fingers for masturbation. When I inquired about this, Nancy offered the rationalization that she used the ball "So my hand won't get tired." Any attempt on my part to get at a prohibition in the use of the hand was met by the strongest resistance I had ever encountered in Nancy. From transference reactions and from her fantasies in which I was represented as a hypnotist, I could see that as I invited analysis of the masturbation and the fetish, I represented to her a dangerous seducer, like her brother Fenton. There was also the fear that analysis would bring her to give up the balls, that the balls would be "taken away" as mother had wanted them to be. I was able to reassure her on the last point by telling her that she could have the balls as long as she needed them. Regarding her fear of seduction, I repeatedly clarified for her that my interest in masturbation and sexual matters was very different from that of another child or even other adults. I was interested, I explained, because we were concerned here about all of her worries, and she appeared to have many worries in connection with masturbation.

As the analysis of the masturbation progressed, Nancy was able to tell me one of the fantasies connected with the use of balls in masturbation. She wished that she could have balls like boys. If she had balls, then she could be both boy and girl and could get seeds from her own balls into her vagina and have a baby. At the same time, I was able to see a preoccupation with breasts in Nancy. Her mother reported to me that Nancy asked repeatedly to see mother's breasts, which mother tactfully refused. Nancy asked numerous questions of mother and me regarding breast development, and expressed her plaintive hope that she would develop breasts soon. The balls, then, were also equated with breasts, although at this point I did not bring this into the analysis.

Arthur

At this point I need to go back in the clinical narrative to pick up the story of Nancy and Arthur as it emerged during the first year of analysis. Arthur, we recall, had been Nancy's "boy friend," and it was he who had given her the bloody nose which figured so strongly in Nancy's persecutory feelings. At the time that I first knew Nancy, Arthur and she were no longer friends. Nancy complained repetitiously that Arthur was mean to her at school, called her names, and made fun of her. She still loved him and wanted to marry him one day, she told me, but he didn't love her anymore. At the beginning of analysis, this story and variations of it were repetitious themes, and always the complaint emerged in a still, toneless voice: "I love him, but he doesn't love me."

It was difficult, at first, to take this childhood love affair seriously, but I soon realized that I needed to. The quality of Nancy's attachment to Arthur could only be described as "enslavement." Loss of Arthur was experienced as a cleavage in her personality. It was as if she had lost the boy-part of her personality, and an unstable bisexual integrity had been shattered in the period before the onset of the seizures. The significance of the bloody nose as castration did not enter analysis until much later.

I was certain that we would not be able to reconstruct in analysis the events that preceded the onset of petit mal without analysis of the relationship to Arthur. But here, again, the defenses against affects were nearly impenetrable for a long period. While she could utter monotonous complaints that Arthur did not love her, she was not aware of grief or anger, or any emotion except a hopeless yearning for him.

For many months I did those things that I could to help her recover feeling, expressed sympathy for her loss, showed that I respected her love, even though others thought it "silly." We dealt with the defenses against grief and anger and, in minute quantities, affect began to emerge. It was months before she could allow herself to cry because Arthur did not love her and she was able to remember the pain she felt when he abandoned her. Gradually, in a restrained, almost timid way, she began to express her anger toward Arthur. She seemed surprised herself to discover that she was angry with him. As the anger mounted over a period of several crucial analytic sessions, something close to rage emerged. In one climactic session, she brought forth a torrent of feeling toward Arthur, blamed him for her bloody nose, and incoherently blamed him for all her troubles. When she left this hour and returned home, she encountered Arthur on the street (he was her neighbor). She got into a fight with him and began to furiously pelt him with mud. Nancy's mother, watching from a window, told me later that she had never seen her child in such a rage. She pelted Arthur and screamed names at him. Arthur, a healthy, strong boy, who could easily have beaten up Nancy, fled before her fury. Nancy came into the house covered with mud and triumphant. Following this episode, Arthur fell in love with Nancy all over again.

With the restoration of the tie to Arthur, there were significant changes in Nancy. There was improvement in all areas of relationship, especially to other children, and greater ability to bring appropriate affect to all experiences. The recovery of affect in this area eventually led to the recovery of memories from the period that preceded the onset of the seizures.

There had been forbidden games between Nancy and Arthur and two other children in Arthur's garage. There had been secret smoking and sex games that were chiefly on the basis of exposure. (Nancy's mother, in her history, had dated these games "about a year" before Nancy started treatment.) From Nancy's material, it appeared that the games had never been abandoned and were still part of the picture at the time of the fight with Arthur that led to the bloody nose. I was never able to reconstruct this time sequence adequately from the analytic material. We only know, through the analytic material, that there was sex play with Arthur, strong reactions from the mothers involved when, at one point, the sex play was discovered, and that furtive games continued until the point of an explosive quarrel with Arthur and the fight that led to the bloody nose.

"To Steal From the King"

If we return now to the masturbation fantasies and the bisexual symbol of the balls, we can trace the threads that led from "the balls" material to a new group of fantasies that was brought into the analysis. Nancy instituted a new series of dramas in her analytic hours. She was a robber who stole into the king's palace at night to steal the king's jewels. In her play, she tried on numerous occasions to bring me into the drama as an accomplice. I declined, but even without my active participation she would sometimes assign me a role and speak parts for me, making me a conspirator. She created a "secret passageway" behind the couch and crawled through the passageway to steal the king's jewels. In my own mind, I assigned the obvious symbolic meaning to the king's "jewels," but I offered no interpretation because the material did not yet suggest how I should handle this. I was surprised, then, when the significance of "jewels" came out in a slip of the tongue one day, after weeks of the king drama. Nancy, the robber, let slip that she knew where the king kept his precious stones. When she named a certain jewel, I recognized a pun on Nancy's mother's maiden name. The jewel name now appeared from time to time as part of the drama. Finally, one day, I drew Nancy's attention to the similarity between mother's maiden name and the jewel. She was startled, and then began to laugh guiltily. She was then able to tell me how she longed to sleep with her mother at night, how lonely it was in her bed, and how she wished Daddy would go away sometimes so that she could sleep with mother.

In subsequent hours, she began to unfold a fantasy in which mother would adopt a baby and she, Nancy, would help mother take care of it. In her fantasy, father was too old to give mother babies, and there was the implication that she wished that she could.

Almost as soon as we began to look into these fantasies, Nancy began to resist their analysis. She resumed the robber games, firmly denied that the games had any meaning whatsoever, and closed out my interpretations. We were approaching the time for my summer vacation. Once during this period of repetitious play of robbing the king, I commented that the robber had many narrow escapes in this play but he never got caught. She said, gravely, "When you get back from your trip North maybe I'll let him get caught."

This summer brings us to the second summer of analysis and the completion of approximately 18 months of analytic work. Before presenting the detailed excerpts from the analysis during the third and fourth years, I shall briefly summarize the seizure picture at this point. Over a period of several months preceding the second summer, the seizures had become rare and, what is still more significant from the analytic point of view, they had become "invisible." Even with trained eyes, it was nearly impossible to identify a seizure now. They were fleeting, momentary, and could not be distinguished from a brief inattentiveness in a normal person. If we thought Nancy had a seizure, we had to ask her. She was usually quite honest in her report, but there was no question now that she could make her seizures a secret. This symptom, which had caused her so much shame, could now join the underworld of those other secrets which can be concealed from grown-ups and carried on "undercover."

All of this played a part in the resistance as the second summer grew near. She could see no point in continuing treatment. She was better in every way, she argued, doing well in school, happy with her family and friends. Since no one could even see her "forgetting spells" any more, why should she continue her analysis? It was not easy to explain to her why I thought analysis needed to continue, that the seizures were still in the picture and might become worse later on, that she still had a strong tendency to keep her feelings buried inside, and that this would make more trouble as time went on. She accepted these reasons with an attitude of passive resignation.

From the analytic point of view, the change in the seizure picture was a puzzle. Analysis of the seizures was fragmentary. The analytic work had apparently diminished and modified the seizures on the basis of discharge. As both erotic and aggressive quantities found normal pathways to discharge, the seizures had diminished demonstrably. The "discharge" aspects of the recovery explained very little that was not already known about petit mal in general, and it remained for us to examine the seizure as a symptom in further analytic work.

Excerpts From the Third and Fourth Years of Analysis

During this period seizures appeared rarely either in or outside of the analysis, but, on several occasions, the occurrence of a seizure with spoken words contributed in large measure to the progress of the analysis.

An EEG in September was summarized in this report:

The EEG is reported as being slightly improved, but it still shows abnormalities, mainly of the petit mal type, but also shows some grand mal components. There is no definite focus. There are many long stretches of entirely normal alpha waves, but there are also occasional bilateral three-per-second spike and wave discharges. There were not nearly as many of these as in the first record. However, then they occurred 60 per cent of the time. Now there were only four periods of discharges, and two of them appeared during hyperventilation and lasted from only four to six seconds.

From the EEG picture, there is certainly suggestion that Nancy has improved, but abnormalities are still present and I think she should continue with medication.

In November of the third year of analysis, Nancy had a seizure at the beginning of an hour in which she mumbled, and the words "my brother" came out distinctly at the end. When she came out of the seizure, she accused me of looking at her in a strange way. I connected this with "the eyes" that she has been seeing in the darkness of her room at night. When I told her the words she had mumbled in her seizure, she began an outpouring against Fenton. She wished he were dead. He always got her into trouble. He made her ashamed and frightened. He has been playing the looking games with her again. Mommy would be so angry if she knew. There was genuine anxiety in her voice.

In the hours that followed, Nancy began to tell me about a looking compulsion that disturbed her. She felt as if her eyes were drawn in two directions toward a boy's or a man's face and toward his genitals. She tried to imagine "how big it is." Her fascination with Fenton's penis emerged strongly at this time. For the first time, Nancy was able to admit her envy of Fenton's penis. There followed a period of acting out in which Nancy engaged in petty thefts. She stole money from

Fenton and her mother, which led us finally to establish the links between stealing and her envy of Fenton's penis.

On the day before Thanksgiving, Nancy complained of nausea and stomach pains during her hour. I was fairly certain from mother's report and my own observations that these were conversion symptoms. I suggested to her that there were very probably some strong feelings inside that were being expressed in these symptoms, and she agreed. We agreed that there might be a point to scheduling an extra appointment on the next day.

On the following day, Nancy arrived for her appointment distraught and close to tears. She had a fantasy that I must be angry at her for "ruining Thanksgiving." With very little help from me, she was able to see this as a reversal, and was able to express her anger toward me. Then, for nearly fifteen minutes, she had a number of seizures. When I told her that the seizures were talking for her, and that something must be bothering her, she said, instantly, "I lost my ball two nights ago." "It must be somewhere in my room, but I can't find it." When I tried to get her to express her feelings, she said firmly, "I don't want the feelings to come out."

At this point she had a long seizure and I could hear her muttering. Then, still in the seizure, I heard her say distinctly, "Fester, it's o.k." When she came out of the seizure, I told her what she had said. She was puzzled, and I asked her to give associations. She said, "Esther, pester, Fenton, Lester, . . . oh! Dexter!" Dexter, she told me, was someone on a television show. There was an episode on one program during which Dexter was given a penalty for something, and the penalty was to eat snails. With this, Nancy put her hand to her stomach, then to her mouth, and looked as if she were about to throw up. "Ugh! Ugh!" she said with loathing. I suggested that some disgusting thought had come up. Yes. She was

thinking of milk. Sour milk. She had some yesterday. "Ugh!"
I suggested there could be another thought or thoughts that
were "ugh." She nodded. Could she tell me? She looked at
me, suffering, and I could tell that she needed help from me.
I reminded her that one of the associations to Fester was Fenton. Was there some connection between the "ugh" thoughts
and games with Fenton? She nodded. Then she said, "Now
I think I want do do something. Get out of here or color or
something. I know why. My next thought is how dirty my
shoes are. I was just looking at them." I said, "Is that a connection, Nancy? Something dirty and Fenton?" "Yes." "What
is the connection with snails?" Nancy, in a very low voice,
"I don't know." I: "Something to do with putting something
in your mouth?" "Yes," in a whisper. "Oh, you know what
came into my mind? It's crazy and I don't want to say it. . . .
Roast penis. Ugh. Roast penis." Tell me about the 'ugh'
part." "I can't say it." I: "Like something one could eat?"
"Yes. Oh, I don't want to talk about this. Please. I'll feel sick
and I won't enjoy myself today." With a powerful effort she
pulled herself out of this mood, began to smile cheerfully
and to talk about holiday plans and trivial observations on
the weather, and banished all the strong feelings from the
picture. I could not reach her feelings again that hour.

There followed a period of strong resistance that lasted for
well over a month. She would not permit me to return to the
material of Thanksgiving Day, although the symptoms of nausea persisted. In the meantime, too, there was a reluctance to
eat at home which involved certain animal foods, most specifically, eggs. Her fantasy was that by eating the egg she was
killing the chicken inside. Most significant was the eruption of
affect which I now observed both within and without analytic
hours. There was strong anger toward me and repeatedly
expressed wishes that I would die. There was rage toward

Fenton over seemingly trivial complaints, and a seething anger toward other children and complaints that nobody liked her. There were hours in which she wept because she did not like herself; she thought she was homely; she hated the way she looked. Any of my efforts to link this material with the Thanksgiving Day crisis in the analysis were firmly put aside by Nancy. When the loathing of her own body was observed in analysis in connection with envy of Fenton and boys, she brushed off my suggestions even though this was material that had been worked with previously in analysis.

During this period there was another episode of exhibitionism on the part of Fenton. He launched a model airplane from his erect penis. This episode and the telling of it in analysis brought on several days of increased seizures. She openly blamed Fenton for her seizures now. "He makes my problem worse. I don't really want to play the games; I mean at the beginning only one little part of me does, maybe a part as big as my little toe; then the feeling gets bigger and bigger and grows 'til it comes out here! [tapping her head significantly]." (At this point Nancy gave me permission to talk with her parents about Fenton's need for treatment. Plans were initiated for Fenton shortly afterward.

The balls came back into analysis now along with a new secretiveness that was not linked specifically to the exposure games with Fenton. She was still using the balls for masturbation. Having one or another of the balls in bed with her was indispensable for sleep. One day, she produced a group of highly illuminating associations to the balls. She began with, "It's like having Mommy with me all the time." ". . . A hand. Mommy's hand." And then she was struck by a thought, "A washcloth . . . when Mommy washed me—I mean *used* to wash me there. That used to give me a good feeling, too." Nancy herself seemed amazed by these associations as they

emerged. Now, for the first time, we were able to see that in
avoiding the use of her own hand in masturbation and substituting the ball, Nancy acquired an imaginary partner in a
sexual game and reproduced in her masturbation the cir-
cumstance under which mother stimulated her genitals. The
sin of masturbation for Nancy, to use her own hand, was partially absolved in the fantasy that another hand, the mother's
own hand, was stimulating her. Later analysis confirmed
through elaborate detail the extent to which the mother's
washing of the child's genitals was experienced as a seduction.

While we were analyzing the prohibition against the use
of her own hand in masturbation, Nancy again became very
resistant. During this period of resistance, there was an increase in seizures and a compulsive finger game made its appearance. The finger game appeared frequently in the course
of analytic hours, and Nancy reported that she found herself
playing with her fingers in the same way at home and at
school. In the finger game, one hand was opened partially
in a clawlike formation; the other hand, with fingers partially
closed, entered the open hand in a rhythmic motion.

Then, one day Nancy came in to her hour with an
announcement: "I have a clue," she said, "I started to figure
it out last night. Last night I was looking at my hands when
I played the finger game and it came to me. First I thought
'claws', then I thought 'mouth', then I thought of putting
something into a mouth. . . . All right, now I think of something else. Now I'm thinking of the word 'cell' and then
'amoeba.' I'll draw a picture. Look, here's the cell and it sort
of swallows another cell. And that goes back to what grown-
ups do. It's like the penis gets swallowed, get it, and the place
it goes into is *like* a mouth." Suddenly she put her hand to
her own mouth. "Ich. I feel sick to my stomach." I asked what
the thought was that made her feel sick. "Ich. A penis." She

could not go on. I said, "And is the 'ich' feeling connected with the thought of the penis in your mouth? Is that the sick feeling?" She said wryly, "Well, why not. After all that's not exactly a tasty dish you know." When I questioned further, she said that there were no memories that came up with these thoughts. She could only think of the cells. And then she brought up one additional association. "Oh, yes. And the stuff that comes out to make the baby. Ich. If that got into the mouth. Ugh!"

When she left this hour she reported that she felt very much better. The next day she announced that the finger game had stopped and that, for the first time, she was able to use her own hand in masturbation. And now for a two-month period we had almost no seizures, no new symptoms, and no reports of anxiety at night.

In the meantime, following analysis of the finger game, some memories began to emerge. The backyard toilet games with Arthur and two other children came into the analysis for a brief period. Nancy told me very gravely that she was sure that these games were connected with the beginning of her seizures. She was not able to recall more than exhibitionism in these games, but some details began to emerge which showed that Arthur's mother had come upon the children, had screamed at them and had taken Arthur into the house for a spanking. (Later in the analysis, there was evidence that the mother had actually made a threat against Arthur's penis in her hysterical outburst.) All of this accounted for the fact that Arthur turned away from Nancy around this time and regarded her as his enemy and temptress. The backyard catastrophe, which was united with the loss of Arthur, gave heightened meaning to the bloody nose that Nancy received at Arthur's hands. I suspect, too, from familiar patterns in Nancy, that the catastrophic end to the sex play with Arthur resulted in loss of genital sensation, that this was interpreted as damage to the genitals, and that the bloody nose that brought this period to a climax was the symbolic proof of damage to the genitals.

"Blackmail—Black Male"

Behind the finger game and a wealth of allusions in the analysis, one felt there was also the memory of a sexual observation, but no specific material in this area had emerged. Some weeks after the analysis of the finger game, Nancy again began to experience resistance in analysis. Finally, one day, she told me that a thought came running through her head on the way to her hour. The thought was: "Selma is a blackmailer." Along with the thought was a fantasy that I would tell her parents that if they did not pay me more money I would discontinue treatment. There was no one else to go to, so her parents had to pay me more money.

She had no associations at first. I reminded her of the criminal games of last spring and the blackmailer who threatened to get the criminal if he didn't pay off. "Yes," she said doubtfully, "but I'm not really afraid that you would tell anyone about anything I've told you, or that you would really blackmail anyone." I tried other leads. I reminded her of a maid who left Nancy's family because she thought she could get more money elsewhere. "Yes," Nancy remembered. Then was I like a maid in this fantasy. "Yes." And the trail broke off again. Then, abruptly, Nancy said, "Now I think of another blackmail. A black *male*." (This had turned up too in a blackmail fantasy last spring.) "And that reminds me of a game Sally (best friend) and I play. She's an all-black horse and I'm an all-white horse, and we love each other." "What do you do?" "Oh, we just run alongside of each other. Play together. See that's where the black *male* comes in." We pursued this further. Were there any other associations to a black male? No. I offered other possibilities. We knew how things can get turned into their opposites in dreams and memories. Black is the opposite of white. Could this have something to do with a white male? She hesitated. Well, that made her think of Daddy. Once she came into his room without knocking. He was just pulling up his pants. She didn't see anything. Another time she came into the bathroom by accident and Daddy was there. "But I closed the door quickly and I didn't see anything." I pointed out to Nancy that from her thoughts today and on other occasions, it appeared that she did once see a man and that it made a very great impression on her. What could it be? She could bring nothing to mind. I asked her if another possibility of a black male was a connection with night. A white male would look like a black male at night. "No!" Nancy said flatly. "You just lost the $64,000 question. I thought we were getting some place before but that doesn't sound right to me. I keep thinking that it was a *black* male." And we could not pursue this further that hour.

Of course my difficulty in analyzing this material is that I could not believe in the possibility that Nancy could have observed "a black male." What opportunity would a protected middle-class child have had to observe a Negro in a sexual act? A few days later, in a conference with Nancy's mother, I asked her if she could shed any light on the mystery. Mother then told me that when Nancy was three and a half years old the parents had taken a two-week holiday in another city. The children were in the care of a Negro maid. When the parents returned, they learned from neighbors and from the children themselves that Cassie's boy friend had visited her at night. Cassie was dismissed shortly afterward. The parents had no evidence that the children had observed the couple in bed; Cassie's room was on another floor, in any case. Since the parents had never considered the possibility that Nancy could have observed a sexual act, they had never told me about this incident.

Our analysis during the next two years proved, without a doubt, that Nancy had witnessed a sexual act between two Negroes, very probably Cassie and her lover. But the details of this observation and the connections with Nancy's neurosis emerged very slowly.

Soon after the revelation of the "blackmail—black male" fantasy Nancy developed an upper respiratory infection to which she was frequently prone and was in bed for nearly a week. When she returned to analysis she reported that the fantasy, "Selma is a blackmailer" had returned. Her associations were "Selma is a robber.... You took my good feelings away." She was very careful to assure me, "These are just my thoughts, you know, I don't really think this." She had lost her "good feelings" and somehow felt I was to blame. There was a fantasy that I would cut off her hands at her wrists so that she could not touch herself. When I inquired about seizures, I learned that this time there had been no seizures for over a week. (This must be noted because, typically, the loss of "good feelings" had always been accompanied by an increase in seizures.)

Then Nancy, still associating, told me for the first time about "a picture" that kept coming into her mind during the time she was ill in bed, a "picture" that she always has when she is ill and sometimes when she is not ill and is alone. The "picture," as she described it to me, had the quality of a hysterical hallucination in vividness and intensity. It was the picture of a chessboard with black and white squares, and on the chessboard were "little creamy, skinny blocks" arranged on the board for a game. When she sketched it for me, she showed a mass of little blocks placed in one corner of the board and two blocks isolated in the opposite corner. Along with the hallucination was a noise, "a noise," said Nancy, "that sounds like a big wh-i--ish."

Now I should mention that Nancy's interest in the game of chess had sometimes bordered on the obsessional. Only two months before, she had described a television dramatization to me of Stephen Zweig's "The Royal Game" which had fascinated her because the imprisoned hero of the story had nearly gone mad with his chess obsession. "It's like he was hypmatized by the game," she had told me. Nancy's own chessboard hallucination predated the television drama by some years, of course.

In this hour and the next Nancy's associations again led in the direction of mutilation fears ("Someone will cut off my hand") and her associations to the chessboard blocks went on in this way: "They're people. It's as if the ones in the corner are a mother and father with lots of children and a couple in the other corner without children." Then the phrase, "Evening Star" came into her mind. "A good horse's name," she reflected. And then a picture flashed through her mind, "A couple in the moonlight kissing. And there's the wh-i--ish sound again. . . . Another picture. A couple riding a horse in the moonlight." And then the associations stopped. There was a trancelike quality in Nancy as she gave these associations. Finally, I asked her if she could ever have seen a couple in the moonlight. She said immediately, "Oh, yes!" I am not sure whether or not she had a brief seizure at this point. When I asked her about her last words, "Oh, yes!" she seemed surprised, as if she had not known she had said this. She assured me she could not remember anything about seeing a couple and could not imagine what made her say that.

It must be noted that these associations that lead back to an observation of a couple were in no way suggested through my analytic handling. From the time of the first revelations of the "black male" fantasies, I did not suggest more than that she had observed a black male, which was a confirmation of her own statement. I never told her, of course, what her mother had told me about the maid and her lover.

For over a month following this beginning analysis of the chessboard hallucination and the couple in the moonlight, we had a nearly impenetrable resistance. Nancy spent her hours in casual chit-chat. She had no problems to report, no conflicts, no fears. During this time, the seizures practically disappeared from the picture (confirmed by parent observations) and something new had taken their place. Nancy now told me that she was "forgetting" all kinds of things and she wanted to make it very clear that these episodes of forgetting were not at all like seizures. She carefully explained the difference. "In my forgetting spells I would blank out. Like the telephone gets disconnected. But this way I don't get disconnected. It's like I hear a person talking but I can't remember what they said." Through careful questions, I ascertained that Nancy was making clear that she never lost consciousness at such moments and that she was actually describing a hysterical absence.

In the two months that followed our partial analysis of the chessboard fantasy, we learned very little more. Resistance continued, and Nancy herself described her despair. At one point the seizures returned for a few days (according to Nancy's own report) and she said, "Oh, I *wish* whatever it is would come out! I wish that that wish was as strong as a horse and my mind was a teensy ant so the wish could push out. But my mind is so strong it just pushes it back." She picked up a pencil and sketched a horse. I asked, "Is that the horse that is pushing its way up? "No. Here is the horse." She drew a huge horse, as large as the sheet of paper, and labeled it "Fury." When I drew her attention to this, she denied stoutly that the horse's name had anything to do with feelings inside. Sometimes I had the strong impression that Nancy was consciously excluding something from analysis, as well. Since Nancy would be leaving for summer camp very soon, it was obvious, too, that she was marking time until the holidays would begin.

Nancy had an excellent summer at camp. Soon after she returned from camp, we had a medical consultation and decided that the phenobarbital would be eliminated following a gradual decrease in dosage for a month. I was never able to learn what magic Nancy attributed to the drug (if any), but its withdrawal was not accompanied by any fantasies that aided me in understanding. The withdrawal of the drug had no effect upon the seizure picture. Nancy, herself, had long ago derided the drug and had pointed out shrewdly that whether or not she had seizures did not seem to have anything to do with the phenobarbital, but had everything to do with how she felt.

During the early fall, resistance continued. I was puzzled by certain features in the transference. More than once I had the feeling that, behind this passive resistance, was a *wish to be forced to do something by the analyst.* This came out most clearly in fantasies in which she would be forced to continue analysis whether she wanted to or not. One had the feeling, too, that there was a certain amount of excitement connected with such fantasies. I began to draw Nancy's attention to this behavior and to raise questions with her. The meaning of this resistance was revealed in dramatic fashion within a short time.

The "Torture Daydreams"

One day, she said to me in musing fashion, "Isn't it funny how so many of my daydreams are torture daydreams?" (It was, indeed, "funny," since she had never told me any torture daydreams during the three years I had known her.") The torture daydreams were associated with certain games that Nancy played with Sally, her dearest friend. The two girls played horses together (which we already know from Nancy's story of last Spring in which Nancy was a white horse and Sally was a black horse.) The details of these games had always been excluded from analysis. In one of Nancy's daydreams, there were two children who were captured by animals and enslaved by them. They were forced to do the work of dray horses. When they were too slow at work, they were tortured. In one of the tortures, a bit was placed in the mouth so that each effort at pulling would cause the bit to cut into the mouth. In another torture, the girl was put in stocks, with head, arms, and legs through holes, while a man behind her threatened her with a whip (but did not actually beat her). The boy, however, was beaten on his arm by the whip. In still another torture, the boy and girl were driven like horses while carrying heavy weights suspended from their backs.

In the next hour, Nancy was nearly inarticulate with shame for having told me the torture daydreams. When we went into the feelings of shame, Nancy told me that the torture daydreams belonged to masturbation, that she needed them to get "a very strong feeling." Now each of the details of the sadistic fantasies came into analysis. She associated to the bit in the mouth of the horse-humans, her own hands in masturbation. "When I tighten up there with my hands." It was an exact displacement from vulva to mouth. The weights on the horses reminded her, she said, of "The balls" . . . "they hang down." The whipping did not yield any associations at this time. She could only tell me that in the fantasy it was the arm that was whipped, at the wrist. Analysis of these fantasies was very slow. Soon after telling me about them, strong resistance emerged. As she herself told me at a later point, "But if I tell you all about the torture daydreams I won't have them anymore, and if I don't have them I can't get my good feelings!"

Gradually, we established the links between the sadomasochistic masturbation fantasies and sex play with Sally, with Arthur, earlier, and still earlier, through the analysis of a screen memory, of oral sex games at the age of four and five with a cousin, Edward. In the sex games, Nancy was usually the passive partner, but it was very clear that she identified with the little boy partner and his excitement. In the games with Sally, the latter was the boy and Nancy was the girl. In masturbation, Nancy was both boy and girl, active and passive, sadistic and masochistic. In the sex games and the masturbation fantasies, I was certain that something was being re-enacted from a sexual observation, but no new material emerged.

Then the chessboard hallucination returned along with hallucinated noises. "It's as if people were talking in another room and saying 'blah-blah-blah! It just sounds like people mumbling or jabbering and I can't make out what they're saying." Yet this yielded nothing new in analysis. It was several weeks before Nancy provided another clue through a game with Sally, and the threads could be picked up again. The game with Sally was one that was confided with deep shame. They pretended they were two dogs, a male dog and a female dog. The male was wrongly thought to be savage and was chained up. Nancy, the female dog, tried to free him. She was to be punished now, by The People. In a climactic scene, the Nancy dog is on her back (tied down) and the

Sally dog is crouched over her legs with his paws under her
while The People lower a heavy metal cast over Nancy's
body. At first she can barely feel it. Then it hurts a little,
then it hurts a lot and Nancy, in the game, "can hardly
breathe." Nancy began to ramble. She confessed that she did
not want to associate to this material: "It makes me
ashamed." Then she said, "There's a word that keeps coming
into my mind and I keep forgetting it." At this moment, she
had a seizure.

The word was "intercourse." When she remembered it
shortly afterward, she said, "I feel ashamed now. I feel like
getting out of here, right now!" As we talked about her feelings, she suddenly interrupted to ask urgently, "What would
happen if something went wrong and instead of the seed coming out of the man, urine came out?" She looked ill again,
and I asked about her feelings. "Like throwing up," she said.

As we worked over this material in this hour and the next,
I drew Nancy's attention to the themes of torture and intercourse, and fascinated looking. I suggested that she may, indeed, have once seen a sexual act between a couple, and that
it seemed to her like a torture. She regarded me wide-eyed,
and then let out a little cry of disgust and horror. Yet, she
did not deny it. "Maybe when I was little." She was silent for
some time. Then I heard her say, "Wa-wa-wa" in a musing
voice, meanwhile blowing her bubble-gum into a large, full
bubble. Then she said, "Look at what I am doing with this!"
She had blown it to its fullest extent, then inhaled and caused
it to collapse. She stopped short in amazement and said, "I
think that's what I saw! a penis, I mean. . . . Now I want to
go home. I feel like getting out of here in a hurry!" I told
her that if she had, indeed, once seen such a thing, she might
have felt like getting out in a hurry.

There followed two hours of blank resistance and two days during which she reported a number of seizures. When I asked what had happened to all the strong feelings, she said, "All gone, I guess. Or maybe I should say they are in forgetting spells now." I then offered the interpretation that the inability to talk might be an important clue in itself. If I was right, she had once seen something between a couple that she could not talk about afterward. She listened to this with interest and then said, "You know what pops into my mind? That maybe someone told me I *mustn't* tell."

It was nearly two weeks later that Nancy brought a report of nausea and stomach pains and a new fear. Her parents had gone out one night and she was alone with Fenton. As she started upstairs to bed, she became afraid to enter her dark room. When she got into her room she realized what she was afraid of. "I kept seeing pictures in my mind, most of all of a man with horns growing out of his head. A horrible monster. And I kept thinking about it and I couldn't fall asleep. . . . But today in class I thought of something. I think it's connected with what I must have seen when I was little, seeing intercourse, I mean. I don't know why, but when I made that connection I was *really sure* for the first time since we've been talking about it that I saw it. . . . He had a black face. Very ugly horns."

Now we had another link between the sexual observation and the "black male" fantasy, and for the first time Nancy was able to see the connections. I had never suggested in analyzing the sexual observations that she may have seen a Negro couple, but now it seemed appropriate to raise this possibility with Nancy. She did not repudiate the idea, but asked very sensibly how this could have happened. I asked if she thought it might have been a maid and a man who visited her. It

could be, she acknowledged, but when and how? I reminded
her that all of our clues, like the man with the horns and the
chessboard fantasy, seemed to be connected with being alone
with mother and father away and also with being sick. Did
anything come to mind? We got no further confirmation from
her own associations.

With the analysis of the "man with the horns" fantasy and
the conviction in Nancy that she had observed a sexual act, the
seizures dropped out of the picture for months. This was in
March of the third year of analysis. There were no seizures observed or reported during the nine months that followed, which
included a summer at camp. In January of the fourth year, the
first seizures observed in months appeared in an analytic hour
in connection with the analysis of a bisexual fantasy.

"The Boy Part of Me"

Now, for many weeks in the analysis, we uncovered no further memories of the primal scene, but instead encountered
a period of formidable resistance. The analytic material centered on horses—Nancy's love of horses, her passionate interest in horseback riding, and a preoccupation with horses
that bordered on the obsessional. Any attempt to establish
the links between the horses and the primal scene material
were futile for a time. She argued that every girl of her age
was "horse crazy," and what was wrong in liking horseback
riding anyway? She was afraid that analysis would deprive her
of her pleasure in horses and riding, and it was with great difficulty that I finally managed to get across to Nancy why we
needed to understand the preoccupation with horses. I told
her quite frankly that there was, of course, nothing wrong
with liking horses, and while a horse is, of course, a horse,
there was something in her feelings and preoccupation with

horses that was beyond—way beyond—what we expect of normal horse lovers. It was like a sickness, I said. To my amazement, this time she agreed. She hung her head and said, "I agree. And Sally's got the same sickness," she said gravely.

In the next hours the horses came into analysis as a symptom. Associations led to masturbation and to a fantasy of child sacrifice in which a child is set upon a pyre and burned alive. Her shame in relating this fantasy was nearly intolerable to her. "Because it gives me a good feeling." Then she switched to a description of new games with Sally. They no longer played "horse" together because this was so "babyish," but they played "riding academy" instead. (I noted to myself that the old horse games with Sally had disappeared with the analysis of the games and of the mutual sadomasochistic fantasies which led to the uncovering of primal scene memories.) In the new games, the two girls pretended that they were taking riding lessons at the academy and they walked and cantered and trotted on make-believe horses. In Sally's back yard there was a tree with a fine, low-hanging thick branch that Nancy used for a horse, "when I canter." All of this was offered innocently, as if no grownup could possibly have any questions about playing "riding academy".

When I drew her attention to the associations that led from the burning child to the riding games, she was defensive at first. When I asked for associations to the details of the game, her face reddened as she came to the thick branch that she used for a horse. Very reluctantly, she said, "a penis." She spent the next twenty minutes alternately rejecting the idea and finding support for it. Finally, she said, "I just thought of something, I just realized for the first time why I like to walk and canter but not to trot. You see you don't post in walking and cantering and you have to post when you trot. And in cantering, for instance, it feels nicer because you do have the horse between your legs all the time, but in posting it would be like leaving the horse."

Toward the end of the hour she turned her thoughts to Sally. Sally, she said sadly, had worse problems than she, Nancy, did. "She's got horses even worse in her head. And Sally's mother doesn't even get help for her. And Sally uses the horses 'for a shield' [her own words] for lots of problems just like I do.... And I think I use Sally for a shield, too. But now I think my shield is cracking a little bit." "Are you glad or sorry?" "Both. But really glad."

But of course, in subsequent hours, the danger that the analyst would take something away from her appeared strongly in the transference. She reported "a day-night dream." "There was a boy who hated Superman just because everyone else liked him. And he dreamed all his life about how he could take away Superman's power. And when he got older he invented something that was like kryptonite in a way because he could do something to Superman's power. It would confuse Superman so that when he set out to find the criminal's hideout he would find it and wouldn't know it." She at first pooh-poohed my suggestions that this fantasy had to do with me. Then, reluctantly, she recalled, how she used to play games with me in which she pretended to be a criminal, and at this point she laughed out loud. "It must mean that I would like to confuse you and do something to your magic power so you won't find my hideout." I linked this to the material that had to do with her wish to be a boy or to have what a boy has, and her reluctance to go into this material with me. She nodded. "That's always been the hardest thing for me, you know."

It was very clear from the material of this period that Nancy needed her "boy part" as she put it for defense, (as "a shield" in her own words). And long before we could analyze the masculine indentification as defense, she was able to put into words her fear of losing "my boy part." She fully accepted my interpretation that she seemed to need her "boy part" as a protection against some danger, but could not pursue this analytically.

She had achieved a kind of bisexual integrity that served her well—from her child's point of view. There were no incapacitating symptoms; the seizures were out of the picture. There was no conflict at home. There was pleasure in schoolwork, pleasure in having friends and being well-liked. But as soon as I began to touch gently on the defensive aspects of her masculinity, "a protection against some danger—we don't know what it is yet" I found that I was creating a disturbance in the ego. There was a transitory return of persecutory feelings ("The kids pick on me; nobody like me") and her school grades began to slip for the first time in two years. (There were still no seizures, however, and no other symptoms.) At the same time, she depreciated her girl's body, complained bitterly that there were no signs of breast development (she was now eleven years old), and expressed her envy of other girls, some of whom were already menstruating and wearing brassieres.

The disparagement of her little girl's body presented an analytic problem. While it was demonstrably connected with the analysis of the masculinity as defense, it had a here-and-now significance in terms of the child's prepubertal concerns and reinforcement from the side of reality. The repetitious features of this disparagement could not be analyzed until there was adequate expression of the conflicts seen by the child as "now." Moreover, the prepubertal character of these concerns presented still another form of resistance to analysis. It was as if the child were saying that if analysis should deprive her of her "boy part" she would have nothing; for analysis could not confer upon her the compensatory signs of femininity; it would take away and give nothing in return.

For a period of several months, we worked on the level of her prepubertal concerns and, as it turned out, with considerable benefit to the analysis. The affective eruptions of prepuberty were, in themselves, repetitions. By centering the analysis on the affects and linking them with current experience, we obtained a considerable advantage for the later analysis of the infantile prototypes. "Envy" which had appeared in the earlier period of analysis in dilute forms was experienced in pre-puberty with an almost savage quality—envy of the girls with breasts, of course. "Hostility toward mother" which had broken through at many points earlier in the analysis, was now experienced with great intensity as Nancy blamed her mother for giving her this poor, skinny, little girl's body. "Self-disparagement" which earlier seemed to "come out of nowhere" now centered in her hatred of her own body. "Fear and envy of males" which had always had an unreal quality when experienced earlier in the analysis was now experienced as "real" and was re-enacted in a variety of ways in the theater of prepuberty. During this period, I did little more than give permission to feel and to listen sympathetically to Nancy's outpourings. There were many hours in which grief, tears, and impotent rage were discharged in a torrent. Still there was no return of seizures.

Then, out of this chaos, I began to identify a theme that provided a bridge between the prepubertal conflicts and the earlier analytic material. Nancy began to report frequent fights with Fenton and with other boys at school. Often these fights began as a wrestling or slapping game with giggles. Then they would move swiftly into a real fight, with Nancy in tears and running. None of this was extraordinary for her age, of course. What was extraordinary was Nancy's fear of Fenton. The fear was out of all proportion to the circumstances. She was afraid that Fenton would kill her, and she experienced this fear as genuine! I was also certain that Nancy was provoking these fights with boys through her teasing. And there was a quality in her excitement as she reported these fights that made me certain that she was acting out a sadomasochistic fantasy. She strongly resisted any attempt on my part to link these fights with her fantasies.

In a dream of this period, a night terror that left Nancy shaken, we saw her terrible fear that analysis would take away her "boy part":

> A girl and a boy were skating and they fall through the ice. They are imprisoned between the water and the crust and they can't escape. They stay for days. Then the boy is given an hour of freedom each day and he can get out and do as he pleases as long as he gets back in time. Then it seemed the boy was being chased by a man who was going to kill him. It seemed like he was shooting pop-corn at him. The boy escaped to a room where he was protected by a closed door. As long as he stayed there he was safe. A very scary dream.

When I suggested the transference implications of the dream, everything began to fall into place. The "hour of freedom" was the "hour of imprisonment," the analytic hour. Nancy was surprised at first, then agreed. Then: "Why everything in that dream was turned around. I am a boy in the dream, too." I agreed, and pointed out that I was the man. Nancy: "Yes. And Fenton. Because you remember the fight I had with him yesterday and how afraid I am of him when he is angry."

Now I pointed out to Nancy how terribly afraid and defenseless she felt as a girl in relation to Fenton. This must be one of the reasons why she would like to be a boy, to feel that she was strong and powerful, too, and could fight back. She agreed. Now I brought her attention to the representation of herself as a boy who is in danger of the analyst, represented as a man, and how terribly afraid she was in the dream. I said, "Now we can see why you are so afraid of analysis at times. You feel that you need your boy part for protection, and you're afraid that I might take away your boy part and you'd be without protection." Nancy: "That's it *exactly!*" And now she could speak more freely of her resistance. "Why I've not even wanted to tell you when I was angry with you. Because if I told you we'd analyze it and if we analyzed it we'd find out something. So I'd just say nothing. It was like the dream. We're really in the same room but I close the door on you and make it two rooms."

Nancy had three seizures in this hour, the first seen in many months. Two appeared in connection with my words, "the boy part of you" and occurred within ten seconds of each other. In each case the sentence was remembered up to the point of "boy part" and then blanked out. When I told Nancy the words that had been blanked out she said soberly, "Well, *that* proves what's bothering me, doesn't it."

And the pop-corn detail in the dream? "Fenton likes to make pop-corn." And then she thought of "the hard little kernels that do not pop" and thought of her hard little nipples that won't "pop," and her unhappiness at being so flat. How she envied Sally for wearing a bra. And since there had been a recent revival of the friendship with Sally, I suggested that having Sally for a friend is also like having what Sally has.

Yet this hour was followed by another period of impenetrable resistance. From a number of details, particularly in her provocation of Fenton and other boys, I could detect the acting out of sadomasochistic fantasies once again, but she firmly closed the door upon my inquiries. Then, one day, she made a confession. She had lied to me all the time about "torture daydreams." She was not ready to tell me yet what they were, she said. Her shame was very evident as she made her confession, and I drew her attention to it. She answered candidly that the torture daydreams gave her a good feeling when she played with herself. "If I tell you, I'll lose the good feeling."

In the following hour she reported a night terror in which she was pursued by Fenton through corridors. There were confused details of secret doors with buttons, and in detail, remembered later, of black and white "checkerboard" tiles on the floor of a room. Her associations led to her fear of Fenton and the old sex games, the torture games with Sally. I drew her attention to the black and white checkerboard tiles and the old chessboard fantasy which we had analyzed earlier in connection with a sexual observation of a couple. Nancy was immediately struck by this. We were able to establish links between "torture daydreams" and sexual observation. Nancy caught, for a moment, the insight that she, as the observing child, had interpreted what she saw as "a torture." But the insight was fleeting and was lost again in subsequent hours.

Now Sally came strongly into the picture again. More and more there appeared to be a bond between Nancy and Sally that could only be described as "enslavement." In fragments, spread over many hours, we saw how Nancy "borrowed through identification" the aggressiveness of Sally, and how Sally played "boy" to Nancy's "girl." And Sally was a cruel and ruthless friend. If Nancy did not comply with Sally's own wishes, she would coldly drop her. She enjoyed seeing Nancy helpless and in tears, and tyrannized her with threats or by coyly turning her favor to other girls. Much of this had been excluded from the analysis in earlier periods of the friendship. Now I could use this to show Nancy how Sally enjoyed cruelty not only in her games, but in everyday life. And then I raised the question, "If you need a girl like that for a friend, what does it say of you?" And Nancy said soberly, "That I must need to be hurt."

Now, for the first time, we began to get material that linked Sally specifically to beating fantasies. There was a game in which the two girls pretended they were runaways from an orphanage. Upon their return, they were beaten. In Nancy's version the "beating" was symbolic, a tapping of each other with a twig. She added later, "We used to have beating as a punishment quite a lot in our torture games, but not any more."

Nancy made an interesting observation in the following hour. "I've been thinking about something. Sally is, like you say, my boy part, but Sally is like a boy to me, too. It's like having a boy friend. . . . You know something else: if part of me wants to be a boy, why do I always choose the girl parts when Sally and I play games?" I: "I've wondered about that too. I think that you satisfy the boy part through a partnership with a girl who plays the boy, and she represents the boy part. But I don't know why you never choose the boy part for yourself. Tell me what comes to mind."

Nancy: "Well, I think being a boy is kind of dangerous. They're rougher. They have to get into fights. They could get hurt." "Like what?" "Well, break a leg. Or cut themselves." "Hurt where?" "I don't know." I suggested that the worst danger to a boy might be injury to his penis. Therefore, to be a boy is dangerous. "Whereas in being a girl there is nothing to lose, so to speak." In this way, she played the girl because it was less dangerous, and played the boy safely through identification with a partner. Nancy was able to see this.

The Dream of the Snake Fight

In the following hour, Nancy brought in "a terrible dream."

> My cat had kittens, but she had four kittens and two snakes. I watched them come out of her. The snakes escape and the whole family tries to get them out of the house. There are three little panels, like doors in the house and if you could get the snakes through the little doors you could get them out of the house. . . . Then the snakes got into a fight. One was a rattler and one a gardener snake [i.e., garden snake], and it was like they were wrestling together. Then the rattler stuck his head right into the mouth of the gardener snake and killed him.

The most scary parts of the dream? "First trying to get the snakes out of the house. Second where the snakes were fighting. It was like who was going to win the fight, the rattler or the gardener." "How did the rattler kill the gardener snake?" Nancy cupped one hand and pushed a finger through the hole! "Like this." I drew her attention to this gesture which was identical with one she used to use during a period of sexual enlightenment in analysis, when she was trying to figure out with my help how the penis could enter the woman. It was a gesture that she used afterward, too, in an unconscious manner when the subject of intercourse would come up in analysis. But this time she denied flatly that her gesture could have anything to do "with what you are thinking." Her resistance was so strong that I dropped the subject. When I suggested that we go on with her associations, that I might be wrong, she was completely blocked. She could not go on.

In the following hour Nancy returned to the dream immediately. And now, curiously, her resistance to analysis of the snake fight appeared to have been dropped overnight. As she pursued details of the dream, she assumed (without any comments from me) that the snake fight symbolized sexual intercourse. She now pursued certain details in the dream. "When the gardener snake was killed it just lay quiet on its back for a while and then it disappeared. And the rattler snake disappeared, too. And all that was left—and this was funny—was the mouth of the gardener snake with its teeth, and the rattler left behind. And then it seemed that the TV set went on in the room and an announcer said something about the snakes disappearing."

> Nancy: What I don't understand is this, If the snake fight stood for two people having intercourse why does the gardener snake lay quietly on her back afterward and then disappear.
> I: What comes to mind?
> Well, something that's finished. It's all over. I guess there has to be a point when people have intercourse when they're all through but I don't know how it ends. Maybe it's like eating. They just have enough.... I don't know if I ever saw the end. I have the feeling I didn't. Couldn't it be that the snake or the lady was just lying quietly while the man was doing that to her and that's what I remembered in the dream, her being so quiet? And the reason I think I never saw the end is the way the snakes disappear and I keep thinking that maybe I ran away. That maybe I stayed and watched because it was so exciting and then got too scared and ran away before the end. Because that's the part of intercourse I can never figure out, how it ends.

As we worked further with details I showed Nancy how the snakes "disappearing" could also be a representation of the penis which disappears into the woman. She confirmed this, then said suddenly:

> I have to tell you something. I made up that whole part about the snakes after the fight was over. The real dream didn't say what happened to the snakes after the gardener was killed. But it just goes to prove something. The parts that I made up came from somewhere inside of me, too, and could be just as important in figuring out the dream and what happened a long time ago as the real dream.

While we were still close to the affectively charged portions of the dream, I stressed the significance of the anxiety experienced in the dream. This was what was most important, I said. Could she understand why? "Yes, because this is how I must have felt when I saw those people. Who was going to win. I wanted the gardener snake to win, but I knew it didn't have much of a chance with the rattler. And I was scared, I guess, because the whole thing must have looked like a fight to me and I thought someone was going to get hurt, the woman."

I pointed out that if this is how she felt at the time, it must have seemed to her that it was very dangerous to be a woman. She nodded. I showed her parallel attitudes in her character today, her fear of masculine aggression, fear of Fenton, and of other boys. I told her that it helped us understand how a little girl could be very feminine and womanly in certain ways, as Nancy was, and still be afraid to be a woman, and to defend against it by keeping a boy part hidden in herself for protection. Nancy agreed. "And that's why I'm timid and shy. Even with girls." And then she said something that I didn't quite understand and never found a chance to explore further: "It's like a girl or a woman who may have had some-

thing like that happen to them and if I get too close to them
it might rub off on me, sort of. I might catch it."

In the next hour she returned to the dream. She commented on the invented portion of the dream. "It just came
to me so naturally that it was like it had been in the dream,
and I didn't realize until later that it wasn't. Next she pursued the details of the mouth and rattle symbols (left behind
by the snake). In associating, she thought that her reaction
was, "he had stolen the penis from the woman." I had the
impression that she was isolating affect again and was simply
translating symbols. I asked if she really felt these things or
was just saying them. No, she thought she felt their right-
ness.

But in the next hour, when she returned to the dream, I
felt strongly that she was isolating affect in connection with
the stolen penis associations that she brought up. Then, mid-
way in a brilliant and empty translation of symbols (she
translated mouth, teeth, vagina, biting off, etc.) she suddenly
switched to talk about Sally and told me, in a casual way, that
Sally had slept at her house last night. Then I learned, that
Nancy had had several seizures outside of analytic hours during the past few days.

Now I had to show Nancy again how her work on the
dream during the past two hours was becoming unprofitable
because she was closing off feeling and working out the dream
as if it were a code. I told her that I had the impression that
she wanted to please me in translating all the details of the
dream, but it had no meaning to her. She was like Little
Black Sambo making sacrifices to the tiger. Was she afraid,
again, that analysis would take something away from her?
Did it have something to do with the fear of giving up the boy
part and something to do with Sally? Nancy smiled sheepishly.

But here the diagnostic picture became cloudy, for something new had entered the situation. There was the possibility that Nancy's father would be taking a new job in another city the following autumn (this was April). It was by no means certain but Nancy knew of the possibility, and all of this came into the transference now. On the one hand, there was concealment of fantasies from me with the sheepish acknowledgement that if analysis were to end by autumn she could keep what was left of her neurosis which, to her mind, wasn't much anyway. The seizures had vanished once again. The pubertal concerns had moderated. Pleasure in learning had returned. And now she behaved as if analysis itself had become a torture. And what had become of the positive feelings toward the analyst, and how would she feel about giving up the analyst? She was cheerfully unconcerned.

Then, one day, when I had canceled her appointment for an out-of-town trip, Nancy appeared at her appointment time and, I was told, appeared quite dazed when she learned I was gone. Then she laughed in astonishment and said, "Oh, of course! I knew that all week!" When I discussed this incident as a symptomatic act, Nancy, for the first time, was able to see how she was handling loss of me through denial. The fear of losing the analyst as "protector" now came into the analysis. One day she said, "Do you think that maybe one of the reasons I hold on to my problems is that it's like holding on to you to make you know I need you? And giving them up would mean giving you up. Because I can't imagine what I would do without you. It would seem awfully strange." I added to this that I thought she might be afraid to give up her symptoms and to give up her "boy part," because if she lost me and my protection and the protection of her symptoms she would feel quite alone. She agreed to this immediately and with feeling. She thought of a story she had been reading of a girl who had no one to love her, and how she had cried and cried as she read it.

A Group of Somatic Memories

Once again external circumstances intervened, and this time served the analysis in an extraordinary way. Nancy's parents planned a two-week holiday for themselves early in May. In anticipation of the parents' absence, Nancy was cheerfully unconcerned and could only think of the fun at being on her own. Would she feel lonely? No. Why should she? Once again there was the denial we had seen in connection with loss of me. (I should mention that I had never in the past successfully captured the feelings of loss in connection with separation from parents. Loss was expressed symptomatically, typically, a cold, an ear-ache, a sore throat. Although we had had a large number of examples of this throughout the analysis, Nancy had consistently denied the connections between these symptoms and loss. It must be remembered, too, that the old chessboard hallucination had established a connection between the primal-scene observation and an upper respiratory infection.) This time I made a prediction to Nancy. I told her I did not know how the loneliness would come out when the parents were gone, but I would take a guess—a cold, a sore throat, an earache, or in some other disguised form. She cheerfully disavowed this.

During the first four days of her parents' absence, Nancy said everything was "wonderful." At the end of the week, she confessed to some slight feelings of loneliness. On Monday of the second week, she called. She had a sore throat, sniffles, no temperature. She thought she should cancel her appointment. I recommended that she come in. When she arrived she looked quite miserable. She complained of a stuffy nose. Her eyes were tearing. "But I don't feel really sick. And the worst thing isn't the cold. I feel *hungry,* terribly hungry, just starving. But not *really* hungry. It isn't like I could eat something and feel better." I was able to show Nancy how the hunger was connected with longing for mother, and how the tearing eyes and congested nose represented the suppressed tears. And now I could encourage the expression of grief and longing more directly. During the next three hours, she was overwhelmed by feelings of love for her mother and a longing for her return. She confessed, with considerable shame, that the longing was only for mother. She wanted Daddy to come back, too, but the sadness was all for mother, In fact—and this was very painful for Nancy to bring out—it was almost, she said, as if Daddy were an interference in her love for mother. As the tears began to come freely in analytic hours, the cold symptoms diminished—an exchange that greatly impressed Nancy. Then, through a piece of acting out and a new set of symptoms, we were able to establish connections between this separation from the parents and an earlier, traumatic separation.

There was a fight with Fenton, not so different from a number of other fights with Fenton, and again there were the fears of Fenton and what he might do to her. But this time Nancy's own destructive rage toward Fenton broke through. Trembling with rage in the analytic hour that followed she said, "I'm afraid I could kill him! I hate him! There will never be enough years to get rid of my hate by talking about it."

And, in a rapid development, during the second week of the parents' absence, a group of facial tics made their appearance. These consisted of a widening of the eyes, a wrinkling of the nose, a distorted grimacing of the mouth, and a stretching of the mouth. When I saw this group of tics in a constellation, I realized that each of these tics had appeared fleetingly at one time or another during the past months, but until the parents' absence we had never seen anything like this. When I drew Nancy's attention to this new group of symptoms, she offered rationalizations ("My glasses were slipping down, etc."), but she became attentive when I began to show her the meaning in terms of body language. When she finally acknowledged the tics as symptoms, she told me that they appeared *only* in her analytic hours. Later, I was able to confirm this.

Nancy could provide no associations to the tics, and I had to suggest the meanings to her, i.e., "to see something frightening," "disgust," "horror," and I suggested to her that the tics represented memories, in the same way that the cold symptoms and the hunger were ways of remembering an earlier time when mother and father were away. When we added this group of symptoms to the fight with Fenton during the parents' absence, and the dream of the Snake Fight which had been incompletely analyzed because of the loss of affective links, we now had a picture, I proposed, of that time that was not remembered, when Nancy had observed the couple. Now we had the feelings that we had lost earlier in connection with the dream of the snake fight.

The tics and the cold symptoms disappeared shortly afterward, but from the analytic point of view, the tics were not satisfactorily explained. We know that they made their appearance only in the analytic sessions during this period (confirmed later by the parents). In my own reconstruction, I saw the tics as a repetition in the analysis of symptoms that had probably followed the original observation of the couple, but I received no further confirmation from analysis. Later, when I checked with the parents they were unable to identify these tics in any way and could not remember ever having seen them.

The longing for mother which emerged so clearly during the period of the parents' holiday now opened up pathways for the analysis of another dimension of Nancy's tie to mother. Nancy reported this dream about two weeks after the parents' return:

> Barbara [older sister] was standing behind me [Nancy]. She reached her hand around my face and under my chin and accidentally struck me in the jaw so all my teeth were loosened and fell out, and I had to have false teeth. I remember how angry I was at Barbara for making me lose my teeth. [Associations led to May, the maid, who recently had her teeth pulled.] . . . A horrible feeling to lose your teeth.

The associations trailed off until I suggested a displacement from mouth to genitals. The gesture of reaching the hand around the face and under the chin led to the association of mother washing her genitals. Then Nancy herself said, with surprise, that she must blame mother for an injury to herself.

Nancy returned to this dream a few hours later. Without any assistance from me, she offered further thoughts on the dream. She thought that it wasn't only that she blamed mother for not having a penis, but must have thought mother took it away from her for a punishment. Barbara's fist in the dream, reminded her of the way in which she used to masturbate with her hand in a fist. The punishment, she thought, was for masturbation. She added grimly: "It's like I have something else to blame mother for now. Because it's as if she made me the way I am and now I'm still so flat and so slow to develop, and it's like she's responsible for that too."

Termination and Some Aspects of the Transference Neurosis

In July, there was definite confirmation that Nancy's father would accept the new job, and the family planned to move in September. Nancy was in camp when the parents brought her the news. After her return from camp, there would be only three weeks (fifteen hours) of analysis.

Nancy had a highly successful summer at camp. She was thoroughly well-liked, received awards for campership, and in horseback riding (!). She enjoyed the camp dances with boys and returned from camp in radiant good health, looking older and very self-confident. There was no homesickness and there were no colds or sore throats either, she assured me.

These were her initial reactions to leaving me: "I feel very sad, of course, but then my next thought is: after all, this can't go on forever, and I can't have you forever. . . . And last night when I was thinking about it I made up my mind I was going to work these last few weeks like I never worked before." She did just that. The temptation must have been very strong to "let things slide" during these last weeks, and yet she very seriously began work on a continuous daydream that led us into further analysis of the transference. The day-dream had begun soon after her parents had visited her at camp to tell her of the plans for moving. It continued almost nightly thereafter:

> A woman is trying to get a man to feel very sexy. She takes him off to a house that is really a whorehouse and then gives him some sweet-smelling stuff that makes him dizzy and he falls into her power. First they put him into a room with a girl and she strips herself for him and he gets her into his power. ["What did they do, Nancy?"] Well, nothing really. They just *looked* at each other. That would be all I could imagine. But when I would come to that part in the day-night

dream, that part always made me want to rub real hard, and when I do that it feels very good. . . . And then, after this girl, they would take him into a room with five hundred girls and he'd get every one of them in his power. And when he was through he'd go into another room with let's say a thousand girls and do the same thing. And that's where it ends. I mean it never really ends.

Nancy's own associations led back to the old looking games with Fenton and fantasies of what a man and woman do in intercourse. She had no associations to "the sweet-smelling stuff," a detail that had appeared in other daydreams in connection with hypnosis or surrender, and which we were never able to analyze. One of the pleasurable highpoints of the fantasy was "the feeling of helplessness" of the woman in which I caught, too, pleasure in surrender and merging with the fantasied object. In the masturbation fantasy, she was both man and woman, active and passive, and the repetitious aspects of the primal scene observation could be pointed out to Nancy.

Yet Nancy, herself, did not see the transference implications of the dream until I drew her attention to the fact that the daydream had begun soon after she had learned that she would be leaving me. Now I drew Nancy's attention to the details, "being in the power of someone" and reminded her of her old fantasies in which I appeared to her as a hypnotist. I reminded her of the passivity we had seen in her during periods of resistance, which suggested the passivity of the woman in the daydream. She saw this with surprise. Then I pointed out, too, that she had told me a great many of her sexual secrets, and that sometimes she had felt that I was a little wicked for encouraging her to speak of such things. Nancy broke in herself, "And *this* must be the whorehouse!" Now I could help her see how I was represented in the daydream

as a man and she as a helpless woman, how the analytic situation had, in certain ways, become symbolized as a kind of sexual situation in which we looked at each other and she was
forced to reveal her sexual secrets.

In the next hour, Nancy provided a continuation of the
daydream. "The man has another woman 'in his power' and
she is forced to do 'something that pleases him.' He rips open
her dress, ripping all the buttons down the front. Another
thing that pleases him: She is only allowed to talk when he
makes a certain sign, crossing her fingers in a certain way.
But when she doesn't do things in just the way that pleases
him, he decides to send her away."

Her associations "You, Selma, again. And me." And she
was able to see how leaving me was represented in the daydream as being sent away, a rejection. I drew her attention
to the details of "stripping" and "undressing" in the daydream, and suggested that this might have a meaning in relation to analysis. Nancy said, "Yes, uncovering all my cover-
up thoughts—like undressing." I asked her if she thought that
maybe, underneath, analysis was exciting to her—like the
games that children play. Nancy thought this over. A few
moments later, she said in a pained little voice, "I just had
the funniest feeling. It was like I was playing with myself
right here!" This gave me the opportunity to show Nancy
how analysis had permitted a kind of undercover acting out
of masturbation and masturbation fantasies, that it was exciting at times and gave her "good feelings," and it must be
very hard for her to tell me this now, and must have been
very much harder to tell me that in the past. Nancy nodded.
"Now Sally pops into my mind. The games with Sally. And
Fenton, too. But mostly Sally right now. Coming here must
be like the games with Sally." We discussed Sally, and I suggested that the relationship with Sally represented, among

other things, the acting out of fantasies and feelings that she had been afraid to bring into her analysis and work out with me. She agreed.

Now, still associating freely, she said, "Now I think of something else. When I play with myself lately I've noticed two things. Sometimes I hear a voice murmuring something that I can't understand—just like it used to be in my forgetting spells. I'm sure the voice is your voice." I: "But how do you know that?" "I don't know how I know it, but it sounds like your voice and that's what I think of." I reminded her that, earlier in the analysis, we had seen how these unintelligible voices had represented something overheard between the couple observed, and suggested that the memory had been transferred to me.

"And the second thing that happens when I play with myself, I can't quite explain. It's a feeling like soft satin with little crinkles in it, then a rougher, satiny kind of material—but very soft, too." I remarked on the obvious representation of her genitals. She agreed, but added, "That isn't all—and I don't know what else it is." She went on in her associations. "Sally again. I'm thinking about how much I've learned from Sally that I would never have known without her. Like going shopping. I usually have to learn things from other people (In the meantime she was stroking her own hand.). Suddenly she said, "Satiny, crinkly—a baby's skin. Rougher, but soft, a grownup's hand." Now she stopped associating. I encouraged her to continue. Very reluctantly she said, "My mother's hand. Bathing me. When I was little." (Recall, that the memory of mother washing her genitals had come up earlier in the analysis.) I suggested to Nancy that mother's bathing her must have seemed to her like the introduction to "good feelings," and I drew her attention to her other associations, Sally, from whom she learned things first. Then I commented on the transference implications, that it must be that she felt I had introduced her to things, that I was like mother in such respects, for although I did not touch her, I talked about such things with her. She agreed, with great discomfort. She began to play with an embroidered watch on her blouse. "Look at me. I'm in a hurry to go. I must be wanting to get out of here in a hurry, right now!" "What are you afraid of?" I asked. "I don't know." "Are you afraid of all the feelings that our talk has stirred up?" "No!" she said laughing. "I'm afraid of the feelings that I won't let myself have right now!"

In the time that remained before Nancy was to move (four analytic hours) I reviewed the transference implications of this fantasy, but we were not able to capture again the intensity and immediacy of the communications of this hour I have reported. It is of some interest to note that there were no recurrences of any symptoms during the last period of analysis, not even the old cold symptoms that had, in the old days, accompanied loss or separation. In her last hour, she was quiet—uncomfortably quiet, I thought—and she talked a little about her sadness at leaving, but her self-confidence was undiminished. She was not afraid that her symptoms would recur. She thought that she could manage on her own, but if she needed further help she knew that her parents would arrange it for her. She was actually kind of excited, she thought, at becoming independent now.

Nancy, at the time of termination, was described by her parents and others who knew her as a tranformed child. She was lively, energetic, an excellent and enthusiastic student at school, and a child with many friends. Her parents have corresponded with me and I have some picture of Nancy during adolescence. She has sustained all of her gains, and the development of one of her gifts has been so extraordinary, that at the age of fifteen she already had achieved a modest local fame. Occasional seizures, brief, fleeting absences "perhaps one a day" have been reported by Nancy. (They cannot be detected by others.) No drugs have been employed. A recent EEG requested by me shows no significant changes since the last record, obtained at the end of the second year of analysis.

Elisabeth R. Geleerd, M.D.

Intrapsychic Conflicts as Observed in Child Analysis

W E CAN CONSIDER PSYCHIC CONFLICT from the moment when, in human development, differentiation into psychic structure has taken place. Theoretically, according to Hartmann, Kris, and Loewenstein (1946), structuralization in rudiment is there from the earliest beginnings. The end results of psychic conflicts vary. They are to a great extent a part of the maturational processes and generally lead to normal development. However, there are many cases in which the conflicts do not reach a satisfactory solution and neurotic symptoms, neurotic character formation, or other manifestations of malfunctioning result from these unresolved conflicts.

In the first eighteen months of life, disturbances in developmental patterns can frequently be corrected when the causative factors are understood and removed. Advice and guidance by a psychoanalytically trained person may be sufficient in the early phases of development. This work can be extended as soon as the capacity of the child to verbalize increases and the treatment is based on a partnership between mother and child analyst. In some emergencies, or in situations where no child analyst is available, a parent may be able to solve a neurotic problem in a child with the help of an analyst.[1]

When a child is ready to become a regular analytic patient depends on the stage of his development.[2] In all cases, we are dealing with disturbances which can be understood in terms of conflict between the ego and the inner or outer world. The disturbances are an indication that the ego is unable to handle a situation of stress. According to A. Freud (1937), these conflicts, in their simplest form, are due to a fear of the loss of the object or body injury. The strength of id impulses and the fear of loss of ego control over them may intensify the conflicts. Early defense mechanisms such as projection and displacement, as well as repression, become operative.

It is the aim of psychoanalytic treatment to bring the unconscious conflicts to consciousness. For the adult patient the method of free association, in the reclining position without seeing the person of the analyst, facilitates the bringing of preconscious thought content into consciousness. With the help of interpretation, repressions are lifted and lost connections are re-established. At the same time, the person of the analyst and the analytic situation introduce new reality factors which become focal points for the revival of old repressed conflicts and affects. Psychoanalytic treatment becomes a field where the interplay of the psychic structures, ego, id, and superego, can be observed from day to day.

In the analysis of children this procedure cannot be duplicated exactly. However, although the child does not free-associate, we find that his play is a partial substitute for this.

[1] See Bonnard (1950), Bornstein (1934), Bornstein (1935), Fraiberg (1952), Sterba (1949), Furman (1957), and Heymann-Gero (1955).

[2] A discussion of the criteria necessary for the treatment to be considered child analysis goes beyond the scope of this paper.

But since his capacity for introspection and self-observation is limited, we need to supplement the free play and the fantasies with observations from the environment. But in child analysis, as well as in adult analysis, the person of the analyst is an important factor in reviving old conflicts insofar as they are already repressed, and making them part of present conflicts as they appear and evolve.

I shall demonstrate intrapsychic conflicts as seen in two cases of child analysis. I shall give examples of how two girls of different character structures and different ages dealt with an id impulse, the wish to smear. I shall then contrast the reactions of each girl in analytic sessions, where the fear of losing the mother could be dealt with analytically.

CASE MATERIAL

The Case of Joanna

Joanna was brought to analysis at the age of four years, eight months. The presenting symptoms were: wetting in the daytime and a change of personality since the birth of a sister when the patient was 18 months old. Before that she had been a bright, lively, charming infant and toddler, advanced in every respect. The mother had started toilet-training just before the birth of the sister. Prior to this, during her pregnancy, the mother had to be hospitalized, and the actual separation of mother and child had been heart-breaking. The child had been pulled out of her mother's arms while the mother was in a wheelchair.

The patient could barely be restrained from attacking the baby sister when she was brought home from the hospital. From that time on, she was cross with the world. She became surly, shy, chronically unhappy, and often hurt herself, seemingly deliberately—e.g., just when she started analysis, she put her foot between the car door and the body of the car; if her mother had not seen what she was doing, the child could have hurt herself badly. On another occasion, she actually burned her hand by putting it on the burning gas stove.

Joanna had been bowel-trained without too much difficulty. However, once, when she defecated in her pants, her mother had been furious with her. She continued to wet in the daytime as well as at night. The night-wetting cleared up through the help of a consultation with a child analyst, a year prior to the beginning of her treatment, who suggested that the parents should not expose themselves to the child. This apparently had created too much sexual excitement. Partial wetting continued in the daytime. The child said that she never knew when she had to urinate; the beginning of urination to her was the signal that she had to go to the bathroom. However, she had enough control so that she would never completely empty her bladder until she reached the toilet.

Joanna was a good-looking child, but her face had a frozen expression. She revealed some of her previous bubbling personality by the fact that she never walked, but always skipped and ran, thus also betraying the underlying sexual excitement. The beginning of the analysis showed two important features. There was a wealth of anal material—"poop all over," as she would say while she looked at me furtively. There was a great deal of mixed-up anal talk, and she had a "Mr. Boo-boo" in her "mind." She made it clear to me that he was not in her head, revealing in this way how acute and astute the self-observations of this four-year-old girl were. She would laugh hysterically, but with a metallic ring, while she talked about "poop" or "slop" being eaten and drunk out of baby bottles. Many ideas were in anal terms, e.g., a baby was bowel movement and the parents would eat it. This was mixed up with ideas about a turtle she had once had, and which had died and been thrown in the garbage. This was also related to thoughts and feelings about a dog which had been run over. She accused her mother of causing his death, without basis in reality. Eating had an anal-destructive meaning but also was the incorporation of love. Thus she pretended to be an animal that ate my flowers. Joanna could grasp the many contradictory meanings of her oral and anal fantasies.

The other trend in the material was her transference, and her real relationship to me which enabled us to analyze her sibling rivalry. She liked to sit on my lap or be close to me and expressed the wish to come also on weekends. She hated to leave when the time was up, and stated that she wished to move into my building. When I discussed her longing for me with her, she added that during the period when we were discussing her intense need to be part of my life, she began to notice my other patients and members of my family. She really wanted to come and live with me in my home. She now became more angry and hostile at home, and at the same time accidents occurred in which she hurt herself. All of this came to a head when she saw another child patient of mine. She became stony and did not want to touch any of the common toys any more, such as the doll house which she had loved before. This period of our relationship dealt with the reliving of her early relationship to her mother, and I repeatedly had to interpret to her disappointment in me for having to share me with other people and children. I connected this with her anger at home and the competition for her parents' love for her baby sister.

In the meantime, the wetting began to diminish temporarily, but increased when she brought primal-scene observations. She became more and more aggressively wild. One time, she kicked me violently and then related a memory of how she had gotten up at night in the country because she had heard her parents on the roof. This was "the worst memory of her life," and she could only hint at it. This memory occurred on a Friday afternoon. She made it clear that she did not wish to spoil her good time over the weekend by having to think of such a bad memory. But on the Monday after, she could tell me "the bad memory," i.e., that on the roof, Daddy had kicked Mommy in the eye with his boots, and Mommy had had a black eye for over a week. Her mother could verify the incident. The parents had rigged up some photographic equipment to take pictures of animals at night on the roof. The father had tried to climb on the chimney and had slipped, accidentally hitting his wife in the face. They never knew that Joanna had witnessed this. They had crowded quarters that summer, and had intercourse when they thought the children were asleep. Thus Joanna could learn to understand that her kicking at me and much of her hostile behavior in analysis and on the outside was an identification with her father in the sexual role as she conceived it.

At this time she had a nightmare of something happening to her mother, and Joanna had to save her. The nightmare dealt with many ideas about her mother's death from many levels. In the meantime, there was much sex play between her and her sister. Joanna resented her mother for getting up early in the morning to stop the sex play. "Mind your own business," she said to her mother, and in many other gruff ways showed that she did not want any interference with pleasureable activities. She began to masturbate more at home, provocatively. She had more accidents which could easily be understood as having been self-inflicted. With me, she was more cross and bossy and told me angrily to stay out of the bathroom when she was there, although I had no intention of entering it. It was then that she was able to tell me that she was wetting her pants a little bit. Thus I had become identified with her mother. Certainly one of the meanings of the wetting her pants was anger toward and resentment of her mother, which were now repeated in the transference. But then came a new contribution.

She started the next session saying, "You know about poop, boo-boo, poop," and then asked, "When do you come to visit me at home? But we all must wear pajamas." I showed surprise. "Yes, we pin them tight" (she showed me how one does it) at the bottom, with a string. "Then you cannot see in," she explained with a shrug of the shoulders, indicating "how could I be so dumb."

I suggested to her, "Oh, when you cannot see in and we all wear pants, then boys and girls and all grown-ups look the same." She nodded her head in agreement. She continued to jump on and off the couch. I said, "You are such a jumper today; I wonder whether you have excited feelings which make you so." She answered, "You could crack your head open, you know, if you jumped in the bathtub." I agreed and said, "I know that hurts sometimes happen to all children, and I know that you often have falls and bumps." She now continued with a memory: "Once I hurt my teeth that way in the bathtub." I answered, "I know how terrible that must have been. Let me see, how are your teeth now?" "All right," she replied and opened her mouth. "How did that happen that time in the bathtub?" "Oh," she said, rather indifferently, "That was the time that Mommy had to leave the bathroom for a moment." While telling me this, she took the doll, undressed her quickly, and then, with red crayon, scratched it vehemently and with great intensity over the whole body, especially in the genital region.

I asked, "Did you bleed when you hurt your teeth?" She answered, "Oh yes, Mommy gave me ice." I then gave her a long interpretation in which I tied up her anger at mother and her fantasy that she had had a penis but lost it through playing with her genital, and that either her mother or I could have prevented it if we had always been present. "You know, Joanne, I believe that in one part of your mind you think that you once had a penis like Daddy and boys. But then you scratched yourself in a pleasant, excited way, and then you hurt it and lost it. And you are so angry at Mommy and me that one of us is not with you so that we could have stopped you—and now I know why you wet your pants. You must think that only people who have a penis can feel that they have to make wee-wee." The wetting stopped after this interpretation. I did not want to deal with the bleeding at that point.

The following is a verbatim report of a painting session which demonstrates the interplay between her id, ego, and superego. This session followed shortly after the discussion of her masturbation and the reproaches she made to her mother.

Joanna played with a wooden train and wanted to paint it because it did not look bright enough. She helped me get the paints out, and carefully put newspaper on the table and then under the table, but not under her chair. She did it as expertly as a grownup would have done. She poured the paints carefully into smaller dishes without spilling any, although she then put the open jars dangerously near her elbow. She selected a brush for each color. I commented on her skill in arranging everything so well: "Joanna, I can see how well you set up the paints and how careful you are to do a neat job." Although she wanted to paint the train in bright colors, she painted the engine black and navy blue. And what happened now was a demonstration of how the sublimation of the partial anal drive gradually broke down and spilled over into other partial drives. One could observe how the patient tried to ward this off by intensification of defenses, succumbed, and finally did something self-destructive.

She called the paint "icky goo," and turned to me saying, "You are Mrs. Icky Goo." Then, "I do not like to mess. I love to clean up, but not when it's a mess." This was a denial of the inner perception of her wish to smear.

Now the dainty, careful brush strokes gradually became less well directed, and I interpreted, from experience of previous painting sessions, as follows: "I know that you like to do a neat job, but I believe you worry that you cannot do that all the time." Her defense against the wish to smear was also expressed by a demand for a lot of clean water for her brushes. When I brought her this, she apparently was preoccupied with another attempt at warding off the breakdown of her defense. She asked, "What happens if you eat turpentine?" I said, "I suppose Daddy uses turpentine to clean off paint. You must be getting very worried that you will mess and you will need turpentine, but our paints can be washed off with water." However, she continued to talk about eating paint. "Is it poison when I eat paint?" I answered, "I guess when you get too excited about painting so that it gets messy, you worry that you even might put it in your mouth. And then you have to worry that bad things will happen from that."

It seemed that the excitation of her anality had excited the orality. Although, apparently, it had started off as an attempt to ward off the anal partial drive with the oral one by the question, "Can you eat turpentine?" it also was a result of a sparking over of the excitement. Again, the impulse became too strong and the fear of punishment was expressed. She painted more and more carelessly, her hands were full of paint now, and she said, "You are Miss Icky Goo; I would want to eat you. You are a sweety pie. I would want to paint forever and ever and ever." Her cheeks were flushed, she was smiling, and most content. The love object who allowed her to do this became a projection of her inner needs. The analyst was "icky goo" for her insofar as she tried to repudiate her behavior, and a "sweety pie" when she accepted the pleasure of it. When a bell rang, she went to the door to see who it was—something she never did before. Her wish to look also broke through now. She put a big black paint mark on the door. It was the next patient and a warning that our time was almost up. Of course, she still wanted to paint more and not stop: "Please let me paint this car." Then, she was almost relieved that her time was up and she could go to wash. "You know, Joanna," I said, "When you have such a good time painting it is very hard to stop." "But," she asked, "will you come to help me wash?" Thus we went to the bathroom and, realistically, she needed my help. She obviously made this into a game with the suds and the soap and water; she also manipulated the water taps and was aware of the hot water tap.

When she was all finished and I was cleaning up a bit, she put her hand under the hot water in a split second, in spite of my warning, "Joanna, we must always mix the hot and the cold water." She stated, "I've been burned much worse before." This was true. "Remember the time I burned my hand?" She reminded us of the episode when she had put her hand over the lighted stove, while her mother, who was cooking, turned her back for a moment. I interpreted: "You know what I think? It looks as if you have to punish yourself because you had such great fun painting. And maybe all this hurting you do to yourself when you burn yourself or fall, or have a cut, or are afraid of getting poisoned, maybe this is to punish yourself for all the exciting fun games— just like when you scratched up the doll with the red crayon and thought she had lost her penis that way." Her answer showed great understanding: "I want *you* to worry about *that*." Here she expressed the wish to enjoy pleasure and not to accept punishment; let the outside world take care of the consequences, but also set limits.

Joanna was now in an inbetween stage. She still committed many self-punishing acts, although not as severe. At the same time, she was a "pleasure-tuned" individual and could tolerate pleasure by balancing it with self-punishment. As mentioned before, when her mother tried to stop sex play with the sister, she frequently answered, "This is none of your business."

The material of the painting session followed two days after Joanna had brought her theory that she had had a penis but had lost it because she had scratched herself. The next day this had been followed by a story of baby hamsters, which had died because the mother had left them. At that time Joanna insisted on going to see the fish in the tank in my other office. She had suddenly been concerned about whether they were alive. I then reminded her again of how she felt, that she lost her penis through scratching. I said that if her mommy or I would always be with her, then she might not harm herself or die. She responded with a radiant smile of feeling understood.

In the painting session, we saw how the ego of this almost five-year-old child had sublimated her anal drive in a wish to paint and to be clean. In the analysis, because of the permissive situation and the analytic process, a struggle ensued between the ego and the id, which ended in a partial victory of the latter, but her superego could not let this go unpunished. Actually, the patient has made an inner bargain to allow herself pleasure at the expense of self-injuries. This child is engaged in a real struggle between internalizing the environmental demands and her need for a protective environment, but she also tries to hold on to id gratification.

Another session of this analysis brings to the fore how an external event, the Cuban crisis, mobilized existing conflicts and brought into play many defenses as well as phobic reactions. This helped us to analyze and understand more fully her fear of separation from her mother.

The week-end of the Cuban crisis in the fall of 1962, the family had gone to the country and decided to prolong their stay because of fear that there might be war and a bombing attack on New York City. As reported by the mother, Joanna was told frankly the reason why they did not return, namely, danger of war. She had cried because she was worried that something might happen to her maid. During her stay in the country, the child had otherwise been very happy except for one night when she could not fall asleep and no one quite understood why.

When she returned for her session, the mother left her with me and went to park the car. Joanna became worried that her mother might be run over—a fear she had never expressed before. She only really settled down when she heard her mother return.

She then asked me: "Did you know that the sun is gradually getting colder and colder and that one day it will burn out and there will be nobody left?" This, to me, sounded very much like the opposite of an atomic bomb. We discussed this bit of scientific information, and I remarked, "That's what some books say, but how do you know all this?" "My daddy told me all about it, and we also read about it in your waiting room." From here our conversation easily led to dying and death, and her worry and concern about it. I said, "I guess these ideas make you worry a lot what will happen to all the people? Maybe you are afraid that everyone will die." She partially confirmed and partially denied this, adding, "But they never do anything to women and children." "Oh, Joanne, now I understand. You are not really thinking about the sun's cooling off, but you are talking about last week. You must have known that something was going on last week when you stayed in the country. And you must have worried whether something might happen to me, as well as to Alice (the maid). I believe that you are also afraid that women and children are not always safe." She beamed at me and nodded her head in assent.

She now switched to another subject—television. "I love TV and I want so many things (she meant the advertising), but Mommy says not to believe everything." "Did you watch TV in the country?" I asked. "No," she replied, "but we had a radio." I continued to question her. "Did you listen much?" "No, but the grown-ups did." I suggested: "Maybe you heard something on the radio which you would rather not believe; maybe you and Mommy and Daddy and Susy stayed away because something might happen to women and children; maybe the grown-ups had listened and talked a lot." "Oh, you mean Cuba," she said, "of course." From here we could really go into her worries and fears, all of which she had denied or turned into the opposite meaning earlier in the session. "But it was safe driving back with Mommy," she insisted. I reminded her of her concern when her mother went to park the car, and she said, "Daddy has not come back with us yet." I interpreted: "Of course, in such frightening times, you worry more, especially when Mommy and Daddy are not together and with the children." This, however, did not encompass the total conflict.

In the next two sessions, Joanna insisted that her mother be in the room with us. Her mother made herself as unobtrusive as possible and found excuses for leaving us alone, such as going for an ashtray or another magazine. This was not easily tolerated by Joanna. She drew a picture of a girl together with her mother and explained that "they lived happily ever after." This fear of separation is a recurring fantasy with meanings from many levels which we had discussed in earlier sessions. Now the fear of losing her mother was predominant. When the mother was in the room, she wanted to be close to her, to have an "affectionate day" like the time, as she expressed it, when she, Joanna, "was the oldest and only one." She referred to the time before the sister's birth. We also knew from previous material about her hostility toward her sister.

In the meantime, the father had also returned to the city and the parents were planning a short business trip together. The grandmother, whom Joanna loves, was to come and look after the children. She continued to stay very close to her mother in the sessions, and I interpreted: "You must hate to be left behind by Mommy and Daddy, even though Grandma is with you." "Yes," she assented. "But remember that last summer you and Susy stayed alone with her and you did not mind," I went on. She said, "How do you know that? You are not supposed to know; it's a secret." "But Joanna," I replied, "you told me yourself, I wonder why you forgot, and why it has to be a secret from me. Maybe you want to keep it a secret from yourself. What is it that someone else and you should not know? Maybe you hate Susy so much right now because you are thinking of the happy times that you and Mommy had before Susy was born. Maybe you wish her to be dead and you don't want to think such a bad thought."

In this instance, the child was unable to face the ambivalence of her feelings, which were dealt with by her by wanting to keep them secret from me, and thus from herself. She went on to talk about a doll, describing the color of its hair and other characteristics, thus ignoring my interpretation. She spoke of this doll in baby talk, and I brought her back to the fact that Mommy was leaving after this hour. She became very quiet, sat pensively, had tears in her eyes, as did her mother, and then she said, "I feel very sad." Thus she could verbalize and experience the distress at her mother's leaving, which had been expressed by clinging and a wish to return to the time before her sister's birth. The hour after this, she played quietly with the dolls and seemed in good spirits. By the following hour her mother had returned, and she finally could tell me why she had been so worried about her. "Mommy might get sick," she said. I remembered that the previous summer, when the whole family was on vacation, the mother had been hospitalized for a few days.

Thus the Cuban affair had mobilized the fear of losing her mother and, in the transference, me. Although, except for the one evening when she had had trouble falling asleep, she had apparently been very happy in the country, anxiety had built up underneath the surface and had reawakened her ambivalent feelings toward her mother. The conflict was revived to one of its earliest roots, the separation anxiety.[3]

The mother's brief hospitalization during her pregnancy with the younger child had occurred at the time when Joanna was experiencing the age-adequate developmental stress of separation anxiety. The mother's hospitalization—perhaps the pregnancy itself and the subsequent hospitalization for

[3] Here again is a warning against believing that children are not affected when they do not seem to show any emotional upset in times of upheaval. Their anxiety operates beneath the surface when the parents act composed. Probably, the parents also experience suppressed anxiety, and old conflicts are aroused which are dealt with successfully on the surface.

the birth of the sister—in addition to her return with the
new baby, had interfered with the process of separation from
the mother.[4] During the summer of the first year of the analysis, when the mother was in the hospital, the child had been
described as being untroubled, but she clung to the mother
a few days after the latter's return. In the analysis, which was
to her a new reality situation, she relived the conflicts about
the birth of her sister in the transference. The interpretations dealt with her wish to have me to herself and her resentment toward my other patients. At this time, we had to
part for vacation and, during that vacation, the mother was
hospitalized again. This must have aroused, in the transference as well as in reality, the not-too-deeply buried fear of
losing her mother, and could account for the temporary regressive behavior of clinging to her mother and talking baby
talk. The improvement in treatment was not affected by
these events. The reality of the Cuban crisis touched off an
intensification of the underlying conflict. There can be no
question that this accelerated the analytic process.

The Case of Sylvia

The second case to be presented here is that of *Sylvia,* who
came to analysis at the age of seven and a half years. She was
an extremely inhibited, shy child who had trouble learning
and making friends. She could only learn at home when her
mother studied with her. While Joanna was a child with a
zest for life, who was caught in a struggle to avoid the demands of her superego, Sylvia was preoccupied with thoughts
about punishment inflicted on "bad people." Gradually, during the analysis, she developed more and more signs and
symptoms of a compulsive character. She and her sister, one

---

[4] I am referring here to the process of separation-individuation, as described
by Mahler (1963). See also McDevitt's paper in this volume, pp. ?

year her senior, had been cared for by nurses in infancy. Therefore, not too much is known of Sylvia's early development.

Sylvia tolerated separation from her mother badly and would often crawl into bed with her at night. We analyzed her homosexual attachment to her mother and sister, her penis envy, her death wishes toward her mother and the older sister. At one session, when she was eight, we discussed war, problems of law, prisons, and medieval punishment She turned to me and said: "You know, if I had been in that garden, I would never have touched that apple." She was, of course, talking about the Garden of Eden and being driven from Paradise—which, according to her, meant becoming mortal and having to die, as a punishment meted out by God.

A painting session exemplifies Sylvia's inability to experience pleasure and the distress which her id impulses caused her. The session occurred at a stage in the analysis when we had already discussed her penis envy and her attachment to her mother. Before the painting session, there was a discussion of "exciting" games which children play with friends —jumping on beds and chairs, throwing pillows, etc. This served as an introduction to a discussion of forbidden bathroom games to which the painting session was directly related.

"I want to paint today," she said, with a glimmer in her eyes. "Sure, go ahead. You know where the paints are," I responded. Like Joanna, she started out neatly and controlled. "What do you want to paint?" I asked. "A mountain and a sunset with a little girl on a horse," she replied. Gradually the colors began to run into each other. "Do you like it?" she asked me, and, before I could say anything, she made a big streak over it. "Oh well, it doesn't matter!" she exclaimed. Then she stood up and made herself a palette from cardboard. The smearing and the cardboard palette were both new ideas for this generally overcontrolled child. I just watched her for a while, and she began a new painting. "You know what it is?" she asked. I could not make anything out of it. "I think it looks like one of those modern paintings," I answered, tentatively. She stood up and became wilder: "I am a mad painter!" she said loudly, and by now she was spattering the paint on her paper and gradually over the table and on me. She became wilder and messier as she went on. But she was not happy like Joanna who so much enjoyed her wild and messy painting. She began to look troubled and anxious, and I felt that her laugh had a forced and metallic quality. I felt she would not be able to tolerate any more loosening of the control of her ego. I remarked, "You know, this reminds me of the wild games that you and your sister and friends play together, and then Mommy becomes mad at all of you. I wonder whether you want me to get mad at you also like Mommy and want me to stop you. I believe you're getting afraid of yourself. And you also have told me about your worries that there will be an earthquake or that Mommy will set the house on fire when she smokes in bed. I believe you now have the same worry that something may happen."

At this point, she dropped her brush and said, "And Mommy is angry when I come home full of paint." I answered, "Yes, you are afraid of Mommy when you think that you do bad things or make yourself dirty, but you also are not sure that you can trust Mommy enough to help you stop when you want to do things which are exciting and Mommy calls them 'bad and dirty.' "[5]

Sylvia's fear of losing her mother was ever-present. Her need for her mother was not only expressed directly in the clinging and searching for her mother at night-time when she went to her bed, but also in the learning situation. Not only real situations, but also those which, by association, could be interpreted as loss of a love object were upsetting and traumatic for Sylvia. Thus she figured out that my children do not have to go to a strange analyst; they could be analyzed by me. She only wanted to be taught by her mother, and in

---

[5] There are legitimate, realistic reasons to account for Sylvia's mistrust of the help she can count on from her parents in the struggle of her ego against her id.

her mind, my children had more ways to hold on to their mother than she had.

In another session, Sylvia came in very much upset. She explained to me, "Mommy has gone back into analysis but with a new doctor." The mother and her former analyst had separated by mutual agreement a few years ago, and it had been left open whether the mother should return or not.

In this hour Sylvia was full of compulsive questions: "Why did Mommy interrupt before she was well? Why do people do that? Why does Mommy go to another analyst? But why did she stop two years ago? How can you stop with your analyst when you are not well?" I tried to answer her questions on a reality basis: "You see, Mommy had improved so much that she did not need an analyst. But sometimes after analysis you find out that a new problem comes up." "But how do you know when you can stop? Why did Mommy's analyst let her go?" she queried.

I finally realized that something deeper was going on. "I think, Sylvia," I said, "that you are worried that I might send you away. Then you will lose me just as you always fear that Mommy will not come back or something will happen to her." She answered, "Maybe Mommy has to go back because Nancy [the sister] and I are so bad." "What are the bad things that you do so you have to think it is your fault?" I asked. "We always fight and jump on the beds and have pillow fights with Tom and Peter [two cousins]." "Yes," I agreed, "I know that you feel very bad about that, but it's one of your problems that you blame yourself for so much, especially for your exciting games, and sometimes even for things other people do."

Now she started again: "But why can't Mommy go back to Dr. X.?" she asked. "You must be worried that I will send you away, and you think that analysts send people away because they tell their bad thoughts. But, I know all grown-ups and children have thoughts and do things which give them a very guilty conscience. And already your mind thinks that you need punishment even when you just *think* something you feel is not right! And there are so many things you thought or did when you were little and which you couldn't understand—you often forget that think-

ing and doing are not the same thing. And everybody has exciting
feelings, and these are just as much part of yourself as that you
know the sun is shining. But you worry that these make you bad.
And you and I both will know when your problems are understood, and then you will know that you don't need to come here."
"But can I visit you?" she asked. "You are so afraid to lose me,
and that's a fear we have to understand. But, anytime you call
me, we'll make a date, and there may always be something you
want to come and tell me. I think you are just as worried about
losing me as losing Mommy."

I felt that, besides the interpretation, she also needed reassurance. Her anxiety was so intense that I did not want to
increase it by remaining "analytically" noncommittal. Also,
it is true that when the time comes to end or interrupt the
analysis I make myself available when it seems indicated for
the particular patient.

The reality event of the fact that her mother went back
into analysis with a new analyst had mobilized her old fear
of losing her mother, which she had relived with me in the
transference. This is comparable to the reactivation of Joanna's old fear of losing her mother which was mobilized by
the political crisis about Cuba. It was not possible for Sylvia to
recall and relive, in the analysis, the earliest fears of separation from her mother. She only remembered that she had
been left with a relative at the age of three, when her parents
had left for the country. Reconstruction in analysis led us to
believe that she considered this a punishment for having
been bad.

DISCUSSION

The difference in the way the material is brought to the
analytic sessions by these two girls must be explained by
more than the age difference between Joanna and Sylvia.

There is a different relationship between ego, id, and superego, and thus the intrapsychic conflicts are different. Joanna's
ego is much less distrustful of id impulses than Sylvia's. Joanna accepts pleasure and tries to bargain with her superego
by paying a price in getting hurt. She could express hostility
to her mother freely, but the fear of losing her mother had
been repressed earlier. She was ambivalent about the need
for mother as a support for her developing superego and
identification with the mother. Sylvia, by contrast, was consciously preoccupied with losing her love object, her mother,
and needed a great deal of analytic work before she could
accept some of her hostility toward her mother. She was
afraid of her "badness" and feared losing control of herself
and being overrun by her instinctual drives. She also needed
the protection of her love objects against her own impulses,
which she feared. This conflict was expressed in her ever-
present fear of disaster. She was always preoccupied with "badness" and punishment and fears of being abandoned.

Joanna, with the help of analysis, became a bubbling personality. She could successfully enjoy her instinctual pleasures by bridling them gradually. With the help of analysis,
she was able to find satisfactory solutions so that she learned
to reduce her need for pleasure and, therefore, did not have
to pay too high a price for it in superego punishment by way
of physical injury. She began to find sublimations, many of
them sound identifications with her mother. She tolerated
her sister better, she learned well in school, she read, she
cared for animals and plants like her mother did, and exhibited many other healthy and constructive behavior features.
One cannot predict whether at a later stage of development
she will be able to maintain this balance.

Sylvia also has improved; she has friends; she does much

better in school; she gets along well at home without clinging to her mother. She is a "reasonable" child, and she, almost too easily, accepts the reality of life and its limitations. She readily makes allowances for the shortcomings of the people in her environment and she excuses them by saying, "He or she needs an analyst." Characteristic for her superego development is the fact that she is inclined to think that analysis helps people to be good, although she has experienced in analysis a greater tolerance and acceptance of what she calls "bad" in herself. She is too realistic, with a tendency to slide over easily into denial of her hostilities because of her fear of losing her love object to some extent, she still has a need for masochistic solution of her conflicts.

Summary

I have described two girls who came to analysis at the ages of four and a half and seven and a half years. Both displayed fears of separation from the mother and fixation in the anal phase of development. Due to the difference between the relative strength of ego, id, and superego, the ways of handling the intrapsychic conflicts were different in these two patients and must be explained not only by the difference in age, but by other factors.

Since we do not have enough data about the early development of one of these two patients (Sylvia), it is difficult to assess the role which their early life experiences played in their later character makeup. But even the more complete early history of the other patient (Joanna) as related by the mother, does not give us sufficient data to enable us to distinguish between what is *Anlage* and what is the reaction to the stresses of life, or what furthered or hindered her functioning. Although we know that Joanna suffered a setback when her mother went to the hospital and when a sister was born, we still do not know to what degree the parents' neuroses contributed to her distress. Also, we have no detailed information regarding Joanna's early life insofar as her nonconflictual development was concerned, and how this contributed to later affective and defensive development. A combination of careful longitudinal studies from earliest infancy on, plus simultaneous analysis of parents and child over a number of years might have given us more precise data from which to draw such conclusions.

REFERENCES

Bonnard, A. (1950), The Mother as Therapist in a Case of Obsessional Neurosis. *The Psychoanalytic Study of the Child.* 5:391-408. New York: International Universities Press.

Bornstein, B. (1934), Phobia in a Two-and-a-Half-Year-Old Child. *Psychoanal. Quart.,* 4:93-119.

Bornstein, S. (1935), A Child Analysis. *Psychoanal. Quart.,* 4:190-225

Fraiberg, S. (1951), A Critical Neurosis in a Two and-a-Half-Year-Old Girl. *The Psychoanalytic Study of the Child,* 7:173-215. New York: International Universities Press.

Freud, A. (1937), *The Ego and the Mechanisms of Defense.* New York: International Universities Press, 1946.

Furman, E. (1957), Treatment of Under-Fives (By Way of Parents). *The Psychoanalytic Study of the Child,* 12:250-262. New York: International Universities Press.

Hartmann, H., Kris, E., and Loewenstein, R. M. (1946), Comments on the Formation of Psychic Structure. *The Psychoanalytic Study of the Child,* 2:11-38. New York: International Universities Press.

Heymann-Gero, E. (1955), A Short Communication on a Traumatic Episode in a Child of Two Years and Seven Months. *The Psychoanalytic Study of the Child,* 10:376-380. New York: International Universities Press.

Mahler, M. (1963), Thoughts About Development and Individuation. *The Psychoanalytic Study of the Child,* 18:307-24. New York: International Universities Press.

McDevitt, John B. (1967), A Separation Problem in a Three-Year-Old Girl.

Rangell, L. (1950), Treatment of Nightmares in a Seven-Year-Old Boy. *The Psychoanalytic Study of the Child,* 5:358-390. New York: International Universities Press.

Sterba, E. (1949), Analysis of Psychogenic Constipation in a Two-Year-Old Child. *The Psychoanalytic Study of the Child,* 3/4:227-252. New York: International Universities Press.